W9-BDY-448

TEXAS BUG BOOK

TEXAS BUG BOOK

THE GOOD

THE BAD

AND THE UGLY

C. Malcolm Beck and John Howard Garrett

HOWARD COUNTY LIBRARY
BIG SPRING, TEXAS

University of Texas Press, Austin

Copyright © 1999 by the University of Texas Press
All rights reserved
Printed in China

Second paperback printing, 1999

Requests for permission to reproduce material from this
work should be sent to Permissions, University of Texas
Press, Box 7819, Austin, TX 78713-7819.

♾ The paper used in this book meets the minimum
requirements of ANSI/NISO Z39.48-1992 (R1997)
(Permanence of Paper).

Library of Congress Cataloging-in-Publication Data

Beck, Malcolm, 1936–
    Texas bug book : the good, the bad, and the ugly /
C. Malcolm Beck and John Howard Garrett.
        p.   cm.
    Includes bibliographical references (p.   ) and index.
    ISBN 0-292-70868-8 (cloth : alk. paper). —
    ISBN 0-292-70869-6 (paper : alk. paper)
    1. Insect pests—Biological control—Texas. 2. Garden
pests—Biological control—Texas. 3. Beneficial insects—
Texas. 4. Insects as biological control agents—Texas.
I. Garrett, Howard, 1947– . II. Title.
SB933.32.U6B435 1999
632'.7'09764—dc21   98-3594

To all the entomologists who tried to keep this book from being published. The delays you caused have forced us to make it a much better book and created more interest in buying it.

PHOTO CREDITS

B   Malcolm Beck
H   Howard Garrett
ARM   *Agricultural Research* magazine, USDA
BD   Bastiaan M. Drees, Texas A&M University
BP   Max E. Badgley, Biological Photography
BS   BioSafe
ENT   Ries Memorial Slide Collection,
         Entomological Society of America
FWNC   Fort Worth Nature Center
RB   Ron Billings, Texas Forest Service
TFS   Texas Forest Service
TDA   Texas Department of Agriculture

CONTENTS

PREFACE

Texas Bug Book is for gardeners, farmers, ranchers, landscape and nursery people, and even those who don't grow plants at all but want a better understanding of nature. It's fascinating to learn why so many different types of creepy, crawly creatures were put here to aggravate us, help us, and offer great beauty.

Yes, we understand that all insects aren't bugs—we wanted a book title that you would remember, buy, use, and recommend to your friends, your family, and your business associates. Our inspiration to do this book really came from customers, readers, and listeners who would ask us about insects or bring them to us in a jar or plastic bag for identification and solutions to the problems they seemed to be causing. We would often find that people had been spraying poisons on beneficial insects that feed on troublesome insects, pollinate flowers, break down organic matter, and perform many other less publicized duties. The so-called troublesome insects are also interesting and quite useful in their own way. They help us understand and improve our agricultural and gardening techniques, and they encourage genetic study of our food sources.

This book concentrates on Texas bugs, beetles, and other critters—those that are the most visible, the most troublesome to humans and crops, and those that are the most helpful. Even this number is almost overwhelming. But read on—you will definitely find this book different, educational, interesting, and an important tool for all growers of plants. Incidentally, in these pages you'll also learn the difference between a bug, a beetle, and an insect.

Being open-minded and willing to share information is a critical part of finding the truth. The following people have helped us greatly by sharing information on the insects covered within these pages and making format recommendations for the book: Dick Richardson, Pat Richardson, Jim Marshall, Richard Fullington, Brian Keeley, Truman Fincher, Dan Clair, Mike Rose, Phil Callahan, Jim Jones, Richard Hogsette, Delbert Weniger, Bart Drees, and Buddy Maedgens. We greatly appreciate their help.

We also thank Texas A&M, entomologists and authors of other books on insects. The books that have been most helpful with our research are listed in the Bibliography.

Malcolm would especially like to thank Del Weniger, Charles Cole, and Buddy Maedgens, who many years ago, before this book was ever conceived, helped him identify and appreciate many of the little creatures described here.

Special thanks to Tracy Fields, Howard's assistant, for entering all the information into the computer so it could be printed out on these pages. Howard or Malcolm would have done the work, but neither of us can type.

Special thanks should also go to Shannon Davies, who, while working at UT Press, not only helped create and edit the *Texas Bug Book,* but also was largely responsible for its successful journey through the approval process to become a reality.

TEXAS**BUG**BOOK

INTRODUCTION

Nature is often seen only from an altered or artificial view. With our modern lifestyle few people take the time to study and know nature's wisdom and perfection or see its beauty and design. Instead, they regard many of the life forms, especially the insects, as having little or no meaning. They see nature as something to be dominated or manipulated. They don't see themselves as part of nature.

To understand nature, walk into the woods or meadows and look around. You'll be in the presence of many living things—plants and animals, large and small. Then look down. You'll find equal amounts of death, many expired life forms covering the soil. Dig into this mulch of dead things and you will find it beginning to decay. The deeper you dig, the more advanced the decay until the individual pieces fade into humus. This makes the soil rich and fertile to grow lusher and healthier plants. Remain for a while in the presence of this cycle of life, death, decay, and new life. Imagine yourself as part of this environment. Then study and think. A good thought to start with is, "Nature is pefectly designed, and everything, even death and insects, are designed for a purpose." Since we are the highest form of life on this earth as far as we know, consider the purpose of even the troublesome insects.

When you study from this approach, you make discoveries and learn things that would otherwise be blocked from view. The aphids, for example, are considred to be our most troublesome insect. They reproduce extremely fast. They can give birth to live young or deposit eggs. When born alive, they are all young females that are born pregnant, and their young are born pregnant. They may grow wings or not grow wings, depending on their needs. They can alter their character to suit almost any environment.

With all of these life- and generation-sustaining abilities, you think they would soon destroy all plant life, but they don't. Organic gardeners and farmers have known for years—and now science is proving—that the aphids are attracted to and can flourish best on plants that are stressed: weak and sick. The aphids act as censors to seek out and destroy the unhealthy and unfit plants. This allows "survival of the fittest," a natural law.

By destroying the unfit, the aphids have kept the plant world healthy so the plants could survive through the centuries to supply us and all other life forms with food, fiber, and energy. This censoring by the aphids makes them and the many other small insects we call trouble-some very beneficial and necessary.

Except for man, nature designed checks and balances so no single living, reproducing creature would get out of control. Nature put the lady beetles and the other predator and parasitic insects here to act as a police force to keep the aphids and other plant-censoring insects in balance and prevent them from overdoing their job.

Instead of letting nature act out its role of destroying the unfit, we put poison on the sick and weak plants to destroy the censoring insects. Then we eat from the poisoned, unfit, nutrition-poor plants and wonder why we get sick. In our failure to properly study and understand nature and our desire to dominate nature, we have caused ourselves much anguish. Poisonous synthetic chemical toxins can now be found everywhere—in most of our food and in the tissue of every human being.

We hope that reading our book about bugs will help you better understand and enjoy not only the little critters but all of nature and help you live without the need of harmful toxins. Let's help protect this beautiful and fascinating planet. It's the only home we have. Let's keep it safe and productive for ourselves and our children.

HOW TO USE THIS BOOK

Source of Common and Scientific Names

Neither of us is university-trained in entomology, and we don't claim that this book is the last word on the subject of insects. We did consult many other books and research papers and several schooled entomologists to help us in the correct identification of the insects, but we were often frustrated to find the experts and the references in disagreement. That's understandable because of the millions of insect species that exist. Many more are out there and still not identified. In addition to the fact that the existing books disagree on insect identification and many of the entomologists disagree on the names, the accepted names keep changing. We had to make a decision on how to give readers some consistency, so here it is. The scientific names in this book agree primarily with *Destructive and Useful Insects* (5th ed.) by Robert L. Metcalf and Robert A. Metcalf.

The common names used by farmers, ranchers, landscapers, pest control people, and entomologists vary even more than the scientific names. Under each listing we have shown the various common names in use, but the primary common names we list agree with the publication *Common Names of Insects and Related Organisms*, published by the Entomological Society of America.

Insect Life Cycles

Throughout the book, you will find references to "complete" and "incomplete" life cycles. A *complete* life cycle or metamorphosis is the type of insect development that has four distinct stages: egg, larva, pupa, and adult. Insects with this development include mosquitoes, wasps, flies, beetles, green lacewings, and ladybugs. An *incomplete* life cycle is a gradual metamorphosis. It is a type of insect development with no prolonged resting or pupal stage.

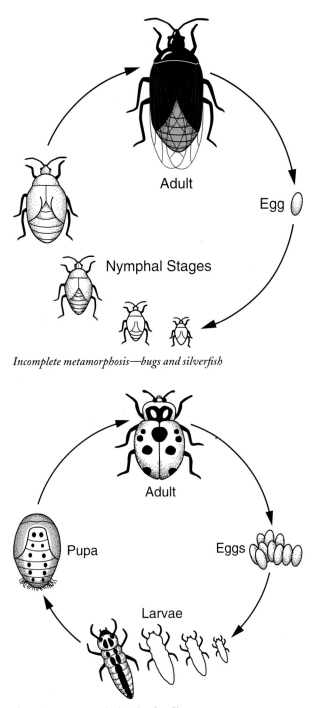

Incomplete metamorphosis—bugs and silverfish

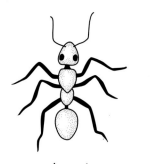

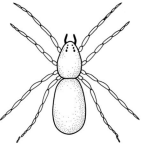

Insect   Arachnid
(spiders and mites)

Distinguishing an insect from a spider

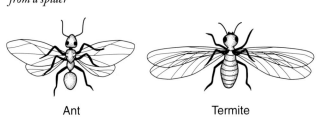

Ant   Termite

Distinguishing an ant from a termite

The three stages are egg, nymph, and adult. Insects with this type metamorphosis include silverfish and the true bugs like stink bugs, boxelder bugs, minute pirate bugs, and squash bugs. Instars are the immature forms of incomplete insects.

Some animals we call insects really aren't. These insectlike critters include spiders, mites, and galls. Galls aren't even animals; they are plant growths that are caused by fungi or insects. Insect galls are the most common. Mites and spiders are different from insects in that they have eight legs instead of six. These critters are included in the book because they are so similar and because of their economic importance and influence on the balance of life.

Why the Stories?

One of the unusual features of this book is the inclusion of personal stories. We both have had many experiences with insects, and our observations serve both to back up our reporting of the insects and to debunk some previously held theories that we have found simply wrong.

During our research, it became overwhelmingly apparent that most of the scientists and university-trained entomologists simply don't agree with us on lots of insect issues. For example, almost no entomologists (among those we've spoken with, anyway) believe that fire ants eat plants. It's simple to establish the truth, however. The fact that they eat plants isn't based on anyone else's book or scientific paper. It's based on our experience of sitting and watching fire ants eat eggplant, okra, and other plants.

Our stories also illustrate how we got our knowledge of controlling troublesome insects with organic tech-

Complete metamorphosis—beetles, flies, etc.

niques and protecting the beneficials with commonsense approaches. The stories might also give readers clues to management techniques that we haven't thought of yet. Getting people to think a little more before blasting away with toxic pesticides is one of the primary goals of this book.

INSECT PEST MANAGEMENT

The known number of insect species is certainly arguable, but there are at least a million and scientists are discovering new species daily. Some scientists estimate the number of species to be as high as 60 million. Of those already discovered, it is our opinion that less than 2 percent should even be considered pests.

Organic growers work under the philosophy that plants growing in their preferred environment and in soil balanced to suit their needs will be healthy, and that a healthy plant's immunity prevents the destructive insects from multiplying into damaging populations. Natural enemies such as beneficial insects and microorganisms are usually able to hold these pests in check. This natural balance can't work when the natural predators aren't present, and that of course is one of the main reasons we are opposed to the traditional practice of spraying broad-spectrum toxic pesticides.

When insects (and diseases) attack plants, organic growers search for the cause of a plant's inability to stand off the attack. Nonorganic growers (those who still use synthetic pesticides and artificial salt fertilizers) treat the symptoms by trying to kill the pests with toxic poisons. These pesticide treatments often worsen the problems by killing off beneficial microbes and insects, thus giving the pests more free rein.

Many so-called pest problems are created by bad land management practices and poor plant selection. We have used compost and natural fertilizers to grow pest-free vegetables and ornamentals, while other plants nearby but not properly fertilized have been heavily infested with pests. Pecan trees that were severely infested with mealybugs, after being mulched with compost, were completely cleared of the pests after two years. Nematodes were gone in one year from a tomato hotbed used to start seedlings after the introduction of compost and earthworms. Peach and other fruit trees with trunks oozing sticky sap healed themselves after being mulched with compost.

When plants in apparently natural conditions become infested with diseases or insects, stressful factors may be quietly at work: the water table has changed, air pollution has increased, or competition is pushing one plant out for others. We have also learned that erratic weather conditions can stress plants and cause insects and diseases to attack. But plants in balanced, fertile soil are not as easily stressed and therefore have a very powerful resistance to diseases and insect pests.

The skeptics will argue, "But we don't have enough compost for all the farms in America." For that reason, really big organic growers don't always use compost. Instead they grow cover crops for additional organic matter. They also test for fertility elements, adding the specifically deficient nutrients to the soil when needed. Organic growers are careful not to use toxic pesticides or any toxic chemicals that harm the living organisms of the soil, such as the beneficial microbes and earthworms that are essential in making a soil fertile enough to grow healthy plants.

Getting rid of all the bugs, beetles, slugs, snails, and other bothersome critters in the farm, garden, or landscape is impossible. It's also a bad idea because most of these living organisms are beneficial. Insects usually do a great job of controlling themselves if we don't foul up the balance by spraying toxic pesticides, using harsh salt fertilizers, or watering too much or too little. Even the insects we would classify as harmful, such as aphids, are helpful in their own way. They attack plants that are in stress from problems of the soil, from unusual climate, or from poor plant selection. In doing so, they help to eliminate unfit plants.

A common misconception about organic farms, gardens, and landscapes is that they are wild looking, more brown than green, and insect-infested. That simply isn't true. Infestations of the allegedly harmful insects can be controlled with organic techniques and products. Pests in the harmful category can include aphids, ants, bagworms, beetles, borers, caterpillars, crickets, chiggers, chinch bugs, fleas, grasshoppers, grubworms, lacebugs, leafhoppers, leafminers, mealybugs, mosquitoes, nematodes, pillbugs, spider mites, roaches, scale, squash bugs, slugs, thrips, whiteflies, and others. These "bad guys" can be controlled by using much safer products than synthetic toxic chemical poisons. Aphids, red spider mites, and other small pests can be controlled with garlic/pepper tea and liquid seaweed while the tougher insects such as beetles and bugs can be controlled with pyrethrum, citrus oil, horticultural oil, or even something as simple as all-purpose flour. We recommend these "killing" organic sprays only as last-resort tools. Spray or dust only when a serious infestation exists because most pesticides, organic or chemical, will hurt or kill more beneficial insects than the targeted pests.

Garlic spray, for example, is an excellent mild insect control. It doesn't kill insects as much as it acts as a repellent. When hot pepper juice is added to the garlic, it becomes a more powerful, yet still mild insecticide. Other good insect repellents include castor oil, neem, liquid seaweed, molasses, citrus oil, and compost tea. However, the best insect control tools are other insects—the ones we call the "beneficials." Protecting native beneficial insects and other animals is critically important for horticulture and agriculture.

There are basically two types of beneficial insects—parasites and predators. Parasites or parasitoids lay their eggs on or in the pest insect's eggs or in the bodies of the pests. The larvae hatch and eat the pests. Predators do the work more directly. They eat the pest insects with powerful chewing mouthparts or they suck them dry by using tubelike mouthparts. Beetles and true bugs are examples of predators. Flies and small wasps are examples of parasitoids. Large wasps are predators. Among our best-known helpful insects are lady beetles, green lacewings, ground beetles, praying mantids, minute pirate bugs, dragonflies, damselflies, fireflies, assassin bugs, spiders, wasps, and predatory mites. Other forms of helpful wildlife include lizards, frogs, toads, turtles, nonpoisonous snakes, and birds. They provide important functions in the balance of nature and should be protected and encouraged. Remember that toxic pesticides can't tell the beneficial animals from the harmful.

Protecting existing native insects is important, but releasing collected or insectary-raised insects to build up beneficial populations is sometimes needed. Springtime is the key time to release most beneficial insects. Soft, succulent new growth on plants often attracts aphids and other critters, especially when high-nitrogen fertilizers are still being used to encourage unhealthy fast growth. Releasing beneficial insects on a regular schedule and fertilizing with soil-improving materials will help provide excellent long-term control. The best beneficials to buy and release include lady beetles, green lacewings, fly parasites, and trichogramma wasps. Keep them cool and watered and don't spray them with any poisons, not even organic insecticides. Their favorite food is juicy, plant-eating insects. If you don't have troublesome levels of plant-eating insects, there's no reason to buy and release beneficials.

Beneficial insects need lots of energy to be active and search for prey. The adults of many beneficials rely on pollen and nectar as food sources. Flower pollen is a source of protein, and nectar is a source of complex sugars called carbohydrates. Therefore, an important part of a successful beneficial-insect gardening program is to plant and maintain a wide variety of flowering plants. In the garden design it is important to use plants that flower in the fall as well as those that flower in the spring and summer.

Lady beetles can be purchased in mesh bags or in small boxes that hold anywhere from 1,500 bugs per pint container up to 70,000 beetles per gallon. The best way to release lady beetles for the control of aphids is to sprinkle or spray the foliage with water and release the beetles directly on the infested plants at dusk or early in the morning when dew is still on the plants. If you apply water, add two tablespoons of

molasses per gallon of water. The lady beetles will definitely appreciate the added sweets.

Green lacewings are excellent broad-spectrum beneficial insects because they control so many different kinds of pests. Containers of eggs or larvae can be purchased for release to control aphids, spider mites, thrips, caterpillars, and other pests. It's best to release them in the cooler part of the day. These insects are very small but aggressive and voracious. The adults are about a half-inch long and feed on honeydew and nectar. The ferocious little alligatorlike larvae actually do the insect control. Green lacewings can be released throughout the spring and summer in a series of releases until natural populations are established.

Trichogramma wasps can be released from small containers or cards attached to plants that are having problems with pecan casebearers, cabbage worms, tomato hornworms, corn earworms, armyworms, and many orchard pests. These beneficial insects are tiny gnatlike parasitic wasps. They should be released in a succession of releases, starting in the spring when affected plants first leaf out. Repeat the release every two weeks. Once established, these beneficials don't necessarily need to be released every year. In an organic program the gnatlike wasps will establish natural populations and be around every year to help control pest insects.

INSECTIVOROUS ANIMALS AND OTHER BENEFICIALS

There are many helpful animals that control insect pests. Some of the most noteworthy are birds, especially purple martins and hummingbirds, bats, toads, frogs, snakes, lizards, and turtles. Here are some stories and details about some of the most beneficial animals that help us with the control of troublesome insects.

Birds

Birds provide important insect control as well as add great beauty and sound to the garden. It is important to encourage wild birds to come to the garden, farm, and

Mud swallows (B)

Purple martins standing guard (B)

Guineas on the farm (B)

Roadrunner on Enchanted Rock (H)

Wild turkeys in South Texas (H)

ranch even though some of our feathered friends can become pests.

Attracting birds with food or shelter to your garden allows you to enjoy their songs and beauty; what's more, their presence helps with the control of many troublesome insects. Hummingbirds, for example, like to eat many flying insects, including mosquitoes and gnats. Purple martins, swifts, and swallows also eat an enormous amount of flying insects. Purple martins are large swallows that are uniformly blue-black. Females have light-colored bellies. They glide in circles, alternating quick flaps and glides, and they spread their tail feathers more than other swallows. They nest in loose masses of debris in tree hollows, barns, other buildings, and purple martin houses. They feed on flying insects, but contrary to popular opinion, mosquitoes make up only about 10 percent of their diet. Sorry about that. Bats are much better for mosquito control.

A Howard Story — Why Feed the Birds?

I feed the birds at my office and at home although some people question the activity. I also end all my radio shows with "Don't forget to feed the birds." Some gardeners from time to time tell me I shouldn't feed the birds at all because it makes them lazy or "it isn't natural." Adding seed and berry-producing plants to provide natural food in the garden is certainly good to do, but supplementing with bird seed mixes is also recommended as a helpful addition to their diets and an effective way to attract more birds to the garden.

My recommendation to feed the birds started as an attempt to get people to slow down and take time to enjoy nature. At the time, I didn't realize how helpful wild birds are at controlling insects. Bird feeding is easy, doesn't take much time, doesn't cost much, and isn't harmful to them in any way. Providing food is simply a supplement to their natural diet. Most bird experts will tell you the same. A good book on the subject of bird feeding is *Attracting Birds to Southern Gardens* by Thomas Pope, Neil Odenwald, and Charles Fryling Jr.

There are times of the year that are better for bird feeding than others. For example, birds will appreciate your help more during the winter and summer than in the spring and fall months. You should feed birds year round, but don't expect to see as many cardinals, sparrows, doves, and others in the spring when the juicy insects are plentiful or in the fall while plants are producing plenty of berries and seed.

Because of their different feeding habits, various birds are attracted to different foods. Some birds are almost exclusively seed eaters while others eat both insects and seeds. Among the seed eaters are cardinals, chickadees, finches, nuthatches, titmice, sparrows, juncoes, jays, doves, pheasant, and quail. To attract juncoes, doves, and other ground feeders, put sunflower seed and smaller seed on the ground or in dishes. Finches, on the other hand, prefer hanging feeders filled with black thistle seed. If sprouting occurs under feeders as a result of feeding birdseed and this is a nuisance, try using safflower or peanut hearts. These seed will not germinate under feeders, and birds love them. Many birds love sunflower seed, but be aware that the raw, uncomposted hulls are toxic to plant growth. Expect a dead spot under the feeder (or put the feeder over a paved or mulched area). Cardinals, chickadees, and even finches like safflower seed. Squirrels, jays, and grackles don't like it. Most sparrows don't either.

Probably the best way to feed the birds is to plant or conserve plant varieties that produce edible seed, berries, or nectar. Good choices include yaupon holly, elderberry, serviceberry, camphor tree, hawthorn, dogwood, persimmon, loquat, fig, eastern red cedar, magnolia, crabapple, mulberry, wax myrtle, Mexican plum, black cherry, hog plum, Carolina buckthorn, barberry, burning bush, cottoneaster, American beautyberry, hollies, mahonia, Chinese photinia, roses, rusty blackhaw, viburnum, coral vine, Carolina snailseed, sunflowers, hibiscus, lantana, Turk's cap, coral honeysuckle, poke salet, blackberries, and nasturtiums. The mockingbirds in my garden definitely have a favorite food—it is chile pequin. They eat the small, hot red peppers like jelly beans as fast as they mature. Chile pequin is a perennial in most of the state. Burning bush (*Euonymus elata*) is another favorite of several bird species. A good resource for what and how to plant is my *Plants for Texas*—even if I do say so myself.

A Malcolm Story—Birds and the Bees

An old gardening friend from the city visited my wife, Del, and me one day in 1957. After I showed him around my little farm, he told me it would be the perfect place to keep honeybees—especially since I didn't use any poisons. It wasn't long before he had brought a dozen or so hives and put them on the farm. Besides being good for pollinating the plants in the garden, the bees were fascinating to watch. Del and I were learning a lot about the art of beekeeping, since our friend had been at it a long time.

The beekeeper always gave us some honey each time he robbed the hives. We enjoyed the sweet amber bonanza, and everything was going great until he came out one day and discovered that I had put up a big purple martin house, where several pair of birds were already in residence. The beekeeper was pretty upset at seeing those birds patrolling the sky. He said I'd better take down the martin houses because he was afraid they would catch and eat all his honey bees.

By then, I was already attached to the friendly martins, and they must have been attached to us too. They acted as if they belonged to the family. They never flew away when we walked near their house but simply gave us a friendly chirp. I just couldn't see taking down the house where our friends were living. Besides, I couldn't believe that such a beautiful and beneficial creature would attack and eat such a beautiful and beneficial insect.

I didn't remove the martin houses, but I did promise to pay the beekeeper for any hive that was lost. As time went by, the martins and bees seemed to be getting along well with each other. One morning on the way to the barn to milk the cow, however, I noticed a martin flying toward its house with swift and erratic maneuvers. It appeared that something was chasing it, as it zoomed right into its house at full speed. I can't imagine how it stopped without slamming into the inside wall of the house. On several occasions, I noticed the same flight pattern by the purple martins and was puzzled. One morning I was close enough to understand. The honey bees were escorting the martins home whenever they accidentally flew through the bees' flight pattern.

Since that discovery, I always watched for the escort bees. Usually there would be three bees, one on each side of the martin about a foot away and one directly behind the bird at about the same distance. I never saw more than three bees, but occasionally there would be only two, one on each side. I'm sure the martins didn't enjoy the escort service, but it was really fun to watch. The bees seemed to fly at the same speed the martins did, and regardless of any evasive move the martins made, the bees kept up and remained in perfect formation.

I knew from then on that I wouldn't be paying for any lost hives, at least not because of anything the martins did. We have always had martin houses on our farm, and my children loved them. The birds would perch on their front porch and look down at the children and chirp to them rather than flying away like the other birds. One beautiful shiny male became our special friend. When we walked out into the barnyard, he would fly high in the air, then fold his wings like a hawk and dive directly at one of us at full speed until he was about six feet above our heads. Then he would spread his wings and flutter to a halt, with a lot of wild chirping sounds as he flew back up into the air. Most evenings, he was ready to put on his show. Usually he came from the direction of the setting sun and tried to sneak up and startle us.

My kids named this dive bomber "Old Dover," and every spring they couldn't wait for him to come back home. He returned at about the same time each year for five or six years. We were all sad to be without him when he didn't return, and no other martin has learned to play like Old Dover did.

Bats

Bats in most regions can outnumber the martins as much as one hundred to one. They come up from their winter homes in Mexico about the same time the martins arrive, but they stay three to four months longer.

Bats are important to the ecosystem, especially in insect control. One bat can eat about 600 mosquitoes and other night-flying insects per hour. Twenty million bats return each year to one Texas cave alone. In a single night this colony eats a quarter of a million pounds or more of

Bats you can see at Bat World (H)

flying insects. Bats also help to pollinate flowers by feeding on plant nectar and pollen.

There are many misconceptions and outright falsehoods about bats. They aren't evil. They don't suck blood from your neck—the only blood-loving bats are the vampire bats that live in Latin America. Bats are quite interesting furry mammals with large wings. They do look somewhat peculiar hanging upside down in caves and under bridges, but their mysterious sleeping habits shouldn't bother anyone, especially since they do all of their beneficial work at night and don't bother anybody during the day.

Bats are intelligent, friendly, gentle, clean, and little if any health threat. They cause less rabies than do cats and dogs. According to bat expert Merlin Tuttle, more people die from dog attacks annually than have died throughout history from contact with bats. Because of the misunderstandings surrounding these wonderfully helpful creatures, their populations have been dwindling all over the world.

The nectar-eating bats aid the pollination primarily of tropical fruits in warm regions but also of the agave plant from which tequila is made. That of course is especially important!

Texas has the highest population density of bats in the United States. There are two particularly interesting bat communities. The first is the largest urban colony, which is estimated at close to a million bats, roosting under the Congress Avenue bridge in downtown Austin. The second, located in a natural cave north of San Antonio, has been proclaimed by the National Geographic Society to be the largest concentration of mammals in a single place on earth. If the one million bats in Austin eat an

estimated 20,000 pounds of mosquitoes each night, imagine the benefit we receive from the 20 million bats that leave Bracken Cave every night from April to October to feed on flying insects.

Merlin Tuttle, in his excellent book *America's Neighborhood Bats*, points out that all bats in the United States and Canada are insectivorous except for three species of nectar-feeders found along the Mexican border of Texas and Arizona. Anyone interested in receiving more information about our furry flying friends can write or call Bat Conservation International, P.O. Box 162603, Austin, TX 78716; (512) 327-9721. Another excellent book on bats is *The Bat in My Pocket* by Amanda Lollar. The book and other educational information is available from the nonprofit organization she runs called Bat World, located at 217 N. Oak, Mineral Wells, TX 76067; 817-325-3404.

To attract bats, you can build or buy specially made houses. Bat houses work best in a location within 1,000 feet of water. Insect populations will be higher around water. The houses should be oriented toward the east or southeast so they warm up quickly in the morning. Hang them in an unobstructed spot about 12 to 15 feet above the ground, but not too close to your living quarters because bat guano will accumulate underneath. Bat guano has a strongly sweet and powerful aroma. It is very high in nitrogen and great for your garden soil. An excellent publication on bat houses is *The Bat House Builder's Handbook* by Merlin Tuttle and Donna L. Hensley. Bat World provides plans in exchange for a small donation and also sells state-of-the-art bat houses.

Malcolm's Poem: "The Bats"

The purple martins get glory by day
As insect eaters while they glide and play,
But in the dark of night
Many bad insects are in flight.
Troublesome bugs of all type,
Moths, beetles, and mosquitoes that bite,
All feel free to fly about,
Bugs know when the birds are not out.
But when the light of day fades away,
Many hungry bats come out to feed and play.
All night they fly and eat,
While the martins are fast asleep.
They are able to catch bugs by the pound
While they navigate using high-frequency sound.
But at light of day they hurry on back
To a dark deep cave or spooky old shack,
And rest up for another night
Of catching bad bugs while in flight,
And return the skies of day
To the martins that glide and play.

Frogs and Toads

Frogs and toads are similar, and both are beneficial. In general, frogs have smooth skin, narrow waists, and long legs for leaping. Toads are wider, have warty skin and short legs for hopping. Both of these amphibians are found on land and in water, but toads can live far from water.

Chorus frogs are not seen as much as heard. During breeding season, they sing day and night near shallow bodies of water. They hide in grass and other vegetation and are extremely hard to spot. Tree frogs are equipped with adhesive-padded toes and long legs and toes to help them cling to twigs and climb trees. Many tree frogs can change color from brown to green to gray to patterned. Some baby tree frogs are bright green. Spadefoots have a small sharp-edged spade on the hind feet, used to dig burrows in the soil. They spend most of their time underground but appear on the surface after heavy rains.

All toads and frogs eat and thus help control insect pests, slugs, and snails. These garden friends can be encouraged by using organic products and avoiding toxic pesticides. They are all very sensitive to pesticides. Toxic poisons are easily absorbed right through their skin and do great damage.

Lizards

The most common lizards in Texas gardens are the anoles, often mistakenly called chameleons. They are usually bright green, and the males have a pink throat fan that they display when showing off for the ladies. They can change color to brown. They eat insects and add beauty to the garden.

Geckos are great lizards for insect control. There are at least three species here in Texas. Asian geckos are smooth-skinned and about 4 to 5 inches long at maturity. The Mediterranean gecko is the same size but has bumps and a ringed tail. Both love to eat young roaches, grasshoppers, katydids, ants, and other insects. They are pale and translucent and have large lidless eyes. Their toes have broad pads and claws extending beyond the

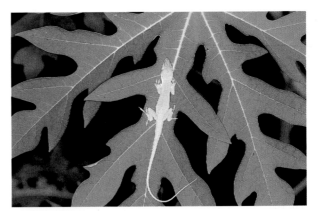
Anole lizard (H)

Gecko lizard (B)

South Texas lizard (B)

Toad (B)

Horned toad (H)

Garter snake (B)

Blind snake (B)

Blind snake worm (H)

pads. The Mediterranean gecko was introduced to Texas several years ago and has now naturalized across at least half the state. This is the most commonly seen gecko because it likes to live around lighted buildings so it can eat the insects that are attracted to the light. Breeding takes place for four or five months in the spring. They lay one to two eggs under shutters or even in the bases of light fixtures. The third species is the tokay gecko, also an Asian import. It is much larger and much more aggressive; although naturalized in some parts of Texas, we do not recommend its release. Unlike the small geckos, it can give you a painful bite. It feeds on insects but also eats small geckos and other animals.

The Mediterraneans can be bought at pet and feed stores. They should be protected and released as an important part of your organic pest control program.

Snakes

There are about 220 distinct kinds of snakes in North America. All are beneficial since they eat rodents and insects. The United States has only four major types of snakes that are poisonous to humans: rattlesnakes, copperheads, water moccasins, and coral snakes, and they all can be found in Texas. Children should be taught the dangers and the benefits of snakes because all others than those mentioned above are harmless and beneficial to humans. Some of the nonpoisonous and very helpful snakes are blackheads, brown snakes, ground snakes, earth snakes, garter snakes, ribbon snakes, patchnose snakes, rat snakes, king snakes, hognose snakes, bull snakes, coachwhips, whip snakes, racers, water snakes,

Turtle (H)

and milk snakes. These benign snakes need to be protected because they help control lots of troublesome insect pests and rodents.

Turtles

Turtles have a long fossil history. Most are carnivorous, but some eat plants as well. Snapping turtles are the most dangerous because they are aggressive and will bite. Don't mess with 'em! Soft-shell turtles look harmless but also bite. Box turtles are the most common in the garden and can be helpful in eating insects, slugs, and snails. They also like the taste of strawberries and other low-growing fruits and vegetables, so they can become pests, especially in the vegetable garden.

Earthworms

Besides the myriad of microscopic plants and animals in each cubic foot of healthy soil, there are lots of macroorganisms, the ones we can see, such as spiders, centipedes, millipedes, springtails, and other insects and critters. But the most fascinating and helpful one is the earthworm. Earthworms inhabit the cool, moist soil in your garden and have a much more important role than that of fishing bait. They are good friends because they provide nutrients, improve the structure of the soil, and benefit other beneficial soil life. There are many species of earthworms, ranging in size, color, soil preference, and life expectancy, but they are all beneficial.

These "Intestines of the Soil," as Aristotle called them, break up soil hardpans, drill miles of burrows that soak up fast-falling rains, help plants root more deeply into the soil, shift chemically unbalanced soils toward a neutral pH, help make soil nutrients available, and loosen compaction.

A single earthworm deposits its weight in castings every twenty-four hours. That may not seem like a lot, but earthworms in an acre of soil are able to produce about fifteen tons of castings in one year. The earthworms also help increase soil microorganisms while they destroy the harmful fungi, bacteria, and root nematodes as they digest them. The earthworm's digestive system also helps neutralize the soil if it is either too acidic or too alkaline. Charles Darwin, who discovered the great

Earthworms (H)

Earthworm castings (B)

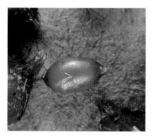

Earthworm eggs (B)

Armadillo (Tom Wood, FWNC)

importance of earthworms, stated that vegetation in many parts of the world would be eliminated without the helpful benefits of the earthworm.

Earthworms are attracted to soils that are high in organic matter and free from pesticides and harsh synthetic fertilizers. Earthworms can be purchased from growers or grown at home in moist compost. In order to confine them to a particular area while you are "raising" them, feed them periodically with cornmeal and molasses. This will prevent them from leaving the compost "nursery" until you are ready to introduce them to your garden or landscaped area. Growing your own earthworms or adding them to your garden can be enjoyable, but they will return naturally and increase in population rapidly if you stop using synthetic chemicals and go organic!

What we organic gardeners should be most concerned about is the level of life in the soil. The best soil test is called the earthworm test. Dig a 12-inch by 12-inch by 6-inch-deep section of soil out of the ground and slowly sift it into a box, bucket, or wheelbarrow. Count the earthworms you see in this half cubic foot of soil. If your test is in turf, there should be at least six earthworms. If the test is in a mulched-bed area, you should see about ten earthworms. They should be big earthworms—about the size of your little finger. If your test doesn't uncover enough worms or if they are puny little worms, your soil needs more improvement.

The presence of lots of big plump earthworms shows that nature has been at work and has filled the soil with life. If you see lots of worms, you can rest assured that the beneficial microbes are there too. If the soil is full of life, the chemistry can't be too far from balanced. If the earthworms are present, the soil will be well aerated and aggregated. Earthworm-rich soil will drain better and also hold just the right amount of water significantly longer. Wait until you see the improved plant growth. The bottom line will be improved soil health, greater biodiversity, and greater plant production.

In conclusion, it could be said that most wild animals are beneficial. Sure, some of them do damage to the soil, eat our plants, and perform other mischief, but they are simply part of that quilt we call biodiversity. The troublesome animals like raccoons, skunks, armadillos, squirrels, and coyotes can be controlled through commonsense management. They can also be repelled with organic products—for example, those that contain hot pepper and castor oil.

Protecting and improving biodiversity is what good land management is all about. It's done by introducing many plant types and allowing insects, frogs, toads, lizards, snakes, birds, and microorganisms to repopulate and flourish. Balanced life and healthy biodiversity are encouraged by introducing beneficial animals and protecting those that exist. Use of native plants and well-adapted plants from other regions also helps. Nature doesn't allow monocultures in the wild. Why should we in gardens and on farms and ranches? If you simply stop using products and techniques that kill, biodiversity will materialize like magic. It is this biodiversity that gives us true pest control.

THE BUGS

THE GOOD

THE BAD

AND THE UGLY

The insects, mites, and spiders that follow are listed alphabetically by common names and cross-referenced for easy access. Each listing includes the most used common name, other common names, scientific names, relative sizes of the insects, physical characteristics to aid in identification, biology and life cycle, habitat, feeding habits, economic importance, natural controls, and organic controls. Under each insect entry there is also an "Insight" section that gives interesting bits of information as well as real-life stories from both of us.

AMBROSIA BEETLE — see Asian Ambrosia Beetle

ANT — see Carpenter Ant, Fire Ant, Harvester Ant, Sugar Ant, Texas Leafcutting Ant

ANT COW — see Aphid

ANT LION — see Doodle Bug

APHID

COMMON NAMES: Aphid, Plant Louse, Greenbug, Ant Cow
SCIENTIFIC NAME: Order Homoptera, family Aphididae, many species
SIZE: Adult — approximately ¹⁄₁₀"
IDENTIFICATION: Small soft-bodied insects of all colors, pear-shaped, with long legs and antennae. The most common color is green, but many species are black, red, yellow, or bluish. Adults are winged and wingless; they usually have a pair of tubes (cornicles) sticking out of the upper end of the abdomen. These tubes spray an oil or waxy fluid on enemies. Aphids also produce a sticky honeydew excretion that ants love; whitish skin casts are left after molts. Some species like the woolly aphids are covered with a waxy white coating.
BIOLOGY AND LIFE CYCLE: In general, eggs are laid in fall and hatch in spring. Nymphs feed in masses by sucking plant sap. These aphids are mostly females that give birth to live young. Sometimes a generation of winged aphids appears and migrates to a new host plant where they feed and produce more wingless females. A generation of true males and females appears in late summer or early fall when temperatures start to drop. These aphids mate, and the females lay eggs that overwinter and hatch the following spring to start the process all over. During warm weather, aphids may go through a complete generation in less than two weeks. They have an incomplete metamorphosis.
HABITAT: You name it. Most ornamental and fruit crops. Foliage of plants, especially the underside of leaves and stems on tender new growth.
FEEDING HABITS: Aphids normally feed in groups on leaves or stems. They pierce foliage or tender stems and suck plant juices, causing leaf curling and stunted growth.

Root aphid (B)

The digested sap is excreted as the honeydew commonly seen shining on foliage. Some feed on roots.
ECONOMIC IMPORTANCE: Aphids reduce the health of stressed plants even further, roll or turn foliage yellow (reducing photosynthesis), and ultimately kill plants. On the positive side, they help to eliminate unfit plants. Some aphids are vectors of disease organisms like viruses.
NATURAL CONTROL: Plant adapted varieties and

Aphid on red oak leaf (H)

Parasitized aphid (B)

Aphid skins after parasites have emerged (B)

Lady beetles feeding on aphids (ARM)

Cabbage aphids (B)

Giant bark aphids (H)

Aphids feeding on plum tree (H)

Winged and nonwinged aphids (B)

encourage natural biodiversity, healthy plants, and beneficial insects such as ladybugs, green lacewings, hover flies, praying mantids, and braconid wasps. Avoid feeding plants heavy amounts of nitrogen.

ORGANIC CONTROL: Strong blasts of water, garlic-pepper tea, liquid seaweed, and the release of ladybugs and green lacewings. Citrus oil spray can be used for heavy infestations. Biological sprays are also now available.

INSIGHT: Aphids, one of the most prolific insects, are considered one of our biggest pests. There are over 200 species. They may produce up to fifty generations per year. Some species produce several generations without mating. The females can lay eggs or give live birth, and those already have within them developing embryos for the next generation. The young can be born with or without wings. It all depends on whether they need to migrate away from a natural enemy or to a better food supply. The life cycle varies widely between different

species and may even vary within the same species in different geographical locations.

With all of their life-sustaining abilities, you would think that aphids would soon destroy all vegetation. But they don't. They have lots of natural enemies in the insect world; more important, healthy, well-grown, and adapted plants have immunity to them. Heavy applications of nitrogen fertilizer will actually attract aphids.

APHID LION — see Lacewing

ARMYWORM

COMMON NAME: Armyworm
SCIENTIFIC NAME: Order Lepidoptera, family Noctuidae, many species
SIZE: Adult — 1½", larva — 1½"
IDENTIFICATION: Armyworms are the immature stage of dull-colored nocturnal moths. Larvae are caterpillars that range in color from pale green to brown or black, often striped with white to yellowish lines from head to tail.
BIOLOGY AND LIFE CYCLE: Complete metamorphosis. One brood per year. Hibernate in the egg or partially grown larval stage. Pupate in the soil.
HABITAT: Grasses, vegetables, and ornamental plants.
FEEDING HABITS: Feed mostly in the spring and early summer on small grains, stems, and foliage. Especially fond of corn, millet, and bluegrass but will also eat other grasses such as bentgrass and bermudagrass.
ECONOMIC IMPORTANCE: Destruction of plant foliage and entire plants. Especially destructive to young seedlings.
NATURAL CONTROL: Parasitic wasps such as trichogramma, parasitic flies, and ground beetles.
ORGANIC CONTROL: Bt (*Bacillus thuringiensis*) products. Citrus and neem products.
INSIGHT: Armyworms are one of the few insect pests that will attack turf grasses; they can be a serious pest on golf courses using artificial techniques. They seem to appear out of nowhere.

Armyworm (H)

A Howard Story

When I worked as an assistant golf course superinten-dent and it was my weekend on call, I got a note from an employee that happened to be the son of the head superintendent. He said that the armyworms were taking the golf course away. I thought it was a joke. It wasn't. The infestation was incredible and required a late-night pesticide spraying to save the greens. It took almost losing my job to get the first lesson on the importance of healthy biodiversity. Golf courses have been notorious for spraying pesticides on a regular preventative basis and destroying beneficial organisms that control pests. Luckily for all of us, especially the golfers that are constantly exposed to those poisons, golf course superin-tendents are starting to learn about the advantages of organic maintenance and natural pest control.

ASIAN AMBROSIA BEETLE

COMMON NAMES: Ambrosia Beetle, Asian Ambrosia Beetle
SCIENTIFIC NAME: Order Coleoptera, family Scolytidae, *Xylosandrus crassiusculus*
SIZE: Adult—⅛"
IDENTIFICATION: Females excavate galleries in stems or trunks and push out plant material, which sticks together and forms narrow protrusions that look like toothpicks. These protrusions are usually the first show of an infestation. One plant can have many such protrusions.
BIOLOGY AND LIFE CYCLE: Larvae bore horizontally into tree trunks. They remain in the tunnels until mature; after they mate, the females leave the host plant. Males are flightless and die in the host plant. A generation may be completed as fast as twenty days or take up to four months. Usually one genera-tion per year. Complete metamorphosis.
HABITAT: Tree and tropical plant trunks. Host plants include over 120 known plants, including pecan, Chinese pistachio, red oak, bur oak, redbud, Bradford pear, and chinkapin oak.
FEEDING HABITS: Females bore into plant trunks and inoculate the tunnel with

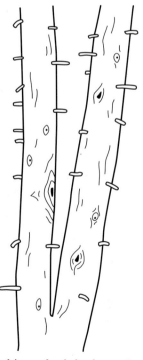
Asian ambrosia beetle and cut lines

fungal spores. Then the females produce a brood. The larvae and the females feed on the developing fungus rather than the host plant.
ECONOMIC IMPORTANCE: Heavily infested plants usually die from the inoculated fungus or a secondary disease.
NATURAL CONTROL: No predators discovered yet.
ORGANIC CONTROL: Keep trees healthy and compost infested wood at earliest detection. You can also cut down the infested tree and let it rot.
INSIGHT: For now, this pest is mostly located in East Texas.

ASIAN LADY BEETLE—see Lady Beetle

ASP—see Puss Caterpillar

ASPARAGUS BEETLE

COMMON NAMES: Asparagus Beetle, Spotted Asparagus Beetle
SCIENTIFIC NAME: Order Coleoptera, family Chrysomelidae. Spotted asparagus beetle—*Crioceris duodecim punctata*. Asparagus beetle—*Crioceris asparagi*.
SIZE: Spotted asparagus beetle—⅓", asparagus beetle—¼", larva—less than ⅓"
IDENTIFICATION: Blue-black cross on the back of adults; looks like four white spots on the wing covers. Eggs are shiny black and laid on young asparagus spears. Larvae are plump, long, off-white, gray, or greenish worms with black head and legs.
BIOLOGY AND LIFE CYCLE: Adults overwinter in plant debris. Multiple generations per year. Complete metamorphosis.
HABITAT: Asparagus plants
FEEDING HABITS: Adults and larvae eat young aspara-gus spears in the spring and summer.
ECONOMIC IMPORTANCE: Severe crop damage.
NATURAL CONTROL: Soil health, adapted plants, and beneficial insects—wasps, lady beetles, and green lacewings.
ORGANIC CONTROL: Spray with citrus oil products and dust plants with all-purpose flour and diatomaceous earth.
INSIGHT: Spotted asparagus beetle has spots instead of the cross marking.

Asparagus beetle (BP)

Asparagus beetle larva (BP)

ASSASSIN BUG

COMMON NAMES: Assassin Bug, Giant Wheel Bug, Wheel Bug

SCIENTIFIC NAME: Order Heteroptera, family Reduviidae, many species

SIZE: Adult—⅜" to 1⅝"

IDENTIFICATION: Various colors and sizes, look like skinny stink bugs or leaf-footed bugs. Abdomen often flares out beneath the wings. Head is elongate with a groove between the eyes. Short curved rostrum (sword-like snout) fits in groove under body. Strong front legs to hold prey. Adults can give you a painful bite but rarely do.

BIOLOGY AND LIFE CYCLE: Eggs usually laid singly or in clusters on branches, in crevices, and under stones and the like. Nymphs are often brightly colored. Incomplete life cycle—with normally one generation per season. Will hibernate in all life forms—eggs, nymphs, and adults.

HABITAT: Many ornamental and food crops.

FEEDING HABITS: Eat adults, nymphs, and larvae of many plant-eating insects. Like to eat troublesome insects from mosquitoes to large beetles. Favorite foods include aphids, leafhoppers, beetle larvae, caterpillars, and small flying insects.

ECONOMIC IMPORTANCE: Control many troublesome plant-eating insects.

NATURAL CONTROL: Spiders and themselves. The young feed on each other.

ORGANIC CONTROL: None needed, highly beneficial.

INSIGHT: Assassin bugs in the genus *Triatoma*, called kissing bugs, bite people at night. They are blood feeders. See Kissing Bug.

A Malcolm Story

Even though the pecan is our state tree, many people are hesitating to plant it because of one unsightly, troublesome pest called webworm. This is a shame, because with just a little study and understanding of nature, the webworm need not be a pest. The webworm has many natural enemies, among them certain birds, but most of its enemies are in the insect world. Wasps are effective at controlling the webworms, but they are not alone. I once saw a praying mantis in a webworm colony holding a worm in each forearm and eating both of them.

While looking out the kitchen window one day, I noticed a webworm colony on a low-hanging pecan branch. Usually I tear these out and throw them on the ground, step on them a few times, then let the fire ants finish them off. But this time, as I started to reach for it, I noticed a member of the assassin bug family, a giant wheel bug, sitting on the outer edge of the webworm colony with a webworm stuck on the end of his snout. Naturally, I didn't destroy that colony but left it alone so that the wheel bug could have a picnic.

Later that day a gardening friend came over, and I took him around the house to show him the assassin bug in action. When we got there, there were two assassin bugs, one on each side of the colony, and each had a webworm stuck on the end of its snout. Early the next day an old friend stopped by. She and I always enjoy discussing nature, so naturally I had to show her the wheel bugs. But, when we got there, they were all gone, and so were all the webworms except one. I made the remark, "I wonder why they didn't eat that last webworm." She replied, "Well, it was left for seed."

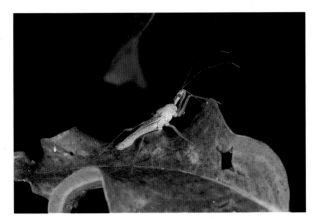

Assassin bug (B)

Assassin bug (H)

BAGWORM

COMMON NAME: Bagworm
SCIENTIFIC NAME: Order Lepidoptera, family Psychidae, *Thyridopteryx ephemeraeformis*
SIZE: Adult—up to 1", bag—¼" to 1½", larva—¾" to 1"
IDENTIFICATION: Larvae hang in bags from twigs of trees. Bags are camouflaged with pieces of twigs and leaves from the host plant. Adult is a black moth. The bag has a small opening at the narrow lower end that serves as a waste exhaust port. A wider opening at the top allows the larvae to crawl out and feed.
BIOLOGY AND LIFE CYCLE: Newly hatched bagworm larvae make conical bags that they carry upright as they move. Adult females are grublike, have no wings or eyes, and are nearly hairless. The rarely seen male adult is a small flying moth. It has clear wings and feathery antennae and is sooty black. The female lays eggs in the bag, then goes through the lower opening and drops to the ground and dies. Larvae hatch and lower themselves on silk threads and attach on limbs where they start building their own silk bags.
HABITAT: Ornamental trees and shrubs like arborvitae, junipers, fruit trees, and many others.
FEEDING HABITS: Eat foliage starting on the upper part of the plant. They live in and feed on willow, cedar, cypress, some pines, boxelder, locust, sycamore, maple, sumac, persimmon, and other ornamentals and fruit trees.

ECONOMIC IMPORTANCE: Defoliation of ornamental plants.
NATURAL CONTROL: Wasps, birds, and several insect parasites and predators.
ORGANIC CONTROL: Bt (*Bacillus thuringiensis*) products sprayed in the spring. Hand picking the rest of the year is by far the best technique.
INSIGHT: Texas has several recorded species of bagworms. Since the female doesn't have wings or ever leave the bag, it is somewhat of a mystery how bagworms get dispersed. While the larvae are attached to single strands of silk thread after hatching, they may be blown a distance by the wind. The silk thread could get caught on an animal such as a bird and be carried a distance.

BANDED WOOLLY BEAR—see Woolly Bear

BARK BEETLE—see Peach Tree Borer

BARK LOUSE

COMMON NAME: Bark Louse
SCIENTIFIC NAME: Order Psocoptera, family Psocidae
SIZE: Adult—less than ¼"
IDENTIFICATION: Adult looks a little like brown lacewing. Protective silvery web on the trunks of trees.
BIOLOGY AND LIFE CYCLE: Silvery web covers the trunk and limbs of trees in the early fall. It

Bark louse (BD)

Bark louse (BD)

Bagworm bag made from agarita foliage (B)

Bagworm bag made from arborvitae foliage (H)

Young bagworms feeding on wax myrtle (H)

happens very quickly, often overnight. More prevalent in South Texas than elsewhere. Web usually lasts only a few days, then disappears.

HABITAT: Limbs and trunks of shade trees.

FEEDING HABITS: Feeds on fungi, scale, aphids, and other insects on tree bark of oaks and other shade trees.

ECONOMIC IMPORTANCE: Beneficial, feeds on troublesome insects.

NATURAL CONTROL: Biodiverse gardens.

ORGANIC CONTROL: None needed.

INSIGHT: Nature will supply these beneficial insects where needed. No need to purchase and release them.

BEE — see Bumble Bee, Honey Bee, Hover Bee, Leafcutting Bee

BEETLE — According to the Coleopterist Society (coleopterists are people who study beetles and their habits), beetles are the dominant form of life on earth. One of every five living species is a beetle! Various beetle species live in nearly every habitat except the open sea, and for every possible kind of food, there is a beetle species that eats it. Beetles appeared before dinosaurs existed, and they now greatly outnumber the dinosaurs' descendants, the birds. Beetles include beneficial and pest species, beautiful and plain, huge and tiny. They have even had a role in human culture, most notably among the ancient Egyptians, who revered the sacred scarab as a symbol of life and rebirth. See Asparagus Beetle, Blister Beetle, Calligrapha Beetle, Colorado Potato Beetle, Cucumber Beetle, Elm Leaf Beetle, Flea Beetle, Ground Beetle, Japanese Beetle, June Beetle, Lady Beetle, Mealybug Destroyer, Rove Beetle, Soldier Beetle.

BIGEYED BUG

COMMON NAMES: Bigeyed Bug, Seed Bug

SCIENTIFIC NAME: Order Heteroptera, family Lygaeidae, *Geocoris* spp.

SIZE: Adult—⅛" to ¼"

IDENTIFICATION: Adults are light yellowish green to

Bigeyed bug hunting for thrips in rose petals (B)

dark gray with small black dots on the head. Have a wider body than chinch bugs and make more rapid movements. Eyes are very large, kidney-shaped, and reddish brown. Football-shaped eggs are whitish gray with red spots. Nymphs are smaller grayish and wingless with irregular patterns of spots on the top of the body.

BIOLOGY AND LIFE CYCLE: Incomplete metamorphosis. Several broods per year in the summer. Adults hibernate in garden debris over the winter. Adults live two to three months after maturity.

HABITAT: Cotton, clover, winter grains, weeds, and alfalfa.

FEEDING HABITS: Often appear when chinch bug populations are high and feed on them. Both adults and nymphs feed on aphids, lygaeid bugs, whiteflies, leafhoppers, plant bugs, small caterpillars, thrips, corn earworm, tarnished plant bugs, and spider mites. All stages of both sexes are predaceous from birth until death, but they can survive on nectar and honeydew when prey is scarce.

ECONOMIC IMPORTANCE: Very beneficial insect that helps control troublesome insects.

NATURAL CONTROL: None needed.

ORGANIC CONTROL: None needed.

INSIGHT: The proboscis (modified mouth structure) of the bigeyed bug extends like a hydraulic piston's ram in stages. This is one of the insects that will naturally reestablish if the toxic sprays are eliminated.

BLACK DUMP FLY

COMMON NAMES: Black Dump Fly, Dump Fly

SCIENTIFIC NAME: Order Diptera, family Muscidae, *Hydrotaea aenescens*

SIZE: Same size as the common house fly, ⅛" to ¼".

IDENTIFICATION: The adult fly is a shiny black fly similar to the housefly. These beneficial flies do not bother animals or people. They have little movement or flight, unlike house flies.

BIOLOGY AND LIFE CYCLE: Females lay an average of 170 eggs over a seven- to ten-day period. Eggs hatch in eighteen to twenty-four hours. There are three larval stages and a pupal stage, which changes into an adult fly. Adults mate after about five days; two days later, the females start laying eggs. The egg-to-adult period is about fourteen days or shorter.

HABITAT: Like dark locations and stay close to the ground. Love manure pits.

FEEDING HABITS: The larvae (or maggots) are predators of the larvae of house flies and other flies.

ECONOMIC IMPORTANCE: Control of house flies resulting from animal manures.

NATURAL CONTROL: None needed.

ORGANIC CONTROL: None needed.

INSIGHT: According to Dr. J. A. Hogsette of the USDA-Agricultural Research Service and the University

Black dump fly (H)

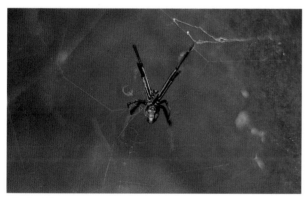

Black widow spider (B)

Black widow spider with recently hatched brood (H)

of Florida, its former name was *Ophyra aenescens*. It is native to the United States as well as Central and South America. Black fly larvae don't need to feed on other fly larvae to live. They can develop naturally on the nutrients from the manure. Dump flies can kill up to twenty house fly larvae a day—a rare example of an animal killing more than it can eat. Dump flies do not feed or rest on animals or humans. Black dump flies have been used successfully in poultry and swine houses, according to Dr. Hogsette. The larvae seem to prefer manures that are comparatively low in fibrous materials. They do not develop well in manures of cattle, horses, sheep, or goats. That apparently means they prefer poultry, dog, and cat manure.

BLACK WIDOW SPIDER

COMMON NAME: Black Widow
SCIENTIFIC NAME: Order Araneae, family Theridiidae, *Latrodectus mactans*
SIZE: Adult—9/16" to 1½"
IDENTIFICATION: Adult females have shiny black bodies and a distinctive red hourglass-shaped marking on the underside of the abdomen. The compact webs are off-white and dense. Males are smaller and have markings on the upper side of the abdomen and large eyes.
BIOLOGY AND LIFE CYCLE: Young spiderlings are whitish when first hatched but darken quickly. Females lay eggs in spring or summer in grayish silken egg balls. Females spin a small, irregular tangled web with a tunnel that she goes into when disturbed. These webs are usually close to the ground. Females eat the males after mating unless they are fast enough to escape. She lays up to 200 to 900 eggs in a sac within the web. The eggs hatch in about thirty days, have one molt, then escape the web and "balloon" to a suitable spot to settle in. Ballooning is done by spinning a strand of silk and letting the wind blow the spiderling to the new location. Young are cannibalistic—only one to twelve young survive from each egg case.
HABITAT: Buildings, rodent holes and burrows, barns, garages, basements, outdoor toilets, hollow stumps, trash, brush, vegetable gardens, and dense vegetation. They particularly like tomatoes and grapes.
FEEDING HABITS: Mostly very small insects.
ECONOMIC IMPORTANCE: Bites can be very dangerous, especially to children and debilitated people.
NATURAL CONTROL: Mud daubers and predatory insects.
ORGANIC CONTROL: Physical removal of webs. Outdoor toilets are the most common place where people are bitten. Spray with citrus products and diatomaceous earth products.
INSIGHT: Bites cause little or only momentary pain, but the poison causes severe cramping and aching pain from ten to sixty minutes after the bite. The pain spreads to all

the skeletal muscles of the body and causes severe hardening of the abdomen. Most deaths are children and the sick and debilitated. Seek prompt medical attention.

A Howard Story

Friends of mine at Marshall Grain in Fort Worth called one day to invite me to see a large black widow they had captured. I had never seen a live one, so I hurried over to take the photo you see in this book. The spider had hatched a brood of young spiders and had been alive for quite a while in the jar. But it was over the next several months that we learned a remarkable fact about female black widow spiders. Not only do they eat the poor puny male after mating, they don't seem to need the male at all, at least not very often. This female continued to produce egg sacs—five, in fact, before she died—and all of them produced baby black widows, lots of them.

BLISTER BEETLE

COMMON NAMES: Black Blister Beetle, Margined Blister Beetle, Silver Blister Beetle, Spotted Blister Beetle, Striped Blister Beetle
SCIENTIFIC NAME: Order Coleoptera, family Meloidae, *Epicauta* spp.
SIZE: Adult—½" to 1"
IDENTIFICATION: Adult beetles are long and slender with narrow necks and heads. They have black or yellow stripes; some are solid gray in color, others blue, purple, green, or brown.
BIOLOGY AND LIFE CYCLE: Complete metamorphosis. Cylindrical eggs laid in the soil in the summer. Larvae vary in appearance with each instar. Younger instars are lighter in color. One generation per year. Overwinter as larvae in the soil.
HABITAT: Many plants, especially food crops. Lower leaves of tomato and potato plants.
FEEDING HABITS: Larvae of some species like to eat grasshopper eggs. Adults eat various plant leaves. Especially a problem on vegetable plants and in alfalfa hay. Like foliage and fruits. Larvae are predaceous.
ECONOMIC IMPORTANCE: Reported to be extremely dangerous to horses if eaten accidentally in hay. Not considered to be a big problem otherwise.
NATURAL CONTROL: Establish strong biodiversity.

ORGANIC CONTROL: Dust all-purpose flour. Spray mixture of manure compost tea, molasses, and citrus oil.
INSIGHT: All blister beetles produce an irritating substance called cantharidin, which can blister the skin. It is also reported that the beetle will kill horses if they eat alfalfa containing the insect.

A Malcolm Story

When still a kid at home, I remember a neighbor who had a swarm of the ash gray (we called them silver) blister beetles that covered an acre on his farm, millions of them. That was one time we didn't argue with our parents when they told us to wear shoes. A couple of the kids got blisters from smashing or rubbing the beetles hard enough to get the oil on their skin.

The beetles always moved into my potato patch first and then into the tomatoes. They fed on the leaves within 6 inches of the ground, and it was late enough in the growing season to sacrifice a few lower old leaves without losing fruit production. If I saw them headed toward smaller plants, I would head them off and chase them in a different direction by banging some pans together. It was kind of fun, like herding miniature sheep.

On our second farm we had a wildflower called Texas poppy. Even though it looks pretty in bloom, it could easily become a troublesome weed. But we have a big beautiful golden blister beetle, a solitary species that feeds on the seedpod of the poppy, keeping it in check.

BLOOD SUCKER—see Kissing Bug

BOLL WEEVIL—see Cotton Boll Weevil

BORER—Borers are the larvae of various beetles, moths, and some flies. In general, they are controlled by having healthy, well-drained soils and adapted plant varieties. Treatment includes releasing beneficial nematodes and trichogramma wasps and applying Tree Trunk Goop (see Appendix C). See Cottonwood Borer, Locust Borer, Peach Tree Borer, Squash Vine Borer

BOXELDER BUG

COMMON NAME: Boxelder Bug
SCIENTIFIC NAME: Order Heteroptera, family Rhopalidae, *Boisea* spp.
SIZE: Adult—½"
IDENTIFICATION: True bugs with grayish brown to black coloring and red highlighting.
BIOLOGY AND LIFE CYCLE: Eggs are laid in cracks of bark and on leaves. Nymphs are bright red. Adult females hibernate in protected spots and produce two or more generations.
HABITAT: Building structures, boxelder and ash trees. Will enter structures especially in the fall.

Silver blister beetle on tomato (B)   *Spotted blister beetle* (B)

Boxelder bugs (H)

Braconid wasp (BP)

Braconid wasp pupae in fully formed cocoon (B)

Naked braconid wasp pupae (B)

FEEDING HABITS: Feed mainly on the seeds of female boxelder trees. They will also eat foliage and flowers of ornamental plants and orchard crops. Injury is usually minimal.

ECONOMIC IMPORTANCE: Little if any.

NATURAL CONTROL: Birds and lizards.

ORGANIC CONTROL: Citrus oil or a mixture of manure tea, molasses, and citrus oil will kill them, but it really isn't necessary.

INSIGHT: Cut down the boxelder trees if you really don't want boxelder bugs around. May become a nuisance in the fall by congregating on trees, porches, and walls. They don't bite or harm anything around the house.

Braconid pupae cocoons on caterpillar larva (B)

Braconid pupae cocoons on caterpillar larva (B)

BRACONID WASP

COMMON NAMES: Braconid Wasp, Parasitic Wasp

SCIENTIFIC NAME: Order Hymenoptera, family Braconidae, many species

SIZE: Adult—1/16" to 5/8"

IDENTIFICATION: Small wasps are black, brown, yellow, or red. They are often metallic and shiny. Pupae can be seen connected to outside of host insects like caterpillars.

BIOLOGY AND LIFE CYCLE: Adult wasps lay eggs in the bodies of host insects, usually aphids and caterpillars. Larvae are white and wormlike and develop within the host. Several generations a year. Hibernate as larvae or pupae in host insect. Silken cocoons in various forms can be seen on the backs of caterpillars. The naked braconid wasp species does not form a cocoon. Complete metamorphosis.

HABITAT: Wherever they can find caterpillar and

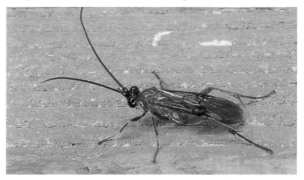
Braconid wasp adult (B)

Braconid pupae on green caterpillar (H)

Braconid larvae emerging from hornworm and starting to pupate (B)

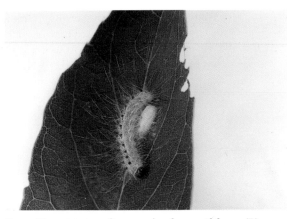

Braconid wasp pupae after emerging from moth larva (B)

Braconid wasp adult (B)

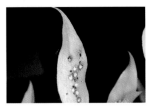

Braconid wasp and parasitized aphids (B)

moth larvae, fly larvae, aphids, codling moths, cabbage white butterfly, and bark beetles.

FEEDING HABITS: Adults feed on nectar and pollen. Larvae eat moth and butterfly larvae.

PREDATORS: Spiders and birds.

ECONOMIC IMPORTANCE: Control aphids, caterpillar and moth larvae, fly larvae, and aphids. Adults help pollinate flowers.

NATURAL CONTROL: None needed.

ORGANIC CONTROL: None needed.

INSIGHT: This little wasp is a classic example of a beneficial insect in that is not widely known but extremely helpful in controlling insect pests. Thousands are killed with every spraying of toxic pesticides. The wasp's pupae stages are greatly varied and interesting. Most have silk cocoons, some just pupate in the hard skin. The silk cocoons vary in appearance. Malcolm photographed one that looks like a cotton ball. We have never seen it recorded in any other book.

A Malcolm Story

For years I was finding silky cotton balls with a half-inch hole through the center and a three-eighths-inch-wide slit across the bottom. It was about two inches long and one and a half inches in diameter. I was finding these balls floating around the upper foliage of my tomato or potato patches but couldn't find them identified in books; experts couldn't even tell me if they were of plant or animal origin. After a few years, the mystery was finally revealed. I found a big tomato hornworm with little white larvae eating holes in its skin and coming to the outside and spinning a silky cotton ball. The shrinking, dying hornworm fell free of the cotton ball and down to the ground for the ants to feed on.

Some braconid species don't bother with the cotton ball—they just spin their own little cocoons. Others don't bother with a cotton ball or spinning a cocoon but just crawl out and attach to the leaf that the hornworm was feeding on and pupate with no cocoon. There are still other species that pupate in individual cocoons, standing straight up on the back of dying hornworms or other big larvae.

Parasitized aphids can be found on almost any leaf infested with aphids. The parasitized aphid will be ballooned, shiny, and a beige or brownish color. When the wasp reaches adulthood in the aphid, it cuts a perfect round door to crawl out.

Adult braconid wasps mate and then deposit eggs in troublesome plant-eating insects of all kinds. Each female can deposit hundreds of eggs. She may deposit all her eggs in one host, but if the wasp species attacks small insects like aphids, she will deposit only one per host.

I had the pleasure of watching a very active braconid female in action one day. She moved so fast I could never get a good photo of her. She was on a weed heavily infested with red aphids. When I first noticed her, she was at the edge of the colony working her way toward the heaviest aphid population. She was parasitizing a very small aphid, skipping the large aphids. She probably avoided them because their skin was too tough, or maybe she realized the adult aphid might die of natural causes and not live long enough for her egg to hatch and reach maturity as an adult wasp.

In nature most all wasps are beneficial; however, the little ones aren't well recognized, probably because they don't draw attention with painful stings.

BROCHYMENA

COMMON NAMES: Brochymena, Rough Stink Bug, Tree Stink Bug

SCIENTIFIC NAME: Order Heteroptera, family Pentatomidae, *Brochymena* spp.

SIZE: Adult—½" to ⅝"

IDENTIFICATION: Stink bug shaped, brown to mottled gray, dull and roughly pebbled. Long head with antennae are located far in front of the compound eyes. Long beak and toothlike projections on side of pronotum.

BIOLOGY AND LIFE CYCLE: Adult female lays clusters of pearl-white eggs on twigs, branches, and leaves in the spring. Nymphs hatch and grow slowly into adults that overwinter in mulch, cracks, and crevices. One generation per year. Incomplete metamorphosis.

Brochymena (B)

HABITAT: Fruit tree orchards, forests, and landscape trees.

FEEDING HABITS: Like to eat juicy caterpillars and other soft insects. Actually they just suck out the juice, using their piercing and sucking mouthparts.

ECONOMIC IMPORTANCE: Beneficial. Control troublesome caterpillars and other insect pests.

NATURAL CONTROL: None needed.

ORGANIC CONTROL: None needed.

INSIGHT: Extremely well-camouflaged insects that blend in with tree bark. First notice of these bugs leads most people to think it's a pest stink bug.

BROWN LACEWING — see Lacewing

BROWN RECLUSE SPIDER

COMMON NAMES: Brown Recluse, Violin Spider, Fiddleback Spider

SCIENTIFIC NAME: Order Araneae, family Loxoscelidae, *Loxosceles reclusa*

SIZE: Adult—1" to 1½"

IDENTIFICATION: Adults are light brown in color and have very long legs. Females are larger than the males and have a distinctive dark brown violin shape on the back. They make irregular webs.

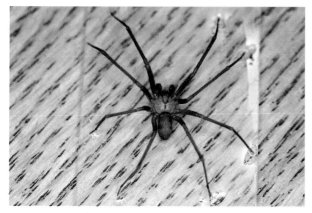

Brown recluse spider (H)

BIOLOGY AND LIFE CYCLE: Incomplete metamorphosis. Females produce one to five egg sacs with a total of 30 to 300 eggs that hatch in one month. Nymphs pass through eight instars (young forms resemble adults). Total life cycle is about one year. Adults can live from two to five years. They bite in defense when they sense pressure (in clothes or bedding).

HABITAT: Under rocks, in loose papers, boxes, clothing, bedding, and shoes. Webs are used as a place to hide rather than to catch prey.

FEEDING HABITS: They hunt at night and feed on various insects.

ECONOMIC IMPORTANCE: Brown recluse spiders help control several pest insects, but their bite can cause a serious wound and in rare cases the loss of a limb.

NATURAL CONTROL: Other spiders, wasps and lizards.

ORGANIC CONTROL: Physical removal of webs. Vacuum often and spray problem areas with citrus products. Freeze boxes of infested papers for forty-eight hours. Use diatomaceous earth outdoors and boric acid products indoors.

INSIGHT: Bites don't hurt at first but become extremely painful later. There is no antivenin. Shake out clothes that have been on or near the ground overnight or hanging in the closet or garage for a long period.

A Howard Story

One of my listeners sent an interesting report on brown recluse spiders. She has been trying to control them for fifteen years and discovered that a similar-looking spider actually kills the recluse. The nonpoisonous spiders have no fiddle on the back but do have black knobs at the joints of the legs. This is apparently what is called the spitting spider. See non-medical device in appendix.

BUG — True bug (Heteroptera) is the correct common name for a group of insects that includes several pest species but also many predatory bugs that attack soft-bodied insect pests such as aphids, beetle larvae, small caterpillars, and thrips. Assassin bugs, ambush bugs, damsel bugs, minute pirate bugs, and spined soldier bugs are beneficial true bugs. As opposed to beetles (Coleoptera), which have a straight-line connection between wing covers, bugs have overlapping wings, which give a diamond-shaped appearance to the back of the insect. See Assassin Bug, Bed Bug, Bigeyed Bug, Boxelder

True bug

Bug, Chinch Bug, Damsel Bug, Flower Bug, Harlequin Bug, Kissing Bug, Lace Bug, Leaffooted Bug, Minute Pirate Bug, Tarnished Plant Bug

BUFFALO GNAT

COMMON NAMES: Black Fly, Buffalo Gnat, Turkey Gnat
SCIENTIFIC NAME: Order Diptera, family Simuliidae, *Simulium meridionale*
SIZE: Larva—¹⁄₁₆" to ⅛", adult is about one-fourth the size of a house fly.
IDENTIFICATION: Eggs are shiny and creamy white, changing to black; larvae are light brown to black, cylindrical, twelve-segmented, with fan-shaped filamentous structures on the head. They attach to rocks with sucker devices on their rear end. Females lay up to 800 eggs on water surfaces or aquatic plants, logs, or rocks. Adults are stout-bodied big flies. Wings are broad and iridescent. Hump-backed, grayish with short antennae. Single pair of wings.
BIOLOGY AND LIFE CYCLE: Found in huge swarms in late spring and early summer where swiftly flowing streams provide aerated water for the larvae to develop. Larvae attach to the rocks and other objects, including vegetation and concrete structures. After several molts, the larvae spin a basketlike cocoon in which to pupate in the water. Adults emerge from T-shaped slits in the cocoon and float to the surface in gas bubbles.
HABITAT: Larvae are found in running water feeding on microorganisms.
FEEDING HABITS: Males and females feed on flower nectar. In addition, the females need blood, which they get from several birds and mammals. Larvae feed on small crustaceans, protozoa, algae, bacteria, and decaying organic matter. The fan-shaped structures on the head are for trapping food from the water.
ECONOMIC IMPORTANCE: Buffalo gnats will attack cattle, horses, mules, hogs, turkeys, chickens, sheep, dogs, ducks, cats, and wild animals.
NATURAL CONTROL: Biodiversity.
ORGANIC CONTROL: Natural diatomaceous earth and citrus products, herbal skin treatments for people. Vanilla sprays seem to be effective.
INSIGHT: Certain species may be gray or yellow. Turkey gnats and similar species have caused severe problems for cattlemen along the Sulfur River in northeastern Texas and Arkansas. In 1990 the pest spread into East Texas.

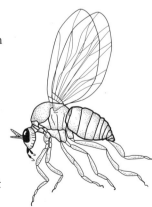

Buffalo gnat

According to Extension entomologist James V. Robinson, turkey gnats have been responsible for large kills of backyard poultry flocks. They also bite people.

BUMBLE BEE

COMMON NAME: Bumble Bee
SCIENTIFIC NAME: Order Hymenoptera, family Apidae. Bumble bee—*Bombus* spp. Carpenter bee—*Xylocopa* spp.
SIZE: Adult—⅓ to 1"
IDENTIFICATION: Adults are fat, black, and fuzzy, with yellow bands on the body and spurs on the hind legs. Carpenter bees can be solid black.
BIOLOGY AND LIFE CYCLE: Eggs are laid in nests in cavities in the soil. They especially like abandoned field mouse nests. They have several broods per year. Larvae are fat, white grubs that stay in the nest's cells. Young queens hibernate, other forms usually die in winter. Carpenter bees or cedar bees are very similar but nest in wooden fences, patio covers, wood shingles, roof eaves, and door and window sills. They like soft cedar wood. Complete metamorphosis.
HABITAT: Wood structures, soil, and in stalks of yucca and agave.
FEEDING HABITS: Worker bees feed on the nectar of many flowering plants.
PREDATORS: Praying mantids, armadillos, and humans.
ECONOMIC IMPORTANCE: Pollination of ornamental and food crops; however, they are less effective than honeybees.
NATURAL CONTROL: Birds, wasps, and praying mantids.
ORGANIC CONTROL: If necessary, can be controlled with soapy water or citrus products or repelled with hot pepper products.
INSIGHT: Bumble bees pack a powerful sting. If you don't threaten them, they usually don't sting, but they can and will if threatened. Plant pollen- and nectar-producing flowers to attract them. Praying mantids catch and eat old, slow, and not very alert bees. Bumble bees living in the ground can sometimes become very aggressive, especially when disturbed by lawn mowers or other

Bumble bee (H)

equipment. To control, go out after dusk when the bees have gone back into the ground. Use a flashlight covered with red cellophane (bees and wasps can't see red). Pour citrus oil, Garden-Ville Fire Ant Control (see Appendix C), or soapy water into the opening and cover it with a large rock (another tip: run away quickly). Remember that bumble bees in the garden are usually not aggressive and are highly beneficial, so hurt these friends only as a last resort. For nests under decks or outbuildings, put honey with a touch of boric acid in a small lid connected to the end of a stick.

BUTTERFLY

COMMON NAME: Butterfly
SCIENTIFIC NAME: Order Lepidoptera, several families, many species.
SIZE: Varies widely.
IDENTIFICATION: Beautiful big wings and long antennae with clubbed tips.
BIOLOGY AND LIFE CYCLE: Complete metamorphosis. Larvae are caterpillars, many of which eat plants and are troublesome.
HABITAT: Many ornamental and food crops.
FEEDING HABITS: Adults eat nectar from flowers.

Monarch butterfly (H)

Swallowtail butterfly in three life stages (B)

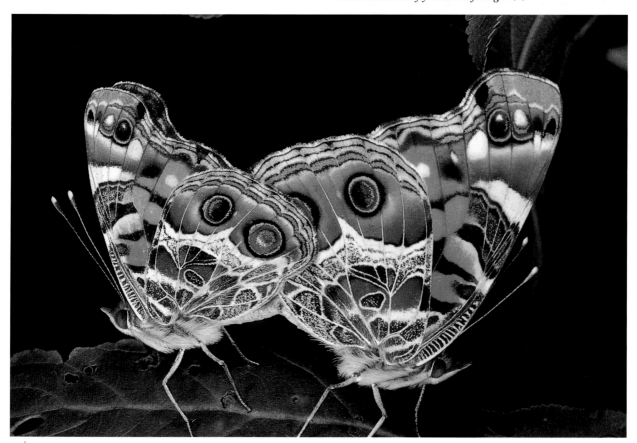

Painted lady butterfly. One of these is no lady . . . (B)

Hairstreak butterfly (B)

ECONOMIC IMPORTANCE: Pollination and garden beauty.

NATURAL CONTROL: Wasps, birds, lizards, and predatory flies.

ORGANIC CONTROL: *Bacillus thuringiensis* sprays if really necessary.

INSIGHT: This is an example of those insects whose life forms are both beneficial and harmful. Adult butterflies pollinate flowers and provide garden beauty, but the larvae or caterpillars can be very destructive pests. Butterflies should be protected because they add beauty and fascination to nature. It would be a dull environment without them. The monarch butterflies have pupal cases that look like jewelry, and the giant swallowtail has larvae that look like bird droppings.

To attract butterflies, plant many varieties of flowering annuals, perennials, vines, shrubs, and trees. Biodiversity with many different flower colors is important for attracting butterflies.

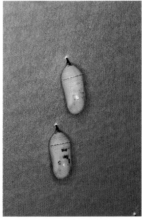

Monarch butterfly pupae (H)

Swallowtail larva (B)

CABBAGE LOOPER

COMMON NAMES: Cabbage Looper, Looper
SCIENTIFIC NAME: Order Lepidoptera, family Noctuidae, *Trichoplusia ni*
SIZE: Adult wing span—1½" to 2", larva—1" to 1½"
IDENTIFICATION: Adults are brownish gray moths with silvery spots in the center of each wing. Active at night. Eggs are greenish white, round and laid singly on the upper sides of leaves. Larvae are green with pale stripes down the back. They form a loop when walking—thus the name.

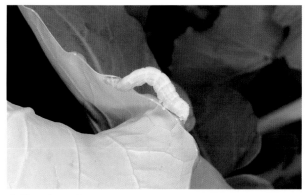

Cabbage looper larva (B)

Cocoon of cabbage looper larva (B)

Cabbage looper adult (ARM)

BIOLOGY AND LIFE CYCLE: Loopers overwinter as greenish to brownish pupae wrapped with delicate cocoons of white thread. The cocoons are so thin that the pupae outlines can be seen. Adult moths emerge in the spring to lay eggs on the surface of leaves. Larvae emerge and feed from two to four weeks and then spin cocoons similar to the ones used to pass the winter. Three to four generations per year or more. The number of worms increases with each generation. Complete metamorphosis.
HABITAT: Vegetable gardens, especially those with brassicas. Enjoy cabbage, broccoli, celery, kale, parsley, peas, potatoes, cauliflower, brussels sprouts, lettuce, beans, radishes, tomatoes, and other garden crops.
FEEDING HABITS: Larvae eat lots of holes in green leaves.
ECONOMIC IMPORTANCE: Destruction of food crop foliage.
NATURAL CONTROL: Trichogramma wasps, birds, paper wasps, and yellow jackets. Loopers are usually controlled by natural diseases and parasites; these function effectively only in an organic program.
ORGANIC CONTROL: Bt (*Bacillus thuringiensis*) products.
INSIGHT: Even the organiphobes recommend Bt because the chemical poisons don't work on this animal. Here is a quote from a 1962 college text: "The looper caterpillars are often almost completely destroyed, usually late in the season, by a wilt disease which causes their bodies to rot." *Bacillus thuringiensis* was the wilt pathogen, but not yet discovered, named, and made available to gardeners.

CABBAGEWORM—see Imported Cabbageworm

CADDISFLY

COMMON NAME: Caddisfly
SCIENTIFIC NAME: Order Trichoptera, several families
SIZE: Less than 1"
IDENTIFICATION: Adults have long legs and four brownish wings covered with hairs. Antennae are nearly as long as the body. Larvae are aquatic and often in cases.
BIOLOGY AND LIFE CYCLE: Larvae live under water, some in cases, some just clinging to stones. Eggs are laid in ropes or masses in or near water, often under stones. Complete metamorphosis.
HABITAT: Sunny areas near water. Adults fly by day.

Caddisfly adult (B)

Calligrapha beetle (H)

FEEDING HABITS: Most adults do not take in food. Larvae feed on small aquatic animals and bits of vegetation.

ECONOMIC IMPORTANCE: Important source of food for trout and other fish.

NATURAL CONTROL: None needed.

ORGANIC CONTROL: None needed.

INSIGHT: Some caddisfly larvae make a delicate silk net that they use to catch various microscopic organisms in the water.

CALLIGRAPHA BEETLE

COMMON NAME: Calligrapha Beetle

SCIENTIFIC NAME: Order Coleoptera, family Chrysomelidae

SIZE: Adult—⅜"

IDENTIFICATION: Adults are oval, similar in shape to ladybugs, but they are leaf eaters. Head and thorax is dark metallic color; wing covers are ivory with dark splotches, dots, lines, and other markings that resemble a Rorschach test. These markings vary greatly. Antennae, legs, and mouthparts are dark in color.

BIOLOGY AND LIFE CYCLE: Complete metamorphosis. Adult females lay eggs on leaves and stems of plants. Larvae hatch and feed on foliage and then drop to the ground to pupate. Adults emerge and also feed on leaves from May to September. Overwinter in the soil as pupae or young adults. At the slightest disturbance, these beetles tend to drop off the tree to the ground to hide, which works well since they are about the color of brown leaves.

HABITAT: Forests, parks, and large commercial properties.

ECONOMIC IMPORTANCE: Not significant. These beetles primarily attack and quickly defoliate sick, stressed trees.

FEEDING HABITS: The larvae and adults feed on the foliage of dogwood, basswood, elm, and other shade trees.

NATURAL CONTROL: Maintain tree health.

ORGANIC CONTROL: Manure compost tea, molasses, and citrus oil spray. Horticultural oil and *Bacillus thuringiensis* products work if sprayed early in the insect's life cycle.

INSIGHT: This very destructive insect is not often seen in Texas. This beetle is a good example of how a sick plant attracts insects that recycle it back into the soil.

A Howard Story

I've only run into the calligrapha one time. During one of my consulting visits to Frito-Lay's National Head-quarters in Plano (the largest organic landscape project currently in the country), I noticed that two of the large American elms had a different look. The foliage was skeletonized and had the look of elm leaf beetle damage. On close inspection, we found these interesting looking beetles. Interesting but ravenous! They were stripping the green out of the leaves in a hurry. The maintenance crew sprayed with pyrethrum, *Bacillus thuringiensis* 'San Diego' and horticultural oil. At the time, we didn't yet know about the power of citrus oil. We were all frustrated about how to control these pests until we finally followed our own advice and realized the cause of the infestation. These old American elms were in terribly poor health. They had in the past been hit by lightning, broken by wind storms, and brutalized by construction activity when the project was built in the 1980s. The calligrapha beetles were just doing their job of helping nature remove these terminally ill trees. We got the message and helped. The trees were removed (improving the look of the area), and we haven't seen a calligrapha beetle since.

CANKERWORM

COMMON NAMES: Spring Cankerworm, Inchworm, Measuring Worm

SCIENTIFIC NAME: Order Lepidoptera, family Geometridae, *Paleacrita vernata*

SIZE: Adult—½" to 1", larva 1"

IDENTIFICATION: Adults are light brown or gray moths with translucent wings. Often called inchworms or measuring worms because of their looping movement. Variable in color, but usually striped longitudinally. Larvae drop from trees on silk threads.

BIOLOGY AND LIFE CYCLE: Female adults are wingless; they climb trees to lay eggs that hatch in the spring just at bud break. Brownish purple eggs are laid in groups in the bark of trees. One brood per year. Larvae hatch in spring when leaves first open, feed for three or four weeks, crawl into the soil to pupate.

HABITAT: Elms, oaks, lindens, sweetgums, apples, and other shade and fruit trees.

FEEDING HABITS: Larvae feed on tree and shrub foliage. They drop down on silk threads to evade predators, then go back and eat some more when danger has passed. Why? Guess they are still hungry.

ECONOMIC IMPORTANCE: Can defoliate broadleaf trees.

NATURAL CONTROL: Trichogramma wasps, birds, and lizards.

ORGANIC CONTROL: Band trunks with sticky material in late winter during egg-laying time. Caution: don't put sticky material directly on the trunk. It will girdle the tree. Put the material on a paper band. Spray with *Bacillus thuringiensis* products as a last resort.

INSIGHT: These little guys will do a lot of damage in the spring to plants like dwarf yaupon holly, but the foliage usually grows back without any long-term injury.

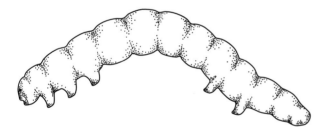

Cankerworm

CANNA LEAFROLLER—see Leafroller

CAROLINA SPHINX—see Tobacco Hornworm

CARPENTER ANT

COMMON NAME: Carpenter Ant
SCIENTIFIC NAME: Order Hymenoptera, family Formicidae, *Camponotus* spp.
SIZE: Adult—¼ to ½"
IDENTIFICATION: Large compared with other Texas ants. Black, reddish brown, or yellowish. May be winged or wingless. Only males and queens have wings. Workers are large infertile females. Thorax in profile is evenly

Carpenter ant (B)

rounded on top. Circle of tiny hairs on the rear end. Red head and thorax, black abdomen.

BIOLOGY AND LIFE CYCLE: Bores into moist, decaying, rotting stumps or logs to form large galleries. Will also infest dry structured wood indoors. Odorous when crushed due to formic acid. Swarms from May to late July. Ant wings seem to function only to disperse the new colonies and prevent close inbreeding. Complete metamorphosis, like all ants.

HABITAT: Nests of excavated galleries in unsound or moist wood.

FEEDING HABITS: Dead and live insects, plant sap, honeydew from other insects, pollen, seed.

ECONOMIC IMPORTANCE: Wood and structural damage; help to break down organic matter.

NATURAL CONTROL: Beneficial nematodes, birds, and lizards.

ORGANIC CONTROL: Boric acid products indoors; citrus products, diatomaceous earth, beneficial nematodes.

INSIGHT: May give you a threatening bite but does not hurt. They do not sting. About the only way to find them is to listen to the walls at night. Where discovered, drill a small hole and dust pyrethrum or boric acid into the wall to kill them. Ants are said to be the most abundant terrestrial animals.

CARPENTER BEE

COMMON NAMES: Carpenter Bee, Wood Boring Bee
SCIENTIFIC NAME: Order Hymenoptera, family Apidae, *Xylocopa virginica*.
SIZE: ⅓" to 1"
IDENTIFICATION: Similar to bumble bees but distinguished by a lack of yellow stripes and by shiny, hairless abdomens. They drill round dime-size holes in wood.
BIOLOGY AND LIFE CYCLE: Live in colonies in trees like cedar, redwood, and pine. Males buzz people within the bee's territory but have no stinger. Females do sting but rarely. After mating in the spring, females build cells in wood and put a small pellet of "bee bread" of pollen and

Carpenter bee (B)

honey in each cell. Each female lays a single egg next to each pellet, and the cells are sealed with plugs of saliva and wood fiber. Larvae hatch and feed on the "bee bread." Usually one generation per year. Complete metamorphosis.

HABITAT: Boards of roofs, wood siding, decks, fence rails, and overhead structures.

FEEDING HABITS: Adults feed on nectar and pollen, larvae feed on "bee bread" made of pollen and honey.

ECONOMIC IMPORTANCE: Pollination of flowers, especially passion flower. Also important for pollinating fruits and vegetables.

NATURAL CONTROL: Birds and microorganisms.

ORGANIC CONTROL: Paint the wood or use wood stain. Treat the wood with castor oil, hot pepper mix, or citrus oil products.

INSIGHT: Carpenter bees are apparently lazy. They don't move around as much as other bees and are even known to puncture the sides of flowers to more easily reach the nectar. This habit is destructive to flowers. The organiphobes recommend Sevin to control these bees. We feel that this toxic poison should never be used.

CASEBEARER—see Pecan Nut Casebearer

CATALPA WORM

COMMON NAMES: Catalpa Worm, Sphinx Moth, Catalpa Sphinx

SCIENTIFIC NAME: Order Lepidoptera, family Sphingidae, *Ceratomia catalpae*

SIZE: Adult wingspan—2½" to 3", pupa—2" to 3", larva—up to 3"

IDENTIFICATION: The larvae are large with a sharp horn at the tip of the abdomen. Larvae have a black streak down their back and are slimmer than the tobacco or tomato hornworms.

BIOLOGY AND LIFE CYCLE: Pupae pass the winter under the soil. Adults emerge soon after catalpa trees are in full leaf. The moths are rarely seen because they fly at night. They are attracted to security lights. Usually two generations per season.

HABITAT: In, under, and within close proximity of catalpa trees.

FEEDING HABITS: Leaves of catalpa and closely related trees such as chitalpa.

ECONOMIC IMPORTANCE: Serious pest on catalpa trees but terrific fishing bait.

NATURAL CONTROL: Parasitic wasps, birds.

ORGANIC CONTROL: Release of trichogramma wasps and *Bacillus thuringiensis* spray as a last resort.

INSIGHT: The adults are big beautiful sphinx moths; the larva is also quite beautiful.

A Howard Story

As a kid in Pittsburg, Texas, I spent a lot of time climbing two catalpa trees in our yard. They are great climbing trees because the bark is smooth. I even tried smoking the long beans after they had dried in the fall. The bean was hard to smoke and didn't taste very good, but it was the cool thing to do at that age. The catalpa worms were always very prolific, and I learned very early that they are one of the very best baits for catching big bluegills or bream.

When I got into landscape design at college, the teacher of my first design class waxed eloquent about what terrible trees these catalpas were. I thought he was wrong then and I still do. Catalpas are good for shade, good for climbing, good for white flowers in the early summer.

CATERPILLAR—see Armyworm, Cabbage Looper, Cankerworm, Codling Moth, Corn Earworm, Cutworm, Imported Cabbageworm, Leafroller, Puss Caterpillar, Tent Caterpillar, Tomato Hornworm, Webworm

CATERPILLAR HUNTER—see Ground Beetle

Catalpa worm (H)

CATOLACCUS WASP

COMMON NAME: Catolaccus Wasp

SCIENTIFIC NAME: Order Hymenoptera, family Pteromalidae, *Catolaccus grandis*

SIZE: Adult—³⁄₁₆"

IDENTIFICATION: Tiny wasp with large red eyes, a broad thorax, short antennae, and an abdomen that tapers to a point.

BIOLOGY AND LIFE CYCLE: Female adult wasp finds a fallen flower bud containing a boll weevil larva. She lays an egg next to the weevil larva. The egg hatches, and the wasp larva eats the weevil larva. The adult wasp may also feed on the weevil larva's blood. Adult wasps live about forty-five days.

HABITAT: Cotton plants. Native to Mexico. *Catolaccus hunteri* is a related species native to the United States.

FEEDING HABITS: Adults and larvae feed on boll weevil larvae.

ECONOMIC IMPORTANCE: Excellent biological control of a major agricultural pest.

NATURAL CONTROL: None needed.

ORGANIC CONTROL: None needed.

INSIGHT: Boll weevil damage in 1994 cost the cotton industry more than $300 million. According to *Agricultural Research* magazine, the figure is probably a lot higher today.

Release 100 to 1,000 catolaccus wasps per acre per week for six to eight weeks beginning early in the spring. Using the beneficial fungus *Beauveria bassiana* also works well on the boll weevil and can be used in concert with the release of catolaccus wasps.

Catolaccus wasp (ARM)

CENTIPEDE

COMMON NAME: Centipede

SCIENTIFIC NAME: Order Chilopoda, several families and species

BODY LENGTH: Adult—¼" to 8"

IDENTIFICATION: These close relatives of insects have thirty legs or more (one per body segment) and range in color from reddish brown to white. House centipedes have extremely long legs extending out all around the body.

BIOLOGY AND LIFE CYCLE: Incomplete metamorphosis. Eggs are laid in the soil; the resulting nymphs are similar to the adults but shorter and with fewer segments.

House centipede (B)

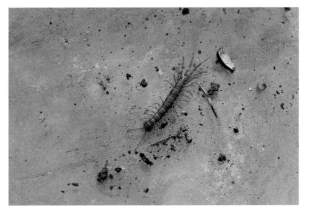

Common centipede (H)

HABITAT: Live in moist, protected places, especially around decaying organic matter—under logs, stones, leaves, bark, and in compost piles, buildings, and basements.

FEEDING HABITS: Feed on small insects, including roaches, clothes moths, and house flies, and sometimes plant roots. House centipedes are predaceous; garden centipedes eat plant roots.

NATURAL CONTROL: Insectivorous animals.

ORGANIC CONTROL: None needed. They are actually beneficial. If they become a nuisance indoors, vacuum them up.

ECONOMIC IMPORTANCE: They have a bite about as powerful as a bee sting, but a bite is rare. They feed on slugs, grubs, worms, cockroaches, ants, and flies, and are considered beneficial around the house.

INSIGHT: The long-legged house centipedes move very rapidly. The large, brightly colored centipedes grow to 8 inches or longer and can inflict a painful bite. We have found them floating in water puddles after rains on top

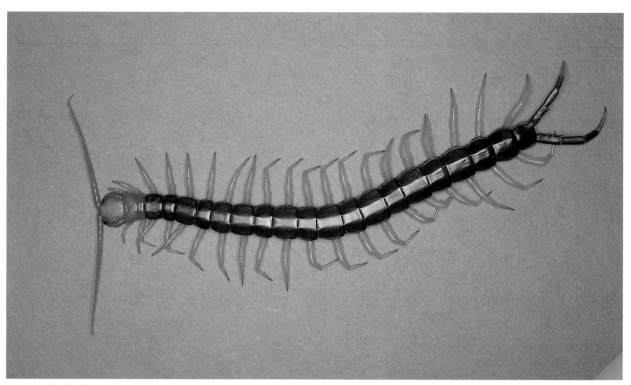

Giant centipede (B)

of Enchanted Rock near Fredericksburg. Millipedes look similar but have two legs per segment and do not have a dangerous bite.

A Malcolm Story

I once took home one of these centipedes in a Ziploc bag, thinking it was dead since it was limp and soggy; but the next morning it was very much alive and clawing to get out of the sealed bag. Could it have been soaking in the water to reconstitute after a drought? It's hard to imagine a big insect like that accidentally falling into a shallow puddle with gentle sloping sides and not being able to swim or crawl out—not with all those feet.

CHEVRON BUG—see Locust Borer

CHIGGER

COMMON NAMES: Chigger, Redbug
SCIENTIFIC NAME: Order Arachnida, family Trombiculidae, *Trombicula* spp., *Entrombicula* spp.
SIZE: Microscopic
IDENTIFICATION: Microscopic animals related to ticks and spiders. Larvae are bright red.

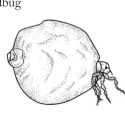

Approximate actual size
Chigger

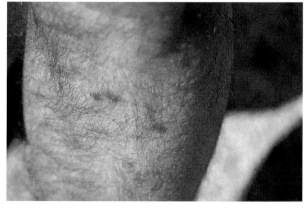

Chigger bites (H)

BIOLOGY AND LIFE CYCLE: Larvae hatch in the spring and are parasites on humans and animals. They inject a digestive juice that dissolves skin cells so they can be more easily eaten. Affected skin will redden and swell. Their numbers are the highest in mid-summer. The adults feed on insects.
HABITAT: Grasslands and weedy unirrigated areas.
FEEDING HABITS: Larvae attach to skin of various animals to feed.
ECONOMIC IMPORTANCE: Cause severe itching and small reddish welts on skin.
NATURAL CONTROL: Increased soil moisture. Some researchers say chiggers have no natural enemies. That may be true, but the imported fire ants will certainly eliminate them.

ORGANIC CONTROL: Sulfur dust is a good repellent. So is lemonmint, also called horsemint (*Monarda citriodora*). Take a hot, soapy bath to remove larvae. Stop the itching with baking soda, vinegar, aloe vera, or comfrey juice.

INSIGHT: If you have to walk through property that's dry and weedy and it's summertime, take a few precautions. First, don't wear shorts. Second, dust your shoes, pant legs, and socks with powdered sulfur. It's available at any nursery or feed store. Rubbing the crushed flowers of lemonmint on your clothing will also repel chiggers.

Chiggers can be controlled with a broadcast application of a diatomaceous earth/pyrethrum product or an application of granular or dusting sulfur at 5 pounds per 1,000 square feet. If you have alkaline soil, the sulfur is also a good soil amendment. If you have acid soil, just don't overdo it. Excess sulfur will kill or severely imbalance the microorganisms in the soil. If your property is watered occasionally, chiggers won't be a problem.

We know one outdoorsman who swears that if you don't wear underwear or socks, the chiggers won't have a place to hide and won't bother you. Sounds a little kinky to us.

CHINCH BUG

COMMON NAME: Chinch Bug
SCIENTIFIC NAME: Order Heteroptera, family Lygaeidae, *Blissus* spp.
SIZE: Adult—1/16" to 1/5"
IDENTIFICATION: Black bodies with white wings with triangular marks on the back. Emit an odor when crushed. Eggs white to dark red, laid in the soil. Nymphs are red with white stripes across the back. Look similar to the beneficial bigeyed bug.
BIOLOGY AND LIFE CYCLE: Incomplete metamorphosis. After hatching, the wingless nymphs are red, then orange, then black, developing a bright-colored band across their back. Two or three generations a year. Adults hibernate in grass.
HABITAT: Lawns; corn and other agricultural crops.

FEEDING HABITS: Feed the most in summer and early fall. They suck the juice from grass leaves through needlelike beaks. They inject a toxic saliva into the plant that causes wilting. Most damage is caused by the nymphs and shows up in circular patterns. They like hot conditions and stressed turf.
ECONOMIC IMPORTANCE: Turf damage. Foliage turns yellow, then brown, then dies. Almost never a problem in well-maintained turf.
NATURAL CONTROL: Healthy soil and turf. When weather turns cool in the fall, a beneficial fungi called *Beauveria* spp. moves in and kills these pests. It appears as a grayish cottony mass of fungal hyphae. Keep lawns moist and don't over fertilize. Bigeyed bugs are a natural enemy.
ORGANIC CONTROL: Diatomaceous earth and compost. Manure tea, molasses, and citrus oil spray.
INSIGHT: Sinking a coffee can with the bottom cut out into the turf and filling with water is supposed to be a way to detect chinch bugs. We question how well this works. Chinch bugs are rarely a problem when turf is kept moist and well maintained.

A friend of Malcolm's spread a lawn with hot compost—some that was still strong with ammonia gas—on a warm summer day; the chinch bugs came to the top by the millions and left the area.

CICADA

COMMON NAMES: Cicada, Dogday Cicada, Dogday Locust, Harvestfly, Harvestman Cicada, Locust
SCIENTIFIC NAME: Order Homoptera, family Cicadidae, many genera and species
SIZE: Adult—1" to 3"
IDENTIFICATION: The big insects that make all the noise in mid-summer. They have wide, blunt heads with big bulging eyes and clear, brittle wings. Empty nymphal skins can be seen attached to trees, shrubs, and buildings in the summer. Skin looks like a hollow June bug skin.
BIOLOGY AND LIFE CYCLE: Males sing in a loud,

Chinch bug (H)

Cicada after emerging from pupal skin (B)

Cicada killer staring down a cicada (H)

sustained, shrill song in the summer. Adults spend about five or six weeks above ground, mate, deposit eggs, and then die. Nymphs have stout brown bodies with large front legs used as scoops. They feed on roots and molt until ready for the last molt. They dig out of the soil, climb a tree, and attach to tree bark or sometimes windows and door screens. Adults emerge during the final molt through a slit in the top, feed for a few weeks, mate, and then lay eggs in slits in tree branches. In two months the eggs hatch and the nymphs drop to the ground and burrow into the soil.

HABITAT: Any treed area, conifers and mixed woods. Also in shrubs.

FEEDING HABITS: Nymphs feed on tree roots. Plant damage comes from the egg-laying slits in stems, which cause tip growth to die.

ECONOMIC IMPORTANCE: Cause little major plant damage. Most serious damage comes from the egg-laying slits in the bark of small branches.

NATURAL CONTROL: Cicada killers.

ORGANIC CONTROL: We know of no effective techniques yet. There are never enough of them in any one place.

INSIGHT: Wrongly called locusts. Females have no sound apparatus. Only males make the sound. They probably defend themselves with their high-pitched sound. The male, which is sometimes called the harvestfly, is responsible for the sad, sustained sound that fills the air on hot summer days. This sound is a mating call and also a means of protection, so loud it hurts the ears of some predators.

CICADA KILLER

COMMON NAMES: Cicada Killer, Cicada Killer Wasp

SCIENTIFIC NAME: Order Hymenoptera, family Sphecidae, *Sphecius speciosus*

SIZE: Adult—1½" to 2"

IDENTIFICATION: Large solitary wasp with black or rusty brown and yellow markings.

BIOLOGY AND LIFE CYCLE: Males can't sting. Females will, but only if forced. Nests are built in the ground. Females dig burrows a foot or so deep where they store adult cicadas that the ladies have paralyzed by stinging. Eggs hatch and larvae feed on the stored cicadas. Fully grown in one week, the larvae pupate into a cocoon, emerging the following summer. Complete metamorphosis.

HABITAT: Active around lawns, vegetable gardens, and oak trees. Nest in the ground.

FEEDING HABITS: Catch cicadas to feed young. Adults eat nectar from summer flowers.

ECONOMIC IMPORTANCE: Little if any other than being a very interesting insect.

NATURAL CONTROL: Encourage biodiversity. All creatures have natural enemies, but at this time we are not aware of any. Probably birds, lizards, and snakes.

ORGANIC CONTROL: None needed; should be encouraged.

INSIGHT: We're asked about this wasp very often, mainly because they scare people when they fly around the garden in the summer. They are actually beneficial and should not be hurt.

A Howard Story

Every year in the summer I get lots of calls and letters about these huge ferocious wasps flying around the garden several feet above the ground. They also seem to be the culprits digging big holes in the garden soil. It's one of my toughest sales to convince people, especially if they are allergic to bee and wasp stings, that this is not a pest but instead a very beneficial inhabitant of the garden. Some people like the sound of cicadas in the summer. I don't. If there were more of these friendly flying beasts, the summer would be much quieter. For a little entertainment, watch a female take a cicada larger than she is back to the nest. She climbs a tree and flies like crazy until she crashes. Then she climbs another tree with her heavy cargo and flies another leg of the trip. Will they sting? Yes. The females can sting if you grab one—so don't.

Adult click beetles mating and eating at the same time. (H)

CLICK BEETLE

COMMON NAMES: Click Beetle, Wireworm
SCIENTIFIC NAME: Order Coleoptera, family Elateridae
SIZE: Adult—½" to 1¼", larva—½" to 1¼"
IDENTIFICATION: Adults are long, slender beetles, usually dull brown or black with bands across the wing covers. Larvae (wireworms) are yellow, orange, or brown cylindrical worms with shiny, hard skin. Eggs are laid in damp soil several inches beneath the surface. Adult beetles can flip in the air to right themselves after being turned on their backs. That's where the click comes from.
BIOLOGY AND LIFE CYCLE: Some species are only a problem in poorly drained soils. Some have a two-year

Click beetle larva (wireworm) (H)

life cycle while others require up to six years to complete a life cycle. Adults overwinter in the soil.

HABITAT: Flowers, leaves, under bark, and in rotten wood. Vegetable gardens and agricultural crops, especially where soil doesn't drain well.

FEEDING HABITS: Wireworms eat small grain seed and seedling roots. Will bore into large roots, stems, and tubers. Will attack beans, beets, carrots, corn, lettuce, onions, peas, and potatoes. Adults of many species don't feed; some eat plant foliage a little.

ECONOMIC IMPORTANCE: Wireworms can severely damage crop production. They are especially hard on newly planted seeds and young root crops.

NATURAL CONTROL: Stimulate beneficial soil life and improve drainage. Spiders, birds, toads, snakes, and beneficial nematodes.

ORGANIC CONTROL: Till the soil and add compost, liquid biostimulants, or a mix of manure tea, molasses, and citrus oil.

INSIGHT: False wireworms are different insects. They are the immature stages of the darkling beetle, a beneficial.

COCHINEAL

COMMON NAMES: Cochineal, Red Dye Bug
SCIENTIFIC NAME: Order Homoptera, family Dactylopiidae, *Dactylopius coccus*
SIZE: Adult female—⅛", adult male—½"
IDENTIFICATION: Females and nymphs are found on the pods of prickly pear cacti under the waxy cotton produced by the insects for protection.
BIOLOGY AND LIFE CYCLE: Incomplete metamorphosis. Only males develop wings.
HABITAT: Desert and arid areas. Prickly pear cacti.
FEEDING HABITS: Juices of cacti, especially prickly pear.
ECONOMIC IMPORTANCE: Juice (body fluid or blood) from the bugs is used as a beautiful red dye.
NATURAL CONTROL: None known.
ORGANIC CONTROL: None needed.
INSIGHT: Clusters of cochineal bugs often feed side by

side, covering large areas of prickly pear like a white furry rug. American Indians used this juice to make a crimson dye. Old drug stores used to sell bottles of cochineal bugs for use as a dye. About 70,000 insects are needed to make a pound of the dye. Cochineal is also used as a food coloring (especially in cake coloring) and permanent dye; it is an ingredient in many beverages, cosmetics, and medicines.

COCKROACH

COMMON NAMES: Cockroach, Roach, Water Bug, Palmetto Bug
SCIENTIFIC NAME: Order Blattodea, family Blattidae
SIZE: Adult—¼" to 1¾"
IDENTIFICATION: Brown, oval and flat-bodied. Antennae are long and slender. Very fast and active at night. Will occasionally fly. You know what they look like. The smaller roaches are German cockroaches; the larger ones are usually American cockroaches or palmetto bugs. Over 3,000 known species.
BIOLOGY AND LIFE CYCLE: Prefer warm, humid conditions. Feed at night on a wide variety of food. Hide in cracks, under floors, and other dark places during the day. They have an unpleasant odor.
HABITAT: Cracks, crevices, cardboard boxes, chimneys, and other dark places that offer protection. Kitchen cabinets, chairs, and tables.
FEEDING HABITS: Will eat any kind of food left accessible. They are attracted into houses for food crumbs and water.
ECONOMIC IMPORTANCE: Ruins food stuff. Most cockroaches live outside and help to decay organic matter. Believed to spread disease, but contrary to popular opinion, they rarely if ever spread human disease.
NATURAL CONTROL: Gecko lizards, scorpions, and beneficial nematodes. Freezing temperatures will kill some species.
ORGANIC CONTROL: Boric acid products, baking soda soap, and sugar baits. Caulking the cracks, crevices, and

Cochineal on cactus (H)

Cockroach being eaten by predaceous stink bugs (H)

Roaches, dead after being attracted to bait (H)

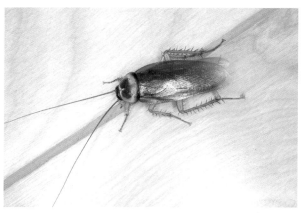

Roach adult (B)

Garden roach (H)

holes in the house so the roaches can't walk right in is the first step in control.

INSIGHT: All creatures were put on earth for a reason, even roaches. They are very important in the breakdown of organic matter. They also eat your food, books, and other possessions, poop all over the place, and may sometimes, although rarely, spread disease.

Howard's Roach Control Program

Roach control is a five-step process:

1. *Exclusion.* Keep them out of your house. Most roaches like it outside until they get hungry, can't find anything tasty there, and walk in through a house's holes or cracks to feast on the water and food crumbs left from dinner. To stop them, use caulking, steel wool, and copper mesh to fill the cracks in masonry, spaces between trim and brick, and holes of all kinds, including spaces around pipes. Put wire screens in air vents and stop up any other entryways.

2. *Elimination of cracks.* Fill cracks and crevices inside the house. One of the best weapons against roaches is the caulk gun. Every time you fill in a crack with caulk, you reduce the number of roaches that your home can

support. Roaches will not mate unless they are nestled in the security of a very small space. A ⅛-inch-wide crack is too wide for roach comfort.

3. *Removal of cardboard boxes.* The honey-combed design of cardboard offers miles of tunnels that are perfect hiding and mating spaces; the glue on cardboard boxes and on paper sacks is attractive food for these critters.

4. *Cleanliness.* Eliminating food and water sources such as dripping faucets, leaks, pet water and food, and dirty kitchens makes your home much less attractive to roaches.

5. *Baits.* Once the roaches are in the house, there's a two-step attack. Boric acid dusted lightly where the bugs are seen is very effective, but use light dustings. If you can see the material after an application, so can the roaches—so you've put out too much. Diatomaceous earth products also work well. Effective homemade baits can be made by mixing one part sugar and one part Arm and Hammer detergent. A pinch of boric acid added to this mix makes it even more effective. This mixture has extremely low toxicity, but it still should be put in bait stations or lids and located in areas where pets and children can't get to them. Stronger baits can be made by mixing two parts flour, one part boric acid, and one part sugar and moistening enough to form little balls or cakes. Add more moisture from time to time to keep them more appetizing. Always keep all pesticides, even these organic home remedies, away from the pets and the kiddos.

6. *Spray.* The best organic sprays for roaches are the citrus products.

A Malcolm Story

I was once asked to give a slide presentation to the San Antonio Pest Control Association. I thought these guys would surely ridicule my philosophy on insect control, but to my surprise they were mostly in agreement. They agreed that without nature's help there is no way we can control insects. During my program I mentioned that I would like to believe all insects are here for a reason but the roaches were causing some doubt. Here they came to my rescue and told this story. When the early English mariners were sailing the high seas into India and Africa, they discovered the African daisy and its magical powers at killing insects. They crushed up the flowers and sprinkled the pieces around the ships to rid themselves of those nasty roaches, which it did. But then a worse pest took over—body lice. With some investigation, they discovered the roaches were preying on the lice. Then the roaches were quickly welcomed back.

CODLING MOTH

COMMON NAME: Codling Moth
SCIENTIFIC NAME: Order Lepidoptera, family Tortricidae, *Carpocapsa pomonella*
SIZE: Adult—¾", larva—about 1"
IDENTIFICATION: Adult moths are grayish brown with lacy brown lines on the forewings. Larvae are pink with brown heads. Eggs are flat, white, and laid singly on leaves, twigs, and fruit buds.
BIOLOGY AND LIFE CYCLE: Two generations per year. Overwinter as a full-grown pink larvae in thick silken cocoon in mulch or on bark.
HABITAT: Orchards and forests.
FEEDING HABITS: Larvae enter apples, pears, quince, hawthorns, crabapples, and walnut at the blossom end. When grown, they tunnel out, leaving brown waste. The second brood eats fruits from any end. They eat large holes from the blossom end or side down to the core and ruin the fruit.
ECONOMIC IMPORTANCE: Destruction of fruit crops.
NATURAL CONTROL: Braconid wasps, trichogramma wasps, and naturally occurring microorganisms. Birds, especially woodpeckers, and ground beetles.
ORGANIC CONTROL: Pheromones and pheromone traps.
INSIGHT: In the past this insect has been one of the hardest pests to control. Pheromones and pheromone traps have mostly eliminated the problem. The codling moth was accidentally introduced into North America. Like other introduced pests, natural enemies didn't come along with them. It may take nature many years to regain a natural balance.

COLORADO POTATO BEETLE

COMMON NAMES: Colorado Potato Beetle, Potato Beetle, Potato Bug, Tater Bug
SCIENTIFIC NAME: Order Coleoptera, family Chrysomelidae, *Leptinotarsa decemlineata*
SIZE: Adult—⅓"
IDENTIFICATION: Striped hard-backed beetles that look similar to lady beetles but are larger.
BIOLOGY AND LIFE CYCLE: Adults are yellow with black stripes on the wing covers and dark dots behind the head. Larvae are reddish with black legs and head. They change color to pink or orange with two rows of black spots on each side. Eggs are yellow-orange laid in rows. Young unmated adults hibernate through the winter in trash piles, old lumber, and other litter on the ground.
HABITAT: Eggplant, potatoes, tomatoes, and other nightshade plants.
FEEDING HABITS: Adult beetles and larvae feed on plant leaves.

Codling moth adult (BP)

Colorado potato beetle adults (B)

Codling moth larva in apple (BP)

Colorado potato beetle depositing eggs (B)

Colorado potato beetle larvae hatching (B)

ECONOMIC IMPORTANCE: Food crop destruction.
NATURAL CONTROL: Ground beetles, assassin bugs, and giant wheel bugs.
ORGANIC CONTROL: *Bacillus thuringiensis* 'San Diego'.
INSIGHT: Malcolm often tells a story about hand-picking potato beetles (see Insight section in Giant Wheel Bug entry) and often gets the argument that this approach is not practical for really large acreage. However, he knows a woman from Germany who tells about her childhood school shutting down for up to two weeks so the students could go pick potato beetles in the big fields. She said they always looked forward to beetle-picking time. We could do the same in this country; it would be a great educational experience for children and organizations like 4-H, FFA, and Boy and Girl Scouts.

CONE NOSE BUG — see Kissing Bug

CORN EARWORM

COMMON NAMES: Corn Earworm, Tomato Fruitworm, Cotton Bollworm, Sorghum Headworm
SCIENTIFIC NAME: Order Lepidoptera, family Noctuidae, *Heliothis zea* or *Helicoverpa zea*
SIZE: Adult wingspan — 1½", larva — ¾" to 1⅛"
IDENTIFICATION: Adult moths are greenish gray or brown with black markings on the forewings. Larvae vary greatly from green to white to red to dark gray. Eggs are yellow or light brown, spherical domed, ridged, usually laid singly on host plants.
BIOLOGY AND LIFE CYCLE: Night flying, up to seven generations per year. Larvae have five or six molts, grow to maturity in a few weeks, then crawl into the ground, burrow to 6 inches, and pupate. Adult emerges in two or three weeks at night and finds a sheltered place to expand and dry its wings. Adults mate, live about two weeks; females deposit up to 3,000 eggs. About three generations a year. The last pupal stage overwinters. Pupae overwinter in the soil.

Corn earworm larva on corn (H)

HABITAT: Beans, corn, peas, peppers, potatoes, squash, tomatoes — even roses and cotton.
FEEDING HABITS: Larvae eat the foliage and buds of many crops such as tomatoes, beans, cotton bolls, lettuce crowns. They enter the corn ears at the tip, eat the kernels at the end, and leave masses of moist castings that cause mold to form. They enter the stem end of tomatoes. Called tomato fruitworm when eating tomatoes. The larvae are cannibalistic if they run into one of their own.
ECONOMIC IMPORTANCE: A cosmetic problem for home gardeners. Not seriously damaging to corn crops, but considered one of the most destructive pests to other agricultural crops.
NATURAL CONTROL: Tachinid flies, trichogramma wasps, and naturally occurring *Bacillus thuringiensis*. Bats, birds, and other insectivorous animals.
ORGANIC CONTROL: Bt products for serious infestations. A drop of mineral oil on top of each ear after silks have wilted (sounds like too much trouble to us). Apply beneficial nematodes to the soil. Organic, healthy corn plants are bothered less, and early plantings are damaged less than late plantings.
INSIGHT: It's good to find one of these worms in the end of the corn ear. It's a sign that the corn is fresh and uncontaminated with poison pesticides. They rarely eat more than just the tip anyway. Corn earworm moths have been intensively studied. They fly high and far to find food and have been detected at 10,000 feet. Bats have been found feeding on them at 3,000 feet. Dr. Phil Callahan did much of his studies for his book *Turning into Nature* using the corn earworm. Cotton farmers have learned to spray a natural, nontoxic garlic oil on their cotton during certain stages of plant growth. The garlic changes the taste of the cotton, causing boll worm to stop feeding and starve. A big cotton farmer we know uses garlic as his only pesticide. He mists the crops with the garlic solution the first time as soon as the plants have six leaves and then again every ten days until the cotton has a full canopy. This gives a four- to six-week residual after

the last misting. He found it is best to spray late in the evening and at night, as you should any foliar spray. This natural program can work to control many plant-eating troublesome pests.

COTTON BOLL WEEVIL

COMMON NAMES: Cotton Boll Weevil, Boll Weevil
SCIENTIFIC NAME: Order Coleoptera, family Curculionidae, *Anthonomus grandis*
SIZE: Adult—¼", larva—½"
IDENTIFICATION: Gray-brown to black, hard-shelled weevils with long, slender beaks. The most characteristic feature is the two spurs on the upper part of the front legs.
BIOLOGY AND LIFE CYCLE: Complete metamorphosis. Generation every twenty-five days. Overwinter in the adult stage.
HABITAT: Cotton fields. Overwinter in all kinds of shelter, in trees, under bark, in trash, in fence rows, and under leaves.
FEEDING HABITS: Feed almost exclusively on cotton. They puncture the squares and bolls with their beaks to feed and lay eggs. The larvae then completely ruin the squares and bolls.
ECONOMIC IMPORTANCE: The most notorious pest in the world, causing enormous financial losses. Makes the manufacture of chemical pesticide very profitable.
NATURAL CONTROL: Catolaccus wasps and some braconid wasps, cultural practices, soil building, and establishing beneficial insect populations.
ORGANIC CONTROL: Garlic spray, neem, pepper spray, catolaccus wasps, and beneficial fungi products such as those that contain *Beauveria bassiana.*
INSIGHT: Cotton is being grown organically by some fifty growers, producing over 20,000 acres over the state of Texas. These pioneering cotton farmers are successful and profitable. If just a small percentage of the research money was spent on studying organic control methods, all cotton could be grown without the use of poisons.

Instead of working with these organic growers and helping them, the USDA and Texas Department of Agriculture tried a boll weevil eradication program using broad-spectrum insecticides such as malathion to spray the southern United States. By late 1995 it had already proved disastrous. On the Mexico side of the Rio Grande, the Mexican farmers with no eradication program harvested more than 500 pounds of lint per acre while just across the river on the U.S. side, which had the same soil, rainfall, and other growing conditions, the cotton was destroyed by other troublesome insects that were normally held in check by beneficial predator and parasitic insects. The beneficial insects had been destroyed by the spraying program.

COTTON BOLL WORM—see Corn Earworm

COTTONWOOD BORER

COMMON NAMES: Cottonwood Borer, Long-Horned Borer
SCIENTIFIC NAME: Order Coleoptera, family Cerambycidae, several species
SIZE: Adult—1¼", larva—1½"
IDENTIFICATION: Large black and white beetle with distinctive markings and long antennae, often referred to as horns.
BIOLOGY AND LIFE CYCLE: In mid-summer female adults gnaw holes in the base of trees to deposit eggs, which hatch in about three weeks. The larvae then bore down into the bark and into a major root by fall. Larvae can live up to twenty years in seasoned wood.
HABITAT: Cottonwoods, poplars, willows, and other soft-wooded trees.
FEEDING HABITS: Adults feed on nectar, pollen, bark, leaves, sap, fruit, roots, and fungi. They sometimes eat tender shoots of young trees, causing them to die. Larvae bore and feed inside trees.
ECONOMIC IMPORTANCE: Destruction of fast-growing trees. Help fallen trees decompose in the forest.
NATURAL CONTROL: Maintain healthy soil and stress-free plants. Birds, lizards, and bats.
ORGANIC CONTROL: Avoid planting fast-growing, soft-wooded trees.
INSIGHT: Be careful—they can bite. Not poisonous, but painful.

COTTONYCUSHION SCALE

COMMON NAME: Cottonycushion Scale
SCIENTIFIC NAME: Order Homoptera, family Margarodidae, *Icerya purchasi*
SIZE: Adult—⅕"

Cotton boll weevil adult on cotton boll (ARM)

Adult cottonwood borer (RB) *Cottonycushion scale* (BP) *Crane fly adult* (B)

IDENTIFICATION: White, ridged masses that hold up to 800 red eggs. Nymphs are red with black legs and antennae. Adults are covered in white hair.

BIOLOGY AND LIFE CYCLE: Three generations per year; overwinter in all three stages: adults, larvae, and eggs.

HABITAT: Apples, apricots, camellias, citrus, figs, peaches, pecans, peppers, potatoes, quince, and walnut and maple trees.

FEEDING HABITS: They attach themselves to and feed on leaves and stems.

ECONOMIC IMPORTANCE: Damage to stressed ornamentals and food crops.

NATURAL CONTROL: Ladybugs, especially vedalia and Australian ladybugs.

ORGANIC CONTROL: Spray dormant oil in late winter before spring. Spray horticultural oil, if needed, year round. Apply mixture of manure compost tea, molasses, citrus oil. Garlic-pepper tea also helps.

INSIGHT: Sometimes confused with mealybugs.

Crane fly pupa shell protruding from soil (B)

CRANE FLY

COMMON NAME: Crane Fly (not Mosquito Hawk)

SCIENTIFIC NAME: Order Diptera, family Tipulidae, *Tipula* spp.

SIZE: Adult—½ to 1", larva—¾"

IDENTIFICATION: Adults are long-legged black, brown, or gray flies with long thin bodies and wings. Legs are long and thin and shed easily.

BIOLOGY AND LIFE CYCLE: Adult flies lay eggs in the soil or in debris. Larvae, called leather jackets, are common in partially aquatic or very moist soil.

HABITAT: Commonly found near water and in tall vegetation.

FEEDING HABITS: Larval food includes decaying plant material, fungi, moss, and rotting organic matter. Adults do not eat or bite, just mate.

ECONOMIC IMPORTANCE: Adults seem to have very little importance other than mating and looking interesting. Larvae can mess up bonsai plant soil and other potted plants.

Crane fly adult, pupal case, and larva (B)

NATURAL CONTROL: Cut back on the watering of container plants.

ORGANIC CONTROL: Neem, citrus oil products, or beneficial nematodes.

INSIGHT: At first glance, you think the crane fly is a giant mosquito. Some people call it a Texas mosquito. Thank God it doesn't bite! Because of its extra long legs and narrow wings, it is a clumsy flyer.

The larval stage is a maggot with the head so poorly developed it almost looks headless. The skin is tough, thus the name leather jacket. When the adult is ready to emerge, the whole pupa case pushes up out of the soil about a half-inch. The case splits open on top, and in about five to eight minutes the adult escapes.

The adults have no apparent economic importance. The larvae prefer wet soils, will eat roots, and have been known to cause problems to bonsai plants. A friend had a bonsai Japanese maple that turned yellow. She counted fifty empty pupa cases and the soil appeared to be greasy wet, caused by the activity of the maggots. A large number of crane fly larvae in one location was a good indication of poor drainage and too much water.

CRICKET

COMMON NAMES: Cricket, House Cricket, Field Cricket
SCIENTIFIC NAME: Order Orthoptera, family Gryllidae, *Acheta* spp.
SIZE: Adult—1"
IDENTIFICATION: Adults are dark brown, gray, or black with long antennae.
BIOLOGY AND LIFE CYCLE: Incomplete metamorphosis. Male crickets are the noisemakers. Like to live and breed in warm protected places. Eggs are laid in moist soil. Hibernate in the nymph stage and have one to three generations per year. Feed at night on insects and plants.
FEEDING HABITS: Eat several kinds of plants, especially long sprouts. Indoors they can damage wool, cotton, silk, synthetic fabrics, carpets, rugs, and furs. They also like food scraps, leather and rubber, beans, cucumbers, melons, squash, and tomatoes.
ECONOMIC IMPORTANCE: Keep people awake at night (although Malcolm says it makes him sleep better).
NATURAL CONTROL: Birds and naturally occurring microbes.
ORGANIC CONTROL: *Nosema locustae* products; diatomaceous earth products. Boric acid products that contain an attractant bait are also effective indoors.
INSIGHT: Crickets are commonly grown for fish bait and food for insectivorous pets. Cricket manure is an excellent organic fertilizer. Mole crickets are less common, live in the ground, and eat plants roots. See Mole Cricket.

Striped cucumber beetle (H)

Yellow and green cucumber beetle (B)

Cricket (B)

Black-spotted cucumber beetle (B)

CUCUMBER BEETLE

COMMON NAMES: Cucumber Beetle, Western Spotted Cucumber Beetle

SCIENTIFIC NAME: Order Coleoptera, family Chrysomelidae, *Diabrotica* spp. Striped Cucumber Beetle—*Acalymma* spp.

SIZE: Adult—¼", larva—½"

IDENTIFICATION: Adult spotted cucumber beetles are greenish yellow with small black heads and eleven (some people say twelve) black spots on the back. Two of the spots on the back of the beetle run together, making one butterfly-shaped spot, so this insect is sometimes called a twelve-spotted cucumber beetle. Larvae are beige with brown heads and a brown spot on the last segment. Eggs are oval and yellow. Striped cucumber beetles have stripes instead of spots and are smaller.

BIOLOGY AND LIFE CYCLE: 200 to 1,200 eggs are laid in the soil at the base of plants. Larvae bore into the roots of plants. One to four generations a year. Adults overwinter in plant debris and mulch. They become very active in the spring.

HABITAT: Beans, corn, cucumber, eggplant, melons, peas, potato, squash, tomato, and several fruit trees.

FEEDING HABITS: Adults chew ragged holes in plant leaves, flowers, and fruits. They like cucumbers and cantaloupe primarily. Larvae eat plant roots and stems.

ECONOMIC IMPORTANCE: Eat plant flowers and foliage and transmit brown rot to stone fruits as well as bacteria wilt and cucumber mosaic.

NATURAL CONTROL: Tachinid flies, soldier beetles, toads, and assassin bugs.

ORGANIC CONTROL: Use cover crops and beneficial nematodes. Garlic-pepper-seaweed spray. Use neem and citrus products for heavy infestations. Plant nonbitter varieties. Inoculate seed with beneficial nematodes. This is the easiest and cheapest control. Cover plants from planting to flowering with floating row cover.

INSIGHT: Spotted cucumber beetle is the adult of the southern corn rootworm and is most damaging to young corn. This larva can severely damage the roots of corn, especially sweet corn in poor growing conditions.

CUT ANT—see Texas Leafcutting Ant

CUTTER ANT—see Texas Leafcutting Ant

CUTWORM

COMMON NAME: Cutworm

SCIENTIFIC NAME: Order Lepidoptera, family Noctuidae, many species

SIZE: Adult—1½", larva—1½"

IDENTIFICATION: Cutworms are the immature stages or larvae of drab gray or brownish moths that are active at night. They curl up while at rest or when disturbed.

Cutworm and cut-off tomato plant (B)

Newly hatched cutworms are brown to black. Feed on seedlings of tomatoes, peppers, eggplant, cabbage, and other food crops, cutting the plant off at ground level.

BIOLOGY AND LIFE CYCLE: Adult moths lay eggs in early summer. Larvae hatch within two days to two weeks and feed on grass and other plants for three to five weeks, then form pupae in the soil. Adults emerge at various times during the summer. One to five generations a year. Overwinter as pupae or young larvae.

HABITAT: Soil dwellers that chew off tender shoots as they emerge. Grassy and weedy fields are attractive to moths for egg laying. Spring-planted ornamentals and food crops.

FEEDING HABITS: Cut off young seedlings at ground level. Some will climb up plants and chew foliage as army worms do.

ECONOMIC IMPORTANCE: Several species of cutworms can damage small grains, tomatoes, peppers, eggplant, and cabbage.

NATURAL CONTROL: Trichogramma wasps, birds, frogs, fire ants, and beneficial nematodes. Plant big healthy transplants.

ORGANIC CONTROL: Cutworm collars around plants. Diatomaceous earth or fireplace ashes around plants. Bt (*Bacillus thuringiensis*) products mixed with moist bran and molasses around plants. Release beneficial nematodes. During daylight hours scratch the soil around damaged or cut-off plants and heavily water the soil. The cutworms will float out, then you can step on them or feed them to the chickens. Crushed red pepper and cedar flakes will also help.

INSIGHT: Malcolm noticed that cutworms destroyed around 10 percent of the vegetable transplants annually until the imported fire ant moved in. Cutworms can be spotted easily at night with a flashlight because they reflect the light.

DADDY LONGLEGS

COMMON NAMES: Daddy Longlegs, Daddylonglegs, Granddaddy Longlegs, Harvestman

SCIENTIFIC NAME: Order Opiliones, family Phalangiidae, several species

SIZE: Body—⅛" to ¼", legs—up to 3" long

IDENTIFICATION: Reddish brown, long stiltlike legs; knees are up in the air but body is close to the ground. Body is oval and compact, not divided by a slender waist like spiders.

BIOLOGY AND LIFE CYCLE: Female inserts individual eggs into the soil. One generation a year. Eggs overwinter. The female can overwinter in the southern part of the state.

HABITAT: In caves, around rock buildings, in knotholes.

FEEDING HABITS: We have never seen them eat anything. Some authors say they eat small insects, some say dead insects or any organic matter. They apparently feed at night.

ECONOMIC IMPORTANCE: Add beauty and fascination to nature.

NATURAL AND ORGANIC CONTROL: No control needed. They are not known to have any bad habits. Insectivorous animals are known to feed on them.

INSIGHT: 200 species in North America, around 3,500 worldwide. The different species are hard to tell apart. The adults are found in large gatherings and look as if they are all tangled up, but they easily move apart if provoked. They resemble spiders but are not.

Daddy longlegs (B)

Damsel bug (H)

DAMSEL BUG

COMMON NAME: Damsel Bug

SCIENTIFIC NAME: Order Heteroptera, family Nabidae, *Nabis alternatus*

SIZE: Adult—¼" to ½"

IDENTIFICATION: Adult bugs are tan, brown, or black; they use their distinctively jointed rostrums (snout or beak) to suck troublesome insects dry. Fast-moving and can fly. Similar in appearance to assassin bugs.

BIOLOGY AND LIFE CYCLE: Adults overwinter in protected spots. Female adults lay eggs on stems. Nymphs hatch and immediately start feeding on pest insects. Two or more generations a year.

HABITAT: On the ground and in vegetation of all kinds.

FEEDING HABITS: They hide in flowers to attack and eat aphids, caterpillars, and many other troublesome insects such as thrips, plant bugs, leafhoppers, and tree hoppers.

ECONOMIC IMPORTANCE: Very beneficial predator. Control plant-eating insects.

NATURAL CONTROL: Biodiversity. Any plant in the aster family will attract damsel bugs.

ORGANIC CONTROL: None needed.

INSIGHT: Can bite, so handle with care. Attract damsel bugs by planting alfalfa.

DAMSELFLY

COMMON NAME: Damselfly

SCIENTIFIC NAME: Order Odonata, many families and species

SIZES: Adult—1" to 1½"

IDENTIFICATION: Adults have long, thin bodies; wings are folded together when at rest (dragonflies hold wings out perpendicular to the body). Most are metallic blue, bronze, or green; blue is the most common color.

BIOLOGY AND LIFE CYCLE: Adults lay clumps of eggs on the surface of water or on plants. Nymphs are very active underwater predators.

HABITAT: Swamps, ponds, boggy places, drainage ditches, and lakes.

FEEDING HABITS: Eat flying insects such as gnats and mosquitoes.

ECONOMIC IMPORTANCE: Eat several troublesome insects.

NATURAL CONTROL: None needed. Birds, frogs, and possibly dragonflies.

ORGANIC CONTROL: None needed.

INSIGHT: One of the most beautiful insects in the garden. And they're beneficial.

Damselfly on lantana (H)

DEVIL'S DARNING NEEDLE — see Dragonfly, Walking Stick

DEVIL'S HORSE — see Praying Mantis

DIRT DAUBER — see Mud Dauber

DOBSONFLY

COMMON NAMES: Dobsonfly, Western Dobsonfly
SCIENTIFIC NAME: Order Neuroptera, family Corydalidae, *Corydalus cornutus*
SIZE: Body — 1½", wingspan — 3½"
IDENTIFICATION: Head is almost round, prothorax is squarish and narrower than the head, wings are translucent and grayish color with dark veins. Mandibles of the male are half the length of the body, are curved and tapering to the tips, and are held crossing one another; the female's mandibles are shorter and capable of biting.
BIOLOGY AND LIFE CYCLE: Rounded masses containing hundreds of eggs are laid on rocks and branches near water. Each mass is coated with whitish secretion. Larvae drop or crawl to water to feed. They crawl out of water to pupate under logs and stones where they overwinter. Adults emerge in early summer.
HABITAT: Live around water, especially fast-moving water.

FEEDING HABITS: Adults eat very little if any; larvae prey on water insects.
ECONOMIC IMPORTANCE: Larvae are good fish bait.
NATURAL CONTROL: Fish.
ORGANIC CONTROL: None needed.
INSIGHT: Fisherman cherish the larvae, called hellgrammites, as bait. Adults are beautiful and fascinating. The male's large crossed jaws look fierce, but are only used to hold females during mating and are useless as weapons. The females have shorter jaws and pack a more powerful nip. Neither is dangerous.

Dobsonfly (B)

DOGDAY LOCUST —see Cicada

DOODLE BUG

COMMON NAMES: Doodle Bug, Antlion
SCIENTIFIC NAME: Order Neuroptera, family
Myrmeleontidae, *Myrmeleon* spp.
SIZE: Adult—1½"
IDENTIFICATION: Adults are nocturnal and attracted to
light. They look like miniature damselflies. Long, clear
wings and skinny bodies. Have antennae with knobs on
the ends. Larvae look like little baby dinosaurs and dig
small cone-shaped holes in sandy soil. They are fat little
guys with huge jaws, and they walk backward. They
camouflage themselves with sand.
BIOLOGY AND LIFE CYCLE: Females lay sticky eggs in
sandy soil. Larvae hatch and a dig a cone-shaped hole
with very smooth interior sides. The cones are death
traps for ants and other insects. When they venture in,
the doodle bug dances and causes a cave-in of the sides
of the cone, grabs the bugs with its powerful jaws, and
sucks 'em dry. Overwinter in a silken cocoon. One
generation a year. Life cycle may require two years.
HABITAT: Sandy soil.
FEEDING HABITS: Food includes ants and other small
insects that mistakenly venture into the cones in the soil.
ECONOMIC IMPORTANCE: Help control several troublesome insects, primarily ants.
NATURAL CONTROL: Birds and spiders.
ORGANIC CONTROL: None needed.
INSIGHT: One of the most curious of all insects. The
larvae are ferocious killers, and the adults are frail and
weak fliers.

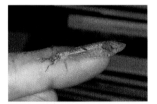
Doodle bug adult (H)

Doodle bug larva (B)

Doodle bug insect traps in sand (B)

A Malcolm Story

As a small child I spent many hours playing with bugs.
The doodlebug occupied many of those absorbing and
intriguing hours. The doodlebug was friendly, it didn't
run away, didn't bite, and it would catch all the ants I
threw into its sand funnel. If the ants tried to escape, it
would throw sand at them and they would slide to the
bottom and get caught anyway.

I would purposely mess up their sand funnel, and
without showing the least bit of anger they would
patiently start rebuilding by going around and around
flipping sand with their head until that sand funnel
would again be perfect. The doodlebug was easy to catch.
I carried them around in my pockets and played with
them all day; when I finally put them back in their sand
home, they would still be there the next day when I
would take them out again and play. Nature must have
put the doodlebug here so children would have something to play with on a long summer day.

DRAGONFLY

COMMON NAMES: Dragonfly, Snake Doctor, Skimmer,
Devil's Darning Needle, Mosquito Hawk
SCIENTIFIC NAME: Order Odonata, several families and
many species
SIZE: Adult—2½" to 4½"
IDENTIFICATION: Adults have huge wrap-around eyes,
long thin bodies, and clear wings that are held out flat
and perpendicular to the body when at rest. Usually dark-
colored—blue, black, and even red. They are fast and
acrobatic fliers. Two pairs of wings. Short, bristlelike
antennae. Tail end of males looks like a grappling hook.
Damselflies are similar beneficial insects, but their wings
are folded on top of the body when at rest.
BIOLOGY AND LIFE CYCLE: Nymphs have large eyes
and slender, cylindrical bodies; they live among weeds
and on the bottoms of ponds. They are very aggressive
and feed on just about anything their size or smaller, like

Dragonfly (H)

Dragonfly (H)

fish and mosquito larva. Nymphs overwinter underwater, where they hide out and feed on other small animals. They crawl up on plant stems in the spring, and the adults emerge from a split in their backs. Nymphs hatch and go through about ten molts. They are vulnerable to birds at this stage. When mature, they can outmaneuver most birds. Eggs are usually laid in water.

HABITAT: Mostly found around ponds and boggy places that have emergent vegetation.

FEEDING HABITS: Its hunting behavior is called "hawking." They eat several flying pest insects, including house flies, gnats, and mosquitoes. They will sometimes eat old, weak, slow honeybees. Can eat as many as 300 mosquitoes a day.

ECONOMIC IMPORTANCE: Beneficial insect.

NATURAL CONTROL: Birds.

ORGANIC CONTROL: None needed.

INSIGHT: Another beautiful creature that adds fascination to nature. The common name devil's darning needle came about because they were supposed to be capable of stitching together the lips of wicked children in their sleep. Adults can fly up to thirty-five miles per hour. They can lift double their weight, take off backward, stop, hover, somersault, and do other impressive acrobatics. They are the most advanced fliers in the animal kingdom.

DUNG BEETLE

COMMON NAMES: Dung Beetle, Scarab Beetle, Tumblebug

SCIENTIFIC NAME: Order Coleoptera, family Scarabaeidae, many species

SIZE: Adult—¼" to 1⅝"

IDENTIFICATION: Small dark-colored beetles that hang around cow and other animal piles. They are usually shiny and brown, green, or black in color, sometimes with a metallic blue or purple luster. Males sometimes have a toothlike projection on the back. Jaws are large and visible. Antennae are very short.

Green dung beetle (B)

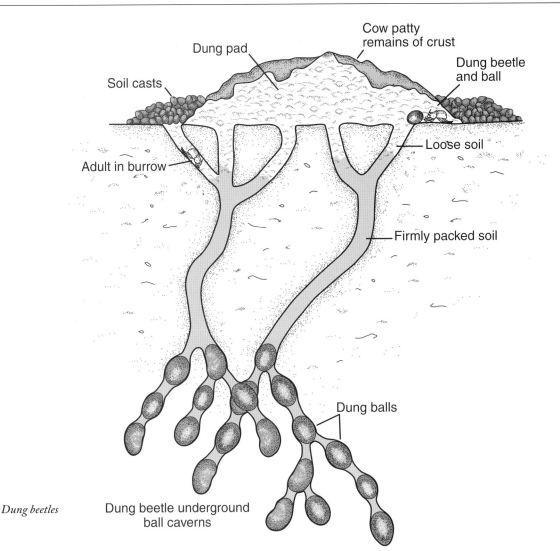

Cow patty
remains of crust

Dung pad

Dung beetle
and ball

Soil casts

Loose soil

Adult in burrow

Firmly packed soil

Dung balls

Dung beetles

Dung beetle underground
ball caverns

Dung beetles, male and female (B)

BIOLOGY AND LIFE CYCLE: Tumblebugs roll manure into balls as large or larger than themselves. Female adults lay eggs in the balls and bury them to supply food for the larvae. Some adults dig burrows below the dung piles. Most dung beetles roll the dung in balls some distance from the piles. A single egg is laid in each dung ball. The larvae hatch and feed on the manure. The male helps in preparing the nest for the larvae. This is the only known case among insects where the male aids in providing for the young.

HABITAT: Soil under and near manure piles.

FEEDING HABITS: Feed on and dispose of fungi, decaying organic matter, dung, and other organic materials.

ECONOMIC IMPORTANCE: Extremely important in the natural cycle of the breakdown of organic matter in the soil.

NATURAL CONTROL: Some species of click beetles, insectivorous animals, robber fly larvae, and fungi.

ORGANIC CONTROL: None needed.

INSIGHT: There are at least 7,000 species. A few species are plant eaters and minor pests.

Dr. Truman Fincher of the USDA-ARS Food Protection Research Lab at College Station has spent a major portion of his career working with dung beetles here in Texas and in many other parts of the world. He calls dung beetles nature's first sanitary engineers. By burying the poop, they cause the following to occur: (1) rapid removal of dung from pasture surfaces so that it doesn't smother the forage or cause a foul area that livestock will not graze; (2) rapid incorporation of the dung into the soil where much less volatile nitrogen is lost to the atmosphere (this buried moist organic matter provides nutrients for teeming masses of microorganisms that turn it into rich, moisture-conserving, healthy soil to grow more healthy, abundant, nutritious forage); (3) breaking the life cycle of many gastrointestinal parasites by burying the dung, in which the eggs and larval stages of the parasite normally incubate; (4) removing the breeding medium (dung) for pest flies like horn flies and face flies, both which cause substantial economic losses in cattle production.

The dung beetles aren't burying the poop as a favor to us and the cows. They are storing it for food for themselves and their larvae and providing a place for their eggs to hatch.

The ancient Egyptians worshipped these insects. The "sacred scarab" can still be found in Egypt and surrounding countries. To the Egyptians, ball rolling symbolized the daily movement of the sun. The tomb of King Tutankhamen contained a pendant depicting the sun god Ra as a scarab beetle rolling the sun across the sky. We don't need to worship these lowly poop rollers, but they are magnificent creatures deserving of our respect.

Incidentally, Dr. Fincher was ordered by the USDA brass to suspend all his experiments on dung beetles during the Ronald Reagan years because a big pharmaceutical company that makes products for controlling flies and parasites complained that his work was interfering with their profit projections. As of press time, Dr. Fincher is still not allowed to continue his research on this beneficial beetle.

A Malcolm Story

While photographing and studying the beetles, I noticed many of them had a number of very small bugs that stayed on their backs. I was watching a smaller black dung beetle and larger greenish one, and each had a different species of bug hitchhiking and licking up the liquids from the manure the beetles were working in. I also noticed that once the pair of beetles had a manure ball rolled a few inches from the manure pile, one of them (according to Dr. Fincher, it was the female) would ride on top and seem to guide the ball around obstacles and in the direction she wanted it to go while the male had his head to the ground and his hind feet pushing. They can move a ball quite fast. I timed them: in a little over two minutes they went 16 feet over some rough terrain, then they both crawled under it to start digging. Soon the ball started disappearing underground. They never remove the dirt from the hole; they just push it above the ball while they keep evacuating under it.

A Dung Beetle Story by Dr. Patricia Q. Richardson

As a child in South Texas, I loved to test the determination of tumblebugs. I was never afraid of them, since they don't spit, bite, or sting. In Freer, Texas, at that time, cows wandered freely through the town. I'd come across a fresh cow pie and watch the tumblebugs arrive. Each would wrestle off a big blob of poop, busily sculpt a ball, and begin to push and roll it away to find a spot to bury it. With curious glee I would create obstacles in their path—a mud mountain over which they would laboriously trudge, a sand valley that they would have to scramble through. Put a stick in the way that was absolutely too big for them to shove the ball over and they would turn and push the ball along the edge until the end where they would return again to their course. They always walked on their front legs, going backwards, using their hind legs to guide the rolling treasure. And they always won, for their tenacity was of longer duration than my four-year-old's attention span.

I was recently delighted to once again observe proliferous dung beetle action in South Texas on a ranch that uses no insecticides. This time it was a big horse plop in front of the ranch house. Within minutes, it was covered with dung beetles—some were tunnelers burrowing straight down through the pile, some were rollers rapidly dividing the loot among themselves. This was about 4:30 p.m. in the afternoon. By the next morning all that was left of the pile was undigested plant debris. The manure was gone, carried underground to provide over time a bounteous feast for many soil life forms. Hail to the "sacred scarab." They are passionate recyclers of one of our most precious resources.

Dr. Richardson is a biologist and researcher at the University of Texas at Austin.

EARWIG

COMMON NAME: Earwig

SCIENTIFIC NAME: Order Dermaptera, several families and species

SIZE: Adult—1⅛"

IDENTIFICATION: Primitive insects with very large pincers in the rear. Usually brown or reddish brown, sometimes with wings.

BIOLOGY AND LIFE CYCLE: Adults lay eggs in the soil from winter through early spring. Nymphs feed on green shoots and plant foliage. Adults like the taste of flowers best; they smell bad when crushed. Nymphs pass through several instars before becoming adults. Eggs are white and round. Two generations per year usually. Hibernation is in the egg stage.

HABITAT: Normal habitat is in ground litter, in soil, under bark, and in crevices, but they will invade homes. They also like young sprouts, flowers, and fruit trees.

FEEDING HABITS: Feed on decaying organic matter, fruit, foliage, mosses, and other insects. They come into homes especially during warm weather. Night feeders primarily as well as scavengers. You may notice some working around your compost pile.

ECONOMIC IMPORTANCE: Earwigs feed on troublesome insect larvae, slugs, and snails, although some do eat food crops and the flowers of ornamental plants.

NATURAL CONTROL: Tachinid flies, spiders, ground beetles, and centipedes.

ORGANIC CONTROL: Citrus products will kill them. Since they are mostly beneficial, we don't recommend it.

INSIGHT: They don't bite, but they do stink! Contrary to the folklore, they don't crawl into your ears. The pincers are used for defense.

ELM LEAF BEETLE

COMMON NAME: Elm Leaf Beetle

SCIENTIFIC NAME: Order Coleoptera, family Chrysomelidae, *Pyrrhalta luteola*

SIZES: Adult—¼", larva—½"

IDENTIFICATION: The adult is a yellow to dull green beetle with black stripes on each side. Small yellow to black larvae.

BIOLOGY AND LIFE CYCLE: Two to four generations a year. Adults feed on emerging foliage and lay eggs soon after. Females lay double rows of yellow eggs on the underside of elm leaves—usually 25 in each spot for a total of 400. Larvae hatch out in about a week and feed on leaves. Overwinter in the adult stage.

HABITAT: Siberian elm, which is commonly misidentified as Chinese elm, is the favorite plant of this insect, although it will eat other elms as well, especially if they are in poor health. American elms are common hosts, and damage will sometimes be present on lacebark elms and cedar elms.

FEEDING HABITS: Larvae eat green tissue from the surface of leaves. Adults eat holes in elm tree leaves and cause a skeletonized look.

ECONOMIC IMPORTANCE: Disfigure elm trees; will sometimes come into the house and be a nuisance. Extremely destructive to ill-adapted elm trees.

NATURAL CONTROL: Birds. Don't plant Siberian elms and cut down the ones you have.

ORGANIC CONTROL: *Bacillus thuringiensis* 'San Diego'.

INSIGHT: Elm leaf beetles are not native. They were brought here from Europe in the early 1800s and have naturalized throughout the country.

Earwig (BP)

Elm leaf beetle adult and eggs (BP)

Elm leaf beetle damage on Siberian elm (H)

FALL WEBWORM—see Webworm

FIRE ANT

COMMON NAMES: Fire Ant, Imported Fire Ant, Red Imported Fire Ant

SCIENTIFIC NAME: Order Hymenoptera, family Formicidae, *Solenopsis invicta*

SIZE: Adults—¹⁄₁₂" to ⅓"

IDENTIFICATION: Four fire ant species are found in Texas. Three are native. The imported fire ant has just about wiped out the natives. The imported fire ant builds its mounds out in the open. Mounds have no visible openings. Stings are painful and sometimes produce a unique white pustule.

BIOLOGY AND LIFE CYCLE: Colonies consist of the brood and several types of adults: winged males, winged females, one or more queens, and workers (which are wingless). The brood is made up of cream-colored eggs, larvae, and pupae. The reproductive winged forms are most prevalent in spring and summer. Mating flights usually happen between April and June. Males die after mating. A queen in a large colony is capable of producing her own weight in eggs every day (1,500 to 2,000). A typical mature fire ant colony will contain 80,000 workers, but some mounds contain as many as 240,000 workers. There can be anywhere from 20 to 500 or more queens per mound. One giant mound was discovered that contained 3,000 queens. Queens can live five years or more. Complete metamorphosis.

HABITAT: Almost any soil but mainly open, sunny areas such as pastures, parks, lawns, meadows, and cultivated fields. Will also infest the vegetable garden. They love eggplant, okra, cabbage, and broccoli.

FEEDING HABITS: Omnivorous, will feed on almost any animal or plant. They eat other insects, oils, sugars, and young seedlings and saplings.

ECONOMIC IMPORTANCE: Tremendous economic problem due to electrical device damage. They also kill baby animals. They do have a beneficial side, however. They eat ticks, chiggers, termites, boll weevils, flea hoppers, cotton bollworms, pink bollworms, tobacco budworms, pecan weevils, hickory shuckworms, flies, fleas, cockroaches, and corn earworms. They are a beneficial predator in controlled numbers.

Fire ants (ARM)

Fire ant mound (TDA)

Fire ant queen (TDA)

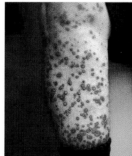

Fire ant stings (B)

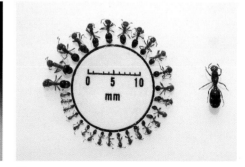

Fire ant measurement (TDA)

NATURAL CONTROL: Lizards, birds, other insects, and microorganisms.

ORGANIC CONTROL: Garden-Ville Fire Ant Control formula, beneficial nematodes, and diatomaceous earth. Beneficial microorganisms in the compost tea and in the gut of nematodes seem to be doing the actual control. Laboratory tests have shown that the beneficial fungus *Beauvaria bassiana* is effective against fire ants. Diatomaceous earth on dry days or mixture of compost tea, molasses, and citrus oil any time. Many gardeners report good results with instant grits and other instant breakfast cereals. Spraying products that contain molasses helps keep them away. Applying ground-up orange and grapefruit rinds to the mounds is another excellent control.

INSIGHT: Research on a parasitic fly from Brazil is being done at the University of Texas at Austin by Dr. Larry Gilbert. It's the native natural control. Texas A&M has also been studying a flylike parasite, *Caenocholax fenyesi*. Spencer Johnson, an entomologist, discovered it while dissecting fire ants.

Howard's Fire Ant Control Program

Fire ants are a blessing and a curse. They kill small animals, foul up electric devices, and bite people. On the other hand, they feed on and thus control fleas, termites, chiggers, ticks, and other troublesome pests. They can only be controlled with an organic program. They are not a natural problem—they are one that we humans created. Fire ants came originally to Alabama from Brazil around 1940. At that time, there was only one queen per mound and the mounds were territorial. Then the "better living through chemistry" people made the brilliant decision to spray a poison called Myrex from airplanes. Instead of forty mounds per acre, the ants began to allow hundreds or more mounds per acre.

To control the fire ants, the first step is to at least try to be smarter than they are. Here's the plan:

1. *Treat individual mounds.* Use citrus compost tea, beneficial nematodes, diatomaceous earth/pyrethrum products, vinegar, or soapy water. A compost tea mixture is the best tool (see Appendix C). Let the mix sit for at least thirty-six hours and then pour the full-strength tea into the center of each ant mound until it is flooded. To make the tea more powerful for fire ant control, add molasses and citrus oil. Garden-Ville Fire Ant Control is the commercial product.

2. *Foliar-feed the site.* Spray all plants, including turf, with a mixture of compost tea, seaweed, natural apple cider vinegar, molasses—known as Garrett Juice (see Appendix C). How does this help with fire ants? Fire ants hate molasses; the microorganisms in the compost

tea attack and kill the ants; and the seaweed simply helps all plants grow, thus establishing biodiversity, which fire ants dislike.

3. *Reestablish biodiversity.* Fire ants love large monoculture fields of bermudagrass or other low-mown grass. They don't particularly like diverse stands of native grasses, wildflowers, forbs, and shrubs. They also don't like other native critters—so stop killing them. Some of the most fire-ant-free properties are those that haven't been sprayed with toxic poisons and have healthy soil conditions. Various microbes, ants, other insects, lizards, toads, snakes, birds, and other animals help keep the fire ants in check.

A Malcolm Story: Ants Away from Home

In all the talks and presentations I give around our part of the country, there is one question that never fails to be asked: "What can we do about fire ants?" The imported fire ant showed up on our farm in the mid-seventies. Right away we noticed they were having an effect on some of our troublesome pests. My wife said she wasn't finding ticks on the kids anymore; about the same time, we stopped losing transplants on the farm.

In early spring we transplanted thousands of tomatoes, bell peppers, and eggplants, and in the fall we planted cabbage, broccoli, and others. We always planted 10 percent more seedlings than we needed because we could depend on the cutworms to destroy about that much of the crop each season. The few mounds of imported fire ants we had then were welcome guests because they were helping control the cutworms and ticks. Before their arrival, we had native fire ants, but they didn't do the complete job of stopping ticks and cut worms.

I didn't see a need to control the ants as long as they were helping me out. But they didn't stop with the ticks and cutworms. They went on to destroy things that weren't pests. Our native fire ants were disappearing, and the red harvester ants were getting fewer and fewer. I haven't seen a single green lizard or horned lizard since 1977. Both were plentiful before the imported fire ants arrived.

The population of the predators rises and falls with the supply of insects they feed on, but not so with the imported fire ants. When their insect prey was depleted, they turned to eating plants. They developed an appetite for okra, tomato, cabbage, eggplants, and any other young tender plants.

I could tolerate the ants as long as they left me alone, but now they have attacked something I use. It's hard to tell what attracts them. They got into an outside extension phone and plugged it so tight with dead ants that it was ruined. They got into an expensive circuit breaker and ruined it, then the water pump pressure switch and finally every light socket and base plug they could get to. They really seem to like electricity.

A Malcolm Story

DE Test on Fire Ants—Disputing Texas A&M

Will diatomaceous earth kill fire ants? It was a question I heard frequently, but couldn't truthfully answer without doing my own testing. I had heard strong arguments both ways.

I got two one-quart fruit jars and put one teaspoon of DE (Brand A) in one jar and one teaspoon of DE (Brand B) in the other. I took my jars and found a healthy fire ant hill. I put a heaping tablespoon of ant hill, including very mad ants, into a jar. Then I put another tablespoon into the other jar. I kept alternating jars until each jar had six tablespoons of ants and soil. I was forced to stop then since the ants were racing up the spoon handle and stinging me. I quickly placed lids tightly on each jar and shook each slightly to mix the DE into the soil.

This test was made about four o'clock in the afternoon. At nine that night, I checked the jars and found all the ants to be healthy and active. At nine the next morning, the jar containing Brand A was full of dead ants. The jar containing Brand B had healthy and active ants. At three o'clock, the ants were still alive, but by eight the next morning, all the ants in the second jar were also dead.

Now I knew that DE would kill ants, but I wanted to know exactly how long it took to kill them. I decided to take the ant samples early in the morning so I could watch them all day. I used the same procedure as before, except that this time I used a third jar without DE as a control. I placed all three jars on my desk so I could watch them throughout the day.

Days went by and nothing happened. The ants were still all alive and appeared healthy. On the ninth day, something finally happened but not what I expected. The ants in the control jar—the one without any DE—were all dead. Not until the thirteenth day did I notice ants beginning to die in the other two jars. By the sixteenth day, the ants in the Brand A jar were finally dead, and on the eighteenth day, the ants in Brand B were dead.

Great! Now I was really puzzled. Instead of proving that diatomaceous earth killed ants, I had proved that it prolonged their lives! More tests were definitely called for, but how? I decided it must have been the difference in the moisture in the jars that caused the difference in the two test results. The first test was taken in the afternoon when the ant hill moisture and humidity were low. The humidity was high in the morning when the second test was taken, so and the ant hill contained much more moisture. Perhaps the moisture kept the ants from losing body fluids and somehow they received energy from the DE to help them survive longer. Another test was needed.

In the third test, I again used three jars, but all contained different brands of DE. All samples were taken from the same mound. I was very careful to get all exactly the same and with as little moisture as possible. The samples were taken on a hot, dry afternoon. By the fifth hour, all the ants in Brand A were dead. The ants in Brand B died by the ninth hour, and those in Brand C were dead by the eleventh hour.

From this test, I learned that DE would kill ants in a low-humidity jar within five hours. But how fast would they die in only dry soil in jars? Back to the drawing board. I used two jars with equal amounts of soil and ants from an ant mound. I shook one jar as if I were mixing in DE, and the other one I disturbed as little as possible. The disturbed ants were all dead in two and a half days. The undisturbed ants took a little longer to die.

All of the jars in all of the tests were kept in the office out of direct sunlight at temperatures between 72 and 82 degrees.

I was ready for one more test to find out if DE alone would kill ants in the field. I found a single big healthy ant hill that had no other hills nearby. I applied about four ounces of Brand A DE and then took a stick and scratched it into the mound. I applied the DE in the afternoon when the humidity was low. The next day at noon I checked the ant mound and found no live ants. Furthermore, unlike many insecticides, the DE appeared to keep other satellite mounds from appearing later. No new mounds appeared in the area.

In summary, all brands of DE tested do kill ants, although some kill faster than others. The method of killing must include dehydration since high humidity seems to limit the effect and even produce beneficial effects. In addition it seemed to me that if given a choice, the ants definitely will stay away from DE. Our latest research shows that DE and citric acid is an excellent fire ant control.

A Fire Ant Story

from One of Howard's WBAP Listeners

Fire ants took up residence in my potted Virginia creeper before I had a chance to plant it. When I discovered the infestation, I immediately moved the plant from my patio to my driveway (using a garden cart, so I wouldn't be stung). I referred to one of your books, then mixed up molasses and a touch of dish soap in a gallon of water. I poured the mixture into the pot and repeated the process once more.

I watched the water run out of the pot and down the

driveway. I didn't see any ants escape that way, and when I turned the pot on its side, *no ants!* I couldn't believe I didn't see any ants. None.

While I am a huge proponent of organic gardening, I'm still amazed when these natural remedies work. Why isn't everyone doing it?

FIREBRAT—see Silverfish

FIREFLY

COMMON NAMES: Firefly, Lightning Bug, Glow Worm
SCIENTIFIC NAME: Order Coleoptera, family Lampyridae, several species
SIZE: Adult—¼" to ¾"
IDENTIFICATION: Small brown and yellow flying beetles that can make controlled flashes of light to attract mates. Head is concealed from above by the shield called the pronotum.
BIOLOGY AND LIFE CYCLE: Complete metamorphosis. Overwinter in the soil as larvae, emerge in the spring. Pupate in early summer. Two weeks later the adults emerge, flying around at night to show off; the females lay eggs just under the soil. The larvae hatch in about a month and feed till fall, when they burrow into the soil for the winter. In the summer the males signal while flying, and the females return the signal from perches on or near the ground.
HABITAT: Nocturnal; live in marshy areas, gardens, and forests. Eggs are laid in moist soil.
FEEDING HABITS: Firefly adults don't eat much of anything, but larvae are carnivorous. They eat other insects, snails, and slugs.
NATURAL ENEMIES: Man—with chemical sprays.
NATURAL CONTROL: None needed—beneficial.
ORGANIC CONTROL: None needed—beneficial.

INSIGHT: Fireflies flash their lights on and off in a distinct pattern. Even the larvae and eggs glow; scientists have no clue about this since it obviously cannot relate to mating. In the adult stage they definitely add beauty and fascination to summer evenings. The larval stage is beneficial. They are meat eaters and dine mostly on young snails and slugs. There are about 130 species of fireflies in this country. In some species the female doesn't have wings. Some researchers claim that fireflies are less active when the moon is full.

FIVESPOTTED HAWK MOTH—see Tomato Hornworm

FLANNEL MOTH—see Puss Caterpillar

FLEA

COMMON NAME: Flea
SCIENTIFIC NAME: Order Siphonaptera, family Pulicidae, *Ctenocephalides* spp. Cat Flea—*Ctenocephalides felis*. Dog Flea—*Ctenocephalides canis*. Human Flea—*Pulex irritans*
SIZE: Pinhead size
IDENTIFICATION: All species are wingless, and all are external parasites of warm-blooded animals. They are flattened from side to side, and their legs are long and adapted for jumping. Bodies are hard and polished with backwardly directed hairs. Their mouthparts are piercing and sucking. The backward direction of the hairs allows the fleas to move easily and quickly through thick fur on animals.
BIOLOGY AND LIFE CYCLE: Complete metamorphosis. Female fleas lay several hundred eggs shortly after a blood meal. Eggs fall off the animal host into the environment and usually hatch into larvae in two to twelve days. Larvae are tiny little wigglers and can live up to 200 days, the pupae up to a year. Legless larvae feed on

Firefly (BP)

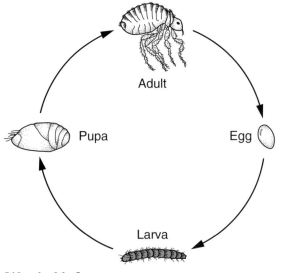

Life cycle of the flea

Flea adult (BP)   *Flea larvae* (BP)

dried blood, flea feces, other animal feces, and other organic matter. The larval stage lasts from one to five weeks. How many times they molt is unclear because they eat their molted skins. When fully grown, the larvae form a small oval cocoon of white silk that sticks to dust and debris. Adults emerge in five days to five weeks and are short-lived.

HABITAT: Dark, moist, cool, dirty areas. Dogs, cats, and other animals.

FEEDING HABITS: Larva feed on dry blood of fleas, mice, rats, and other animals, excreta, and other organic matter. Adults feed on fresh blood.

ECONOMIC IMPORTANCE: Hard to control; expensive pest. Can cause severe skin problems for dogs and cats. Flea allergy is the most common skin disease of pets. Fleas can transmit tapeworms.

NATURAL CONTROL: Keep sites clean and animals healthy. Beneficial nematodes and fire ants.

ORGANIC CONTROL: Beneficial nematodes and citrus products. Flea control requires a comprehensive program. Use banana stalks under decks. The most effective flea control device is the vacuum cleaner, which will remove flea eggs, flea larvae, and flea food. Put towels down where pets lie, and wash those towels weekly. Use diatomaceous earth. See Howard's control program below.

INSIGHT: A female flea can lay over 1,000 eggs during her lifetime. A pair of fleas can produce 20,000 fleas in three months. During the cocoon stage they are invulnerable to typical pesticides. Optimum conditions for egg hatching and flea development are 65 to 80 degrees and 70 percent humidity. When it is 95 degrees this summer and you have fleas, the problem may be in the house, not out in the yard. Fleas like dark, damp, cool spots. The most common flea is called the cat flea. It attacks cats, dogs, rats, chickens, opossums, raccoons, squirrels, and other warm-blooded animals.

Howard's Comprehensive Flea Control Program

No, there are still no silver bullets for fleas or ticks — no magic organic or chemical product exists that will completely control these pests all the time and leave the beneficial insects, your pets, and your family alive and healthy. Control does, however, continue to get simpler and more effective.

Holistic or comprehensive programs work and are less trouble in the long run. Trouble comes from continuing to spray toxic materials and poison yourself, your property, and your animals — and yet never get the pests under control.

The secret to controlling fleas is to control the eggs and larvae. They are far more numerous than adults. Adult fleas usually make up only about 2 percent of the total population. Larvae don't feed on animals, as do the adults. Flea larvae feed on organic debris, primarily dry blood. That's why keeping the pets and the environment clean is so important. Flea larvae live wherever the eggs have fallen, not on the animals. They do not bite animals or humans. They do, however, grow up to be adults unless you murder them while they're young.

1. *Organic grounds maintenance*. Allow biodiversity to reestablish to create competition. Insects and microbes compete with each other for territory and food. When toxic pesticides are used, the competition is reduced.

2. *Diet*. Nutrition is an important part of a comprehensive flea control program. Feed your pets a balanced, nutritious diet of your own cooking or an organic pet food. Avoid processed foods, especially those that contain chemical preservatives. Ethoxyquin, for example, is a pesticide used as a preservative in many pet foods. BHT and BHA are other chemical preservatives to avoid. Vitamin C is a more acceptable preservative to look for.

I give my dogs food supplements daily — garlic, natural diatomaceous earth (DE), food-grade kelp, and essential fatty acid products. Garlic helps repel fleas, and the DE is a natural wormer and aids in digestion. If the mixing sounds too complicated, just use natural food-grade diatomaceous earth daily. Use about a teaspoon for small dogs and cats and a tablespoon for large dogs. For livestock, about 1 to 2 percent of the food ration should be DE. It can also be fed free choice along with salt blocks and mineral supplements.

3. *Cleaning*. Vacuum frequently, rake and sweep dog runs and sleeping areas regularly, pick up and thoroughly compost pet waste. Flea larvae must have organic matter. Keeping the pet areas clean helps to starve out fleas. Remove trash, lumber, and other debris that can harbor fleas. It's best to establish a regular sleeping area for your pets and restrict their access to areas that can be cleaned easily and often. Carpeted areas are the hardest to keep clean.

4. *Grooming*. Bathe pets weekly or as needed but only with mild, nontoxic soaps. Herbal shampoos and neem shampoos are the most effective, but any low-phosphate, biodegradable soap will work. I like products that use a coconut base. Shampoos containing citrus oil (d-limonene) and tea tree oil (melaleuca) are also effective. Avoid all soaps containing harsh pesticides. Leave

shampoo on pets for five minutes before rinsing.
If not done too often, bathing pets helps greatly because
soap kills fleas. Brushing regularly is even better because
it cleans and stimulates the natural oils in the pet's coat.
These oils help to repel fleas and other pests. The regular
use of a flea comb is another effective aid. Its small tines
remove fleas, and the comb can be dipped in a bowl of
soapy water between strokes to kill the fleas caught in
the tines.

5. *Exercise.* Make sure the pets get plenty of natural
exercise from running and playing, or walk them around
regularly. It's good for the animals and for you.

6. *Pet treatment.* Apply herbal powders of pennyroyal,
lavender, eucalyptus, and rosemary. Pennyroyal is too
strong to use on cats. Diatomaceous earth is an inexpen-
sive and effective tool to use as a dry powder on the pet's
fur. Don't use it regularly because it's very drying to the
skin. Citrus oil products can also help control fleas.
Citrus oil products are available commercially, or you
can make your own mixture (see Appendix C). Pour into
the animal's fur and cover the skin thoroughly. Pay
special attention to areas that are hard for the pet to
reach. All types of citrus work, but oranges seem to work
best. This treatment is also effective for skin rashes
caused by flea bites.

7. *Indoor treatment.* Treat infested carpets with
diatomaceous earth or boric acid, but don't overdo it. For
heavy infestations, spray d-limonene (citrus) products on
carpets and furniture. Baking soda dusted on carpets will
also help. Dirty, infested carpets should be water-
extraction cleaned or completely removed from the
house.

8. *Outdoor treatment.* Dust or spray diatomaceous
earth and pyrethrum on infested areas. Light dusting is
better than heavy globs. In liquid sprays, add 2 to 4
tablespoons of DE/pyrethrum to 1 gallon of water. Use
about 90 percent DE and 10 percent pyrethrum. Use
only as needed to avoid killing beneficial insects.
Concentrate on dark, damp spots where fleas hang out.
DE and pyrethrum are nonselective and, like all dusty
materials, can cause problems if inhaled. (Remember
that diatomaceous earth for pets and horticultural use is
not the same as swimming pool DE. Buy natural DE
only from your local organic retailer. Pool filter DE has
been heated and chemically treated. It does not kill
insects and is much more dangerous to breathe because it
contains a higher level of crystalline silica dioxide.)
Citrus oil, molasses, manure compost, and garlic are
even more effective and less toxic. Apply beneficial
nematodes to the entire property and keep the treated
areas moist so that the microscopic worms don't dry out
and die. There are several brand names of beneficial
nematodes. These beneficial animals also help control

fire ants, roaches, termites, and grubworms. For more
information, see Nematode.

A Malcolm Story

As a child on the farm and now on my own farm, I have
always had dogs. They are part of the family. I have never
known our dogs to be without some fleas. My dad said a
dog needs to scratch to be happy. I know now that was
just his excuse so he wouldn't have to spend money or
take time to treat the dogs. About 1983 we started taking
paunch manure from a slaughterhouse and using it as an
ingredient in making compost. Soon our dogs and all the
free-roaming dogs of the neighborhood and even the
coyotes learned when the paunch truck was due and they
would be waiting. They loved to eat this stuff. Soon after
that, we noticed all the dogs' coats were getting slick and
shiny, even one that had had some bad skin problems.
One day a neighbor mentioned that his dogs no longer
had fleas. I remembered seeing his dogs at the paunch
pile, so I decided to check our dogs. Sure enough, there
wasn't a single flea on any of our dogs. Why? I don't
know. I thought it was the awful smell until a discussion
with a medical doctor who researched nutrition told how
in the wild a carnivore always eats the gut section first
after a kill. They now feed the guts and paunch to sick
carnivores in zoos. The gut from herbivorous animals
has special nutrients, vitamins, and enzymes not found
other places in nature. We dumped the paunch in the
same location until 1995. During those twelve years
none of the dogs eating from the paunch ever had a
single flea. We now dump the paunch at our new
compost yard miles away. The dogs here, which can no
longer snack on paunch, have fleas—and the dogs there
have shiny coats and no fleas. This proves nutrition is the
most important factor in controlling parasites in
animals, as it is in plants.

FLEA BEETLE

COMMON NAMES: Flea Beetle, Leaf Beetle
SCIENTIFIC NAME: Order Coleoptera, family
Chrysomelidae, several species
SIZE: Adult—$\frac{1}{10}$" to $\frac{1}{16}$"
IDENTIFICATION: Shiny black, blue-black, or brown-
black beetles about the size of a pinhead. Some have
stripes or other faint markings. They jump like fleas
when approached, due to enlarged hind legs. Adults are
black, brown, or bronze. Larvae are legless grubs with
brown heads. Have chewing mouthparts and eat little
round holes. Larvae look like thin white worms.
BIOLOGY AND LIFE CYCLE: Adults overwinter in the
soil and emerge in the spring. They feed, lay eggs on
plant roots, and die by mid-summer. Larvae hatch and
feed for two or three weeks, then pupate in the soil.

Adults emerge in two or three weeks. There are one to four generations a year.

HABITAT: Most vegetables, some flowers, and weeds. Soil and plant foliage.

FEEDING HABITS: They eat small round holes in the leaves of potatoes, peppers, beets, brassicas, and other crops. Young sprouts are often a target. Leaves are skeletonized, giving plants a bleached appearance before they wilt and die. Larvae feed on roots and tubers below ground. They leave brown snake-looking marks on potatoes.

ECONOMIC IMPORTANCE: Adult beetles chew holes in leaves, especially in the early spring. Larvae damage plant roots.

NATURAL CONTROL: Beneficial nematodes control the larvae in the soil. Encourage biodiversity in the garden: plant a varied mix of crops along with susceptible plants.

ORGANIC CONTROL: Neem, citrus oil, and row covers. Garlic spray will often control if applied early and often.

INSIGHT: To help control this pest on susceptible crops, plant them about two weeks later than normal and use large transplants to encourage quick maturity.

FLEA HOPPER

COMMON NAMES: Flea Hopper, Garden Fleahopper
SCIENTIFIC NAME: Order Heteroptera, family Miridae, *Halticus bracteatus*
SIZE: Adult—$\frac{1}{12}$" to $\frac{1}{10}$"
IDENTIFICATION: Small black insects that move around very fast on leaves after being disturbed. They look like tiny little marbles rolling around on leaves. They have long legs and long antennae; they resemble flea beetles but are smaller. Their damage to plant foliage looks similar to spider mite damage.

BIOLOGY AND LIFE CYCLE: Females insert eggs in the leaves or stems of plants they feed on. Greenish nymphs appear on the underside of leaves in the early spring and grow rapidly into blackish adults. Five nymphal instars (nymph stages between molts).

HABITAT: Garden plants such as beans, beets, cabbage, celery, cowpeas, cucumbers, eggplant, lettuce, peas, peppers, potatoes, pumpkins, squash, sweet potatoes, tomatoes, legumes, ornamentals, and many weeds.

FEEDING HABITS: Piercing, sucking mouthparts; impart a molted look to foliage and destroy the green surface of leaves.

Flea hopper

Flea hopper (H)

ECONOMIC IMPORTANCE: Cause severe damage to many crops when allowed to develop into serious infestations. Compost tea and neem are effective.

NATURAL CONTROL: Biodiversity, proper garden conditions.

ORGANIC CONTROL: Garlic-pepper tea when young insects first appear in the spring. Citrus-based sprays for heavy infestations.

INSIGHT: This is a classic indicator insect. It becomes a pest only when the plants are not healthy or when site problems exist. We don't see the pest often.

A Howard Story

This is the one insect that I have had consistent difficulty controlling in my own vegetable garden. One problem is that I don't always spray early in the season, as I recommend others do. The other problem is that my vegetable garden is too shady because I've planted too many trees. The best long-term control of the flea hopper is excellent light, excellent drainage, healthy soil, and well-adapted plants.

FLOWER BUG—see Minute Pirate Bug

FLOWER FLY—see Hover Fly

FLY—see Crane Fly, Damselfly, Dragonfly, Horse Fly, House Fly, Hover Fly, Longlegged Fly, Robber Fly, Syrphid Fly, Tachinid Fly

FLY PARASITE

COMMON NAME: Fly Parasite
SCIENTIFIC NAME: Order Hymenoptera, family Pteromalidae, *Muscidifurax* spp. and *Spalangia* spp.
SIZE: Adult—approximately $\frac{1}{8}$"
IDENTIFICATION: A small black wasp.
BIOLOGY AND LIFE CYCLE: This wasp deposits its eggs in the larvae of flies or soon after the fly larva has gone into the pupa stage. The wasp egg soon hatches, and the wasp larvae feed on the developing fly and destroy it.

Fly parasite adult (B)

Fly parasite newly hatched from fly pupa (B)

House fly larvae (B)

Parasitized house fly pupae (B)

After the larva reaches maturity, it then pupates and soon emerges from the dead fly pupa as an adult to start the generation over. One generation every three weeks. Complete metamorphosis.

HABITAT: Wherever flies are attracted to moist, decaying organic material such as rotting vegetable waste, manure, or dead animals.

FEEDING HABITS: Larvae feed on developing flies in the larva and soft pupa stages. Adults draw fluid from fly pupae.

ECONOMIC IMPORTANCE: Controlling flies and keeping them from becoming a big nuisance.

NATURAL CONTROL: They serve as their own control, as they reduce the population of their host.

ORGANIC CONTROL: None needed.

INSIGHT: These parasitic wasps have biological radar for finding fly pupae. They can be your best friend if you operate a dairy, feedlot, or stable or if you simply maintain a compost pile. If released properly, they can completely eliminate the need for chemical fly control—and at a lower cost. Here are instructions for an application of fly parasites.

The parasites will be shipped in fly pupae with wood shavings to insulate the pupae against damage. Place the shipment in a warm area out of direct sunlight until you observe hatching—approximately two to ten days, depending on the temperature and the stage of wasp's development at the time of shipment. In the warmer days of summer, it is not unusual for the parasites to be hatching aggressively upon arrival. In this case, they should be released shortly after you receive them.

Scatter a small amount of the fly pupae in the problem areas. Apply some around watering and feeding receptacles, taking care that they are out of the way of the paths where your animals routinely walk. Use the remaining parasites around any damp, cool spots that make good breeding areas for fly populations. Make scheduled follow-up applications.

A Malcolm Story

At Garden-Ville's first compost yard, we didn't use fly parasites because they weren't available at the time. We fought the fly problem every way we knew, short of using toxic sprays. We were using nontoxic sprays until it got to be too much trouble for what it was costing. We stopped using anything at all and the flies didn't get any worse, even though a new batch came with each daily load of manure.

After a time, we (and the neighbors) learned to tolerate the flies. When we were finally able to purchase fly parasites, we released them all around the compost yard but didn't get the results we were hoping for. Then we realized that the fly adult, pupa, and larva were being brought in with the daily loads of manure. So we went to the source and began releasing fly parasites at the stables where we were getting our manure. Soon the stable operators saw the benefits of this approach and began releasing the fly parasites on their own. Now all our waste suppliers, including dairies and feedlots, are releasing fly parasites. We now have three compost yards, and the flies at these locations are no worse than in any park or picnic area. The loads of manure and vegetable waste now have the fly parasites coming in with all the various life stages of the fly. We have no more new flies hatching at our locations.

Since we use no toxic fly control at our compost locations, we also get help from many other natural controls. In the evenings we have a lot of barn swallows, dragonflies, and other insects and animals patrolling and catching any flies the parasites have missed.

We don't want to completely eliminate flies, however. We need a few to help keep the beneficial decomposing microbes moved around so our compost piles will always be properly inoculated. The fly parasites also parasitize and control other flies.

FOREST ARMYWORM—see Tent Caterpillar

FOURLINED PLANT BUG

COMMON NAMES: Fourlined Plant Bug, Plant Bug
SCIENTIFIC NAME: Order Heteroptera, family Miridae, *Poecilocapsus lineatus*
SIZE: Adult—¼" to ⅓"
IDENTIFICATION: Adult is yellowish green and black with four jet black lines on the pronotum (shield behind the head) and forewings. Nymphs are bright red with a black spot on the thorax (midsection) and yellow stripes on wing pads. Damage by this insect looks more like disease infection than insect damage.
BIOLOGY AND LIFE CYCLE: One generation a year. Very active insects. Eggs overwinter in soft tissues of plant stems. Incomplete metamorphosis.
HABITAT: Meadows, gardens, and crop fields. These insects love mint, hyssop, other herbs, roses, and small fruits.
FEEDING HABITS: They suck plant juices, nectar, and sometimes liquids from freshly killed insects. White or dark spots appear on upper sides of leaves where these bugs have sucked juice. When severe, the entire leaf will wither and drop. The spots look more like a fungus disease than insect damage.
ECONOMIC IMPORTANCE: Cosmetic damage early in the growing season. They are rarely around after it gets hot.
NATURAL CONTROL: Birds, assassin bugs, and other insectivorous animals.
ORGANIC CONTROL: Treat before the insects mature with the Garden-Ville Fire Ant Control formula.

Fourlined plant bug, side view (H)

Fourlined plant bug, top view (H)

INSIGHT: We didn't see these insects for many years. During the spring of 1995 they were more visible, and we had many calls about their damage. They are beautiful insects.

A Howard Story

For years I had seen a dark spotting on the foliage of mint and other herbs that looked like a fungus disease. It wasn't until recently that I finally spotted the real culprit. It was a spring that was very wet. I guess that caused the plant bugs to be more plentiful and easier to see—about the time I finally noticed these colorful bugs, several of my listeners had sent me examples of the same bug and the same damage. The mystery had been solved.

FROGHOPPER—see Spittlebug

FUNGUS ANT—see Texas Leafcutting Ant

FUNGUS GNAT

COMMON NAME: Fungus Gnat
SCIENTIFIC NAME: Order Diptera, family Mycetophilidae, *Sciara* spp.
SIZE: Adult—1/10" to ⅛"
IDENTIFICATION: Black, brown, or dull yellow,

mosquitolike flies. Some are more brightly colored. Humped thorax and long legs.

BIOLOGY AND LIFE CYCLE: Adults lay eggs that hatch into slender, cylindrical larvae that eat fungi in decaying organic matter. The larvae of some species eat small insects, worms, and plant roots. Adults live about one week and lay up to 200 eggs that hatch in about four days.

HABITAT: Grain plants, cucumbers, potted plants, and bonsai plants. Commonly found in moist wooded areas but also in indoor house plants. Often troublesome in indoor atriums.

FEEDING HABITS: Larvae eat fungal matter and decaying organic matter. They will also do some damage to plant roots and stems.

ECONOMIC IMPORTANCE: Can damage plant roots but are more of an irritation that anything.

NATURAL CONTROL: *Bacillus thuringiensis* 'Israelensis'. Water potted plants and courtyards less often.

ORGANIC CONTROL: Neem or citrus oil products. A drench of citrus, compost tea, and molasses, Garden-Ville Fire Ant Control, and beneficial nematodes.

Fungus gnats near penny (H)

INSIGHT: Mulching potted plants, just as you would outdoor beds, helps with pest control. Add lava sand and earthworm castings and cover these materials with aged pecan shells or cedar flakes. Adding a tablespoon of natural apple cider vinegar to each gallon of irrigation water will also help keep plants healthy and control pests like fungus gnats.

GALL

IDENTIFICATION: There are many different kinds of galls. They are primarily caused by wasp, fly, and aphid insects and are usually more cosmetic than damaging.

HABITAT: Many ornamental and food crops.

FEEDING HABITS: Wasp, fly, or aphid gall insects "sting" a plant, which causes a growth that the insect uses as a home for its young. The gall serves as a shelter and food supply.

ECONOMIC IMPORTANCE: Although unsightly, most are not considered very damaging. Tannic acid from galls has been used for centuries to tan skins of animals. Many galls contain materials that make the finest inks and dyes. Some galls contain products that have been used in medicine since the fifth century B.C.

NATURAL CONTROL: Biodiversity.

ORGANIC CONTROL: None needed, although healthy plants seem to have fewer galls.

INSIGHT: Science does not yet know what makes the plants grow the curious, elaborate, and at times even

Puffy insect galls on red oaks (H)

Phylloxera galls on pecan leaves (H)

Wasp galls on live oak (H)

Marble-like galls from red oaks (H)

Mysterious gall on red oak leaf (H)

Woolly Oak Gall (B)

Giant wheel bug adult (B)

beautiful structures that are absolutely foreign to the plant in the absence of the gall insect. The same species of gall insects on different species of plants causes galls that are similar while different gall insects attacking the same plant cause galls that are different. The galls also become homes for other than the initial insects.

GARDEN FLEAHOPPER—see Flea Hopper

GIANT BEETLE—see Rhinoceros Beetle

GIANT WHEEL BUG

COMMON NAMES: Assassin Bug, Giant Wheel Bug, Wheel Bug
SCIENTIFIC NAME: Order Heteroptera, family Reduviidae, *Arilus cristatus*
SIZE: Adult—1" to 1⅜"
IDENTIFICATION: Adults are large, dark gray or gray-brown insects with a distinctive gearlike raised area on their backs. Nymphs are red with black markings. One generation per year.
BIOLOGY AND LIFE CYCLE: Eggs are laid on branches. Incomplete metamorphosis.
HABITAT: Shrubs and trees above ground, seldom found on the ground. Meadows and field crops.
FEEDING HABITS: Insect eaters; suck juices from many troublesome insects such as moths, squash bugs, cucumber beetles, and webworms.

Giant wheel bug in final molt (B)

ECONOMIC IMPORTANCE: Beneficial insects that feed on several pest insects.
NATURAL CONTROL: None needed.
ORGANIC CONTROL: None needed.
INSIGHT: Giant wheel bugs look ferocious, and they are. Although beneficial, they will give you a painful stab if you handle them roughly.

A Malcolm Story

My first-ever experience with beneficial insects involved the giant wheel bug. Every year, potatoes were a large part of our vegetable crop, and some years the potato beetles were bad enough to warrant some control. Since I wanted to stay organic, I really wasn't sure what to do. When I was a child at home, our dad made us pick the potato beetles by hand. Now that I owned a farm and had responsibility, I figured I'd better find an answer. I just couldn't believe picking a few beetles was the answer I needed.

I bought a bug book and learned that the first potato beetles to appear in the spring were the young unmated adults that hibernate through the winter. If you get them before they deposit eggs, you have knocked them out for the season.

One thing I remember from picking the beetles as a child is that the beetles didn't seem dumb. A lot of them would see us coming and fall to the ground and play dead. I wanted to destroy as many as I could, so I squashed them between my fingers. Every now and then I found one on the ground with no juice. They were already dead. As I continued down the row, I soon found the answer: a giant gray bug with half of a cogged wheel sticking up on its back and a long snout. The snout was used to stab the potato beetles and suck their juices. It wasn't long before I found several more of these big wheel bugs that were sucking the potato beetles.

After that, I didn't bother to pick any more beetles. Almost daily I watched the potato beetles decrease in number. At the same time, the lady beetle population remained strong and kept the aphids from getting a toehold. I think that gradually improving the soil each year may have given the plants some immunity, and by hand-picking and not using poison, I didn't kill any of their natural enemies such as the giant wheel bug. Each year I watched the giant wheel bug, and never once did I see it capture a beneficial insect. In addition to the potato beetle, they captured and killed striped and spotted cucumber beetles and various pest moths.

We stayed on that small farm for eleven years, and the potato beetles never came back. On our new farm, the potato patch was bigger, and with the first planting the potato beetles came in droves. My two oldest sons were eight and ten, and I decided it was time they learned about potato bugs. With the size of the patch, however, I figured they would need help, so I recruited two little neighbor girls. I took all the kids out into the field and explained the good bugs and bad bugs and their life cycles. The kids found it fascinating.

I said I would pay the kids a penny for each bad bug they picked. I gave them each a can with soapy water to drop the bugs into and explained how soap alone would kill the bad bugs. The kids picked with enthusiasm about as long as you would expect, then came to the house to show me and count their bad bugs. Surprisingly, no good bugs had been picked. Together, I owed those kids almost five dollars.

The next day the little neighbor girls were back, asking if they could pick bugs again. One of them said she wouldn't even charge me if I would let them pick. My two boys didn't offer, but it took much less persuasion than I thought it would, even for them. Each year thereafter, the kids had their bug-picking party. As with the first farm, each year as the soil was built up to better and better fertility and we killed only bad bugs and protected the good ones, the potato beetles became less and less a problem. They were eventually gone completely.

GLOW WORM—see Firefly

GOLD BUG—see Tortoise Beetle

GOLDEN TORTOISE BEETLE—see Tortoise Beetle

GRAIN BEETLE—see Grain Pests

GRAIN MOTH—see Grain Pests

GRAIN PESTS

COMMON NAMES: Grain Beetle, Grain Moth, Grain Weevil
SCIENTIFIC NAME: Many orders, families, and species
SIZE: Varies greatly.
IDENTIFICATION: Varies greatly.
BIOLOGY AND LIFE CYCLE: Insects whose larvae and adults eat grain. They are particularly a problem in large grain-storage vessels and buildings.
HABITAT: Stored raw grain such as rice, milo, corn, soybeans, peanuts; also stored processed products such as cereal grains, cake mixes, flour, and cornmeal.
ECONOMIC IMPORTANCE: Destruction of large volumes of grain.
NATURAL CONTROL: Beneficial predators and parasites can be purchased to control grain pests.
ORGANIC CONTROL: Pheromone traps, spraying the walls of storage vessels and the top of grain with *Bacillus thuringiensis*. Treating grain with diatomaceous earth. Releasing trichogramma wasps and other beneficials. Use Bt for moths and DE for beetles and weevils.
INSIGHT: Grain beetles, moths, and weevils are all troublesome insects. One problem with the use of DE in stored grain is that it is abrasive to the grain-handling equipment.

Xylocoris flavipes, the warehouse pirate bug, is used for control of larvae, eggs, pupae, and adults of all species of beetles and moths (except the larvae and pupae of the Angoumois grain moth, which develop inside the seed).

Trichogramma pretiosum, a moth egg parasite, deposits eggs within the eggs of moths. The complete life cycle of these parasites occurs within the host eggs. On the ninth day following parasitism, the adult parasites emerge from the host egg.

Bracon hebetor, a moth larval parasite, deposits eggs on the exterior of all moth larvae (except those of the Angoumois grain moth). Hatching larvae consume the fluids of the pest larva and form cocoons adjacent to the carcass of the expired host or pest insect. Adult parasites hatch from the cocoons in twelve to fourteen days to repeat the beneficial cycle.

Anisopteramalus calandrae, a parasitic insect referred to as AC, stings the weevil larvae within the infested seed and deposits her eggs there. Hatching larvae consume the body fluids of the pest (host) larvae, form a cocoon, and emerge from within the seed in twelve to fourteen days as adult parasites to repeat the cycle.

GRAIN WEEVIL—see Grain Pests

GRASSHOPPER

COMMON NAME: Grasshopper
SCIENTIFIC NAME: Order Orthoptera, family Acrididae, many species
SIZE: Adult—1" to 3"
IDENTIFICATION: Adults are black, brown, yellow, or green. Enlarged hind legs for jumping. Many have brightly colored underwings. Nymphs are similar but smaller.

Grasshopper young eating plants (H)

Immature grasshopper (B)

Grasshopper adult (H)

BIOLOGY AND LIFE CYCLE: Female adults deposit masses of elongated eggs in burrows in the soil or on weeds. Eggs hatch in the spring; nymphs grow and molt for forty to sixty days. Adults feed until cold weather.
HABITAT: Cereals, grasses, and other agricultural crops. Grasshoppers like sterile, unhealthy areas.
FEEDING HABITS: Chew foliage of many crops.
ECONOMIC IMPORTANCE: Can destroy crops in a hurry.
NATURAL CONTROL: Natural enemies such as blister beetles, ground beetles, predatory flies, parasitic flies, and especially birds. Beneficial fungi that inhabit healthy soil.
ORGANIC CONTROL: Floating row cover or biological controls such as *Nosema locustae* or *Beauvaria bassiana*. Garlic-pepper tea. All-purpose flour from the grocery store works as well. A mixture of molasses, compost tea, and citrus oil also works. Build soil health and mulch bare soil. Drench soil with neem products.
INSIGHT: Important in the food chain for fish and small animals. Grasshoppers need bare soil for egg laying. Blister beetle larvae eat the eggs.

GREENBUG—see Aphid

GREEN LACEWING—see Lacewing

GREEN STINKBUG—see Stink Bug

GROUND BEETLE

COMMON NAMES: Caterpillar Hunter, Ground Beetle, Tiger Beetle
SCIENTIFIC NAME: Order Coleoptera, family Carabidae
SIZE: ⅛" to 1"
IDENTIFICATION: Dark, sometimes metallic-colored, shiny, fast-moving, ground-dwelling, long-legged beetles. Adults have long threadlike antennae. Some stink when handled. Many have prominent eyes. Some have grooves or pits on the forewings. Those active at night are often black. Day hunters are sometimes brightly colored. Head and thorax often smaller then abdomen. Larvae are slender, slightly flattened, and tapered at the tail, which has two hairlike projections.

Ground beetle (B)

BIOLOGY AND LIFE CYCLE: Eggs are laid in the soil. Predaceous larvae are segmented and tapered toward the tail. Larvae have large jaws and eat insects, as do the adults, which may live two to four years. Overwintering adults emerge from the ground in the spring from a pupal cell and lay their eggs. Larvae hatch and feed on insects and slugs for two to four weeks and then pupate in the soil. One generation per year.
HABITAT: Most vegetable crops, especially root vegetables, onions, and potatoes. Under stones and debris. Active mostly at night. Like perennial beds and permanent plantings.
FEEDING HABITS: Both larvae and adults eat caterpillars; the Colorado potato beetle; larvae, pupae, and eggs of root maggots and flies; larvae of imported cabbage worm; diamondback moths; cutworm and cabbage loopers; aphids; asparagus beetles; slugs; flea beetles; and snails. Come to think of it, they feed on many of our most noxious insects.
ECONOMIC IMPORTANCE: Control of many troublesome pests.
NATURAL CONTROL: None needed. These are very beneficial insects.
ORGANIC CONTROL: None needed.
INSIGHT: Hedgerows are important habitat for ground beetles. Over 2,000 native species. Ground beetles can be attracted by planting perennial beds to give them stable habitats. White clover also provides excellent habitat.

GRUB—see June Beetle

GRUBWORM—see June Beetle

GUANO BEETLE

COMMON NAMES: Guano Beetle, Lesser Mealworm
SCIENTIFIC NAME: Order Coleoptera, family Tenebrionidae, *Alphitobius diaperinus*; family Dermestidae, *Dermestes carnivora*.
SIZE: Adult—¼" to ⅜", larva—⅜" to ⅝"

IDENTIFICATION: *Alphitobius* spp.—corrugated wing covers on the adult beetles, wireworm-looking larvae. *Dermestes* spp.—beetles have slight wing covers with some coloration, larvae look like fuzzy lady beetle larvae.
BIOLOGY AND LIFE CYCLE: Complete metamorphosis.
HABITAT: Bat caves.
FEEDING HABITS: The meat eaters eat dead and sick bats and other animals in caves. The others eat bat droppings. Both foods are digested into a clean, natural fertilizer.
NATURAL ENEMIES: Cave mice, other predator animals, and predator insects.
ECONOMIC IMPORTANCE: Keep bat caves more sanitary; very beneficial insects.
NATURAL CONTROL: None needed.
ORGANIC CONTROL: None needed.
INSIGHT: According by Brian Keeley of Bat Conservation International, Bracken Cave in San Antonio serves as home for one of the densest populations of mammals on the earth. Every spring an estimated 20 million Mexican freetailed bats (*Tadarida brasiliensis*) return to this cave to raise their young. Scientific studies show that a female freetailed bat that is nursing a pup will consume her weight in insects every night. For 20 million bats that's an estimated 250,000 pounds of insects nightly all summer. Why doesn't the cave fill up with guano?

The number of different insects involved in the biology of the cave is too great to discuss in detail. However, two different beetles, the guano beetle and the dermestid beetle, play a major role in the "processing" of the bat guano.

The guano beetle, also called the lesser mealworm, is the major processor of the guano. The entire life cycle of the guano beetle from adult to egg to larva to pupa stages is carried out in the cave. The larvae look similar to, but smaller than, the mealworms for sale at the pet store. Because of the vast quantity of guano that is available during the summer, the population of the beetles increases dramatically, causing the floor of the cave to look like a seething mass of life.

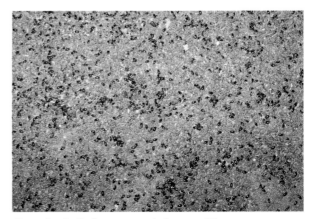

Guano beetles feeding on guano in bat cave (B)

Freetail bats leaving cave at dusk (H)

The dermestid beetle (*Dermestes carnivora*) also attains very large populations and plays an important role in the processing of the debris collecting on the floor of the cave, but they do not eat the guano. As the scientific name of this species indicates, the larvae of this beetle eat flesh. With that many bats in the same area, some are bound to fall to the floor and die, and these bats are promptly consumed. Researchers entering the cave have to wear special protective clothing to avoid being attacked by the dermestid beetles. A freshly fallen bat can be consumed by the dermestids in minutes.

The combination of these two beetles keeps caves from rapidly filling with the guano and debris that results from this massive population of bats. These beetles serve as the cave janitors. Humans have been taking advantage of the guano for use as fertilizer and, in earlier times, for the manufacture of gunpowder. Thanks to Brian Keeley from Bat Conservation International for this information.

HARLEQUIN BUG

COMMON NAME: Harlequin Bug

SCIENTIFIC NAME: Order Heteroptera, family Pentatomidae, *Murgantia histrionica*

SIZE: Adult—¼" to ⅜"

IDENTIFICATION: Adults are red (or yellow) and black, shiny, flat and shield-shaped true bugs. Eggs are very distinctive. They look like tiny white barrels with black rings and are laid in two straight rows. Nymphs are red, black, and oval.

BIOLOGY AND LIFE CYCLE: Breed year round and can have several generations a year. Adults hibernate in plant debris.

HABITAT: Many food crops such as beets, brussels sprouts, squash, cauliflower, cherries, citrus, collards, horseradish, kohlrabi, peas, mustard, radishes, turnips, tomatoes, and corn. Vegetable garden vegetables, especially mustard, broccoli, cabbage, turnips, and radishes.

FEEDING HABITS: Both the nymphs and adults feed heavily on all members of the cabbage family, causing light splotches, shriveling, and deformity.

ECONOMIC IMPORTANCE: Can destroy a garden in a hurry.

NATURAL CONTROL: Biodiversity. Plant in the proper season—the fall. Encourage birds. Plant "trap" crops of mustard, turnip greens, and the like.

ORGANIC CONTROL: Spray with manure compost tea, seaweed, molasses, vinegar, and citrus oil.

INSIGHT: The harlequin bug migrated up from Central America and became a big pest in the garden. The best control is planting mustard, cabbage, turnips, and related plants early in the spring season so they are out of the garden before the middle of March. Or better yet, plant them in the fall.

Harlequin bugs are ranked as the biggest pest of the mustard family, but they rarely ever appear in the fall of the year. When planted in the fall, the mustard and cole crops will not bolt and go to seed or turn bitter as fast. In the fall, these plants mature as the days are getting cooler and shorter, which gives them a better flavor. When planted too late in the spring, these bugs move in fast. Could this bug be telling us

Harlequin bug eggs (B)

Harlequin bug (B)

"Look, dummy, you are planting these plants in the wrong season"? If we would just pay attention, maybe all of the little critters have something helpful to tell us. When studied, all the insects, even the troublesome ones, are interesting.

The most fascinating thing about the harlequin bugs is their eggs. There are always ten in a bunch, two rows of five side by side, and they look just like little wine barrels. You can see the "hoops," the "cork" in the center, and the "staves" casting a shadow across the top. It is worth growing at least one mustard plant in the late spring just to get a look at the eggs.

HARMONIA LADY BEETLE—see Lady Beetle

HARVESTER ANT

COMMON NAMES: Big Red Ant, Harvester Ant, Red Ant

SCIENTIFIC NAME: Order Hymenoptera, family Formicidae, *Pogonomyrmex* spp.

SIZE: Adult—⅕" to ¼"

IDENTIFICATION: Large red to dark brown ant. Thorax with one pair of spines. Long hairs forming beard under chin. Mounds are completely different from fire ant mounds. They are large and flat and have an opening.

BIOLOGY AND LIFE CYCLE: Swarming is usually in June and July. Nests are always located in exposed soil, never indoors. Complete life cycle—eggs, larva, pupa, and adult.

HABITAT: Large bare areas free of all vegetation around the nest.

FEEDING HABITS: Eat seeds, especially small ones.

ECONOMIC IMPORTANCE: Not considered a troublesome insect if plenty of native seed is available. The red ants are actually quite beneficial. They are in competition

Harvester ants (B)

Harvester ant mound made of fine gravel (H)

Harvester ant mound made of earthworm castings (H)

Shuckworm larva damage (B)

Shuckworm hole in pecan (B)

Shuckworm larva (B)

Shuckworm (H)

for space with fire ants and important for biodiversity by spreading seeds of various species.

NATURAL CONTROL: Mulch and green cover crop. Birds, lizards, frogs, toads, horned toads, and other lizards. Biodiversity.

ORGANIC CONTROL: None needed.

INSIGHT: Very interesting and beneficial ants. Be careful; they have a powerful bite and a powerful sting that injects formic acid. They bite only when you disturb their mound. They are not as aggressive as fire ants, but their sting is more painful than a fire ant sting. When treating fire ant mounds, avoid treating these ants. They should be protected.

HARVESTMAN CICADA—see Cicada

HERCULES BEETLE—see Rhinoceros Beetle

HICKORY SHUCKWORM

COMMON NAMES: Hickory Shuckworm, Shuckworm
SCIENTIFIC NAME: Order Lepidoptera, family Torticidae, *Cydia caryana*
SIZE: Adult—⅜", wing span ½", larva—⅜"
IDENTIFICATION: Adults are brown to black moths. Larvae are small white worms with brown heads.
BIOLOGY AND LIFE CYCLE: Eggs are deposited on leaves and young nuts. Larvae infest the shucks covering the nuts and then overwinter in the fallen debris on the ground. They pupate in late winter to early spring and emerge as adults in the summer. As many as five generations a year.
FEEDING HABITS: Larvae feed in developing young nuts. In the late summer and fall the larvae tunnel into the shucks of hickories and pecans, preventing the kernels from filling out.
ECONOMIC IMPORTANCE: Can cause severe injury to pecan and hickory crops. Nuts are damaged and shucks fail to open.
NATURAL CONTROL: Bats, green lacewings, trichogramma wasps and other wasps.
ORGANIC CONTROL: Beneficial nematode soil treatment. Throw compost on top of infested shucks. Larvae are unable to mature in decaying shucks and adults cannot emerge from the soil. Successive releases of trichogramma wasps.
INSIGHT: In mid-season it is sometimes hard to tell the difference between the pecan casebearer and the hickory shuckworm. When the nuts get too hard for the casebearer to penetrate, the casebearer will also tunnel in the shuck. The casebearer frass or castings will be pushed to the outside of the shuck. There it tends to build up and stick. When the casebearer is found, there is usually one per nut. The shuckworm keeps the castings in the tunnel because it eats itself a new hole to escape after it pupates into an adult moth. Usually the pupal skin can be seen hanging halfway out of the hole after the moth has flown away. Two or more shuckworms may be found in the shuck of each nut. The shuckworm is creamy white while the casebearer has an olive or gray-green color.

HONEYBEE

COMMON NAME: Honeybee
SCIENTIFIC NAME: Order Hymenoptera, family Apidae, *Apis mellifera*
SIZE: Male drone—½" to ⅝", queen—¾", female worker—⅜" to ⅝"
IDENTIFICATION: Adult bees are fuzzy, gold- and

Honey bees outside hive on warm day (B)

Varroa mites on honey bees (ARM)

black-striped, with two pairs of transparent wings. Larvae are white grubs that stay home in wax combs in the hive.
BIOLOGY AND LIFE CYCLE: Bees are social insects that live in colonies numbering up to 80,000 or more. Queens lay eggs in wax cells, and workers feed and care for the larvae. Royal jelly is fed to certain larvae, causing them to

New swarm of honey bees (B)

become queens. Mated queens leave with a swarm of workers to start a new colony. Bees overwinter in hives and live on stored honey. Workers are sterile females and the most numerous. The sole function of males bees, called drones, is to mate with the queen—but only once; they die immediately after mating. Unmated males are killed and dumped from the hive. And they say it's a man's world!

HABITAT: Hollow trees and hives kept by beekeepers. Many flowering plants.

FEEDING HABITS: Workers feed on nectar and honey and gather pollen. Larvae feed on honey and royal jelly.

NATURAL CONTROL: Mites and the unnatural synthetic pesticides. Sevin is one of the worst pesticide choices left on the market. It is extremely toxic to bees.

ORGANIC CONTROL: None needed.

ECONOMIC IMPORTANCE: Honey production and pollenation of many ornamental and food crops.

NATURAL CONTROL: None needed.

ORGANIC CONTROL: None needed.

INSIGHT: Worker bees are able to sting but only once because the stinger is left inside the victim. The African bee or "killer bee" is closely kin but much more aggressive. The latest research suggests that our nonaggressive bees breeding with the "killers" is resulting in moderately aggressive bees that produce a lot of honey.

Tracheal and varroa mites have caused great destruction of honeybee colonies since the 1980s, but painting the hives a dark brown color helps. As the temperature of the hive increases, the bees fan more and their bodies heat up, killing the mites. Tracheal mites are microscopic and responsible for about 10 percent of the mite destruction to honeybees. Varroa mites are much larger and more destructive, causing about 90 percent of the mite damage. Planting lots of flowering plants, especially those rich in essential oils, such as mints or other fragrant herbs, helps to eliminate the mite problem.

HORNET—see Texas Yellowjacket

HORSE FLY

COMMON NAME: Horse Fly
SCIENTIFIC NAME:
Order Diptera, family
Tabanidae, *Tabanus* spp.
SIZE: Adult—¼" to 1"
IDENTIFICATION:
Larger than house flies,
usually darker with larger
eyes. Some horse flies are

Horse fly (B)

jet black. Hair is all short and fine, Not bristly. Eyes are often brilliantly colored.

BIOLOGY AND LIFE CYCLE: Eggs are laid on vegetation in marshy areas. Larvae are predaceous on small insect larvae, worms, and crustaceans.

HABITAT: Flowers, excrement, and decaying organic matter.

FEEDING HABITS: Females are animal-blood feeders. Bites are painful. Males eat nectar from flowers.

ECONOMIC IMPORTANCE: Horse flies are vectors of several diseases and can be troublesome to livestock and humans.

NATURAL CONTROL: Fly parasites, flycatchers and other birds.

ORGANIC CONTROL: Fly swatters and diatomaceous earth fed to animals. Releasing the beneficial insect called the fly parasite, or dump fly, will eliminate any infestation. Citrus oil sprays will also kill them.

INSIGHT: These stout, broad-headed flies that are usually dark-colored and often have brightly colored eyes. Their flight is usually silent, unlike that of house flies, and they deliver a painful bite in search of a blood meal. Only the females bite; the males feed on nectar and pollen.

Compost offers powerful biological fly control. Composting organisms like bacteria, fungi, mites, insects, and even small animals add in the decomposition of animal dung and attack immature flies in the manure.

A Malcolm Story

These flies were a big nuisance on the farm. After working in the fields on hot summer days, we would go swimming in the stock tanks. The horse flies would always wait until we were in the water before they would attack. For some reason, they would rather bite a wet body than a dry one, and they were always smart enough to land on our backs so we couldn't swat them. Our only defense was to quickly dive under the water before the fly could bite. If one did manage to bite, and usually they did, it was a pretty sharp sting; but the sensation lasted only a moment and there was no swelling or other aftereffects.

HOUSE FLY

COMMON NAME: House Fly
SCIENTIFIC NAME: Order Diptera, family Muscidae, *Musca domestica*
SIZE: Adult—⅛" to ½"
IDENTIFICATION: You know what a house fly looks like. Round, lots of bristles, long legs—lovely! Mouthparts are spongelike.
BIOLOGY AND LIFE CYCLE: Eggs to larvae to pupae to adults in just eight days. House fly eggs are laid in masses

House fly (H)

in dung or rotting organic matter. Maggotlike larvae develop fast and pupate in about a week.

HABITAT: Flowers, excrement, and decaying organic matter.

FEEDING HABITS: House flies feed by lapping up liquids with their spongelike mouthparts.

ECONOMIC IMPORTANCE: Vectors of several diseases and can be troublesome to livestock and humans.

NATURAL CONTROL: Fly parasites, flycatchers and other birds, dragonflies, and beneficial microorganisms.

ORGANIC CONTROL: Fly swatters and diatomaceous earth fed to animals. Releasing the beneficial insect known as the fly parasite will eliminate almost any fly problem. Spray with citrus oil products.

INSIGHT: House flies don't bite as horse flies do. Fly larva maggots are important in helping to dispose of organic waste.

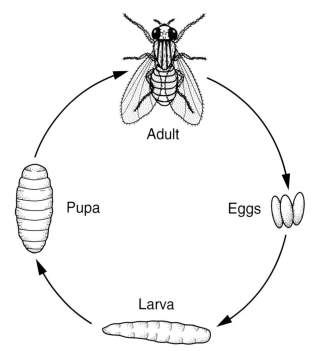
Life cycle of the house fly

Hover fly (H)

A Malcolm Story

During the seventeenth century, the belief prevailed that every living thing possessed some special usefulness to humans. If we took this approach today, there is no telling what we would discover. Instead we spend most of our resources making toxins designed to destroy many of the little creatures that share the planet with us.

The lowly house fly has virtues that have been recognized but not given due credit. The people making compost understand how the housefly is constantly moving the decomposing microbes around, which keeps the materials being composted well inoculated. Probably the fly's greatest benefit to man was discovered during World War I, when the medics noticed that wounds of soldiers lying on the battlefield for hours did not develop infection, as did those that had been treated and dressed promptly. The difference was due to the fact that the older wounds were always infested with maggots, which were larvae of the house flies. The remarkable discovery that these maggots were much better than any known surgical or medicinal treatment for cleaning up the infection in deep-seated wounds has lead to the practice of rearing maggots of the housefly and introducing them into wounds to eat out every microscopic particle of putrid flesh and bone. A secretion of the maggots has also been found to even help to heal wounds. As the maggots eat the infected, rotting tissue, they also kill the pus-forming bacteria by digesting them, and they continually apply minute quantities of the healing secretion to the depths of the wound more effectively than instruments can.

HOVER BEE—see Hover Fly

HOVER FLY

COMMON NAMES: Flower Fly, Hover Bee, Hover Fly, Sweat Bee, Sweat Fly, Syrphid Fly
SCIENTIFIC NAME: Order Diptera, family Syrphidae
SIZE: Adult—less than ½", larva—⅛" to ¼"
IDENTIFICATION: Adults look like bees or small wasps and are usually seen hovering around flowers. Males have a distinctive hovering and darting habit and shorter antennae than wasps. Some are very small, others are

Hover fly larvae (B)

larger than house flies. They commonly raise and lower their abdomen when resting. They have two wings whereas bees and wasps have four. Wings are held out to the side at rest; bees fold theirs in. Hover flies don't bite or sting.

BIOLOGY AND LIFE CYCLE: Larvae are maggots that are usually whitish, but one species is green with a red or white stripe down the back. Maggots are tapered toward the head and usually found near aphids. The female lays tiny single eggs near aphids, and larvae hatch in two to three days. Small cylindrical legless maggots become sluglike and later turn into pear-shaped pupae attached to leaves or stems. Some drop to the ground to pupate in the soil. Adults emerge after two or three weeks. The life cycle (from egg to adult) takes two to six weeks. From one to seven generations a year. Overwinter as larvae or pupae.

HABITAT: Vegetable crops attacked by aphids, especially cole crops and sweet corn. Also plants in herbal and ornamental gardens. Hover flies love flowers.

FEEDING HABITS: Adults are attracted to and feed on the nectar and pollen of many flowers. Larvae are predators on aphids, caterpillars, mealybugs, scale, thrips, corn borers, and corn earworms. They especially like small flat flowers such as carrots, Queen Anne's lace, horseradish, and wild mustard. They can often be seen on roses. The grublike green larvae love aphids. They hold them up and suck their juices as if drinking soda from a bottle and then toss the dry skin aside. They eat about one aphid per minute.

ECONOMIC IMPORTANCE: Larvae are effective predators of aphids and other troublesome insects. Adults are important pollinators. The hover fly hurriedly floats from flower to flower, drinking nectar. By doing so, they are excellent pollinators, which we now need since so many of our honey bees are being destroyed.

NATURAL CONTROL: None needed.

ORGANIC CONTROL: None needed.

INSIGHT: Not commercially available yet. Hover flies can remain absolutely motionless in air where bees and wasps bob up and down. When syrphid flies land on flowers, their wings stop moving, but the buzz keeps buzzing. Attract these insect friends with plants that produce lots of pollen and nectar—such as sweet alyssum, buckwheat, caraway, chickweed, dill, fennel, wild lettuce, morning glory, silver lacevine, yarrow, and other plants in the daisy and carrot families. Coreopsis, coriander, sunflowers, scabiosa, blue-eyed grass also help to attract hover flies.

HUMMINGBIRD MOTH—see Tobacco Hornworm

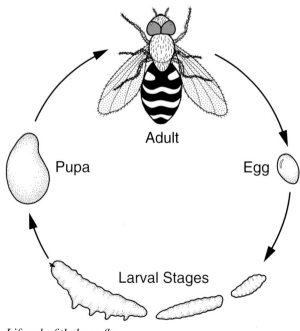

Life cycle of the hover fly

Adult

Egg

Larval Stages

Pupa

ICHNEUMON WASP

COMMON NAMES: Ichneumon Wasp, Ichneumon
SCIENTIFIC NAME: Order Hymenoptera, family Ichneumonidae, many species
SIZE: Adult—⅒" to 1½"
IDENTIFICATION: The largest of the parasitoid wasps. Tan, brown, or black wasps with big, slender bodies and long antennae. Some species have long thin ovipositors (for egg laying), often mistaken for stingers. Distinctly thin waists and long legs. Larvae are tapering white grubs that are parasitic on other insects.
BIOLOGY AND LIFE CYCLE: Adults lay eggs in host insects such as caterpillars, sawflies, beetle larvae, and others. Female adults also control insects by killing them and sucking their juices. Overwinter as mature larvae in cocoons. Several generations per year. Complete metamorphosis—eggs, larvae, pupae, adults. Distinctive cocoons sometimes colored or striped. Some adults sting and some don't.

Ichneumon wasp (ENT)

HABITAT: Natural gardens, forests, and fruit orchards.
FEEDING HABITS: Larvae feed on insect hosts like corn borers, corn earworms, cabbage maggots, asparagus beetles, moths, and sawfly larvae.
ECONOMIC IMPORTANCE: These beneficial wasps control several troublesome insects and are highly beneficial.
NATURAL CONTROL: Insectivorous animals.
ORGANIC CONTROL: None needed.
INSIGHT: This is the largest family of insects. Attract them by planting pollen and nectar-producing flowers such as wild carrots and yarrow. These extremely beneficial insects should be protected. They are important to the lumber industry. The adults of some species can penetrate through an inch of wood and deposit their eggs directly on a wood-boring larva.

IMPORTED CABBAGEWORM

COMMON NAMES: Cabbageworm, Imported Cabbageworm
SCIENTIFIC NAME: Order Lepidoptera, family Pieridae, *Pieris rapae*
SIZE: Adult—1½", larva—up to 1¼"
IDENTIFICATION: Adult is a fast-moving, pretty, small white butterfly with black tips on its wings. Eggs are tiny yellow cones. Larvae are pretty little light green worms.
BIOLOGY AND LIFE CYCLE: Pupae overwinter in garden debris. Adults emerge in the spring and lay eggs on plant foliage. Larvae feed for two to three weeks. Several overlapping generations per year.
HABITAT: Broccoli, cabbage, brussels sprouts, cauliflower, and other leafy garden plants.

Imported cabbageworm larva (B)

Imported cabbageworm adult butterfly (H)

FEEDING HABITS: Larvae eat ragged holes in leaves and heads of cabbage, cauliflower, broccoli, and other leafy vegetables. They leave a trail of droppings.

ECONOMIC IMPORTANCE: Destruction of garden crops.

NATURAL CONTROL: Parasitic wasps, yellow jackets, insectivorous animals. Plant early-maturing varieties.

ORGANIC CONTROL: *Bacillus thuringiensis* products, floating row covers. Release of beneficial wasps. The time to release trichogramma wasps is when you see the pretty little white butterflies fluttering around and landing on your vegetable plants. Make a release prior to this time for even better control. These beautiful little female butterflies lay a translucent egg on foliage every time they light. Don't let their delicate beauty fool you. These little green worms are very destructive.

INSIGHT: Will often hide in the heads of cut broccoli. Soak heads in salty water to drive pests out—unless you like a little protein with your veggies. It's easier to see the light green worms on plants with purple foliage.

IMPORTED FIRE ANT—see Fire Ant

INCHWORM—see Cankerworm

INSIDIOUS FLOWER BUG—see Minute Pirate Bug

JAPANESE BEETLE — These beautifully iridescent beetles were accidentally introduced into this country in 1916. In 1933 government entomologists isolated a bacteria called milky spore disease that produces a fatal blood disease in this grub. It brings about an abnormal white coloring in the infected insects. We don't have Japanese beetles in Texas, and the milky spore disease does not seem to work on our pest grubs. Beneficial nematodes will also help to control them. See June Beetle.

Japanese beetle (ENT)

JUNE BEETLE

COMMON NAMES: Grub, Grubworm, June Beetle, June Bug, May Beetle, May Bug, White Grub
SCIENTIFIC NAME: Order Coleoptera, family Scarabaeidae, *Phyllophaga crinita*
SIZE: Adult — ¾"
IDENTIFICATION: White grubs are the larval stage of May or June beetles. Larvae are characteristically C-shaped with a white body and tan to brown head. The last abdominal segment is clear, allowing dark digested material to be seen. Larvae vary in size with age and species. Adults are medium to dark brown.
BIOLOGY AND LIFE CYCLE: Females lay up to forty eggs, which hatch 2 to 5 inches inches deep in the soil in three to four weeks. Three instars. They feed the first summer on decaying vegetation, hibernate through the winter, and feed on organic matter and plant roots the second summer. Adults emerge in the spring. The process can last from one to three years. The adult beetles show up in late March. There are over 100 species of June bugs in Texas, but this one is responsible for almost all the damage to lawns. In Texas this four-year cycle is cut to two years and even down to one year in the southern part of the state because of warmer soil conditions. Green June bug larvae are primarily organic-matter eaters and actually beneficial.

Green June beetle larvae (B)

Green June beetle larva crawling on its back (B)

HABITAT: Adults fly around and land on door screens. Larvae (grubs) live in the soil. Pest grubs are found primarily in turf. Those found in planting beds are usually feeding only on decaying organic matter and are not troublesome. Beneficials and pest grubs are hard to tell apart when found in the soil, but if you lay the grubs on a smooth surface, the larva of the green June beetle will turn over on its back. With its feet in the air, it scoots away at a surprisingly fast pace.
FEEDING HABITS: Larvae feed on plant roots or decaying organic matter. Feeding decreases as soil temperatures decrease in the fall when the grubs migrate deeper into the soil. Adult beetles chew leaves at night but are not highly destructive.
ECONOMIC IMPORTANCE: Can cause reduced plant production and even plant loss. Damaging to lawns. Grubs are rarely a problem for organically maintained gardens with healthy, biologically alive soil.
NATURAL CONTROL: Grow nectar and pollen plants to attract native predators and parasites. Beneficial nematodes, cats, skunks, opossums, armadillos, raccoons, foxes, coyotes, and other insectivorous animals.
ORGANIC CONTROL: Beneficial nematodes, compost, sugar, and light traps for adults. Milky spore disease does not seem to work on our Texas grubs. *Heterohabditis* nematodes seem to be the most effective nematodes for grubworms.
INSIGHT: According to entomologists, only one in 100 grubs is destructive to plant roots.

A Howard Story

In mid-summer, the chemical pushers say that it's time to broadcast the Diazinon or Oftanol granules. There are several reasons why this is a bad idea. For starters, most people, especially organic gardeners, don't have grub infestations heavy enough to treat. If only two or four grubs per square foot exist, there's no need to treat. It's perfectly natural for some grubworms to exist in the soil. Most species of grubs don't even damage plants. Since I first became involved in organic projects, I've seen only two projects with enough grubworm damage to warrant treatment. One project was commercial, the other residential. In both cases the grubworm infestations were symptoms of the problem — not the actual problem. Both sites had fescue grass in shady areas and soil that didn't drain well. In other words, both turf areas were in stress. Organic pesticides such as nicotine sulfate, rotenone, and soaps were used heavily to try to eliminate the problem. In retrospect, I now know that those organic pesticides

June beetle adult (B)

June beetle light trap (B)

Light trap catch of June beetles (B)

Green June beetle adult (H)

were not only unsuccessful in stopping the pests, they were actually making the problem worse. They were killing the beneficial soil life. Chemical pesticides kill even more of the beneficial organisms in the soil. Few organic gardens have grub problems because the balance of life in the soil usually prevents any one particular animal from becoming a problem. Balance is the key.

Beneficial nematodes are an excellent treatment for grub-infested soils. Beneficial nematodes are microscopic, nonsegmented roundworms that enter the pest through the mouth or other natural body opening. Some just drill right in. Once inside the host, nematodes feed, reproduce, and emerge to find new hosts. They also introduce other microbes that help in the destruction of the pest. Nematodes are purchased from insectaries or organic suppliers. Once applied to the soil, the area must be kept moist and cool. Ideal soil temperature is 75 to 80 degrees. Plan to apply the nematodes in early fall or spring. University testing shows the beneficial nematodes to be very tough and able to stand high temperature. Moisture, however, is critical.

Sugar is an excellent treatment for grubs and other soil pests. White sugar works, but dry molasses is better. Both should be applied in problem areas and watered in; use 10 to 20 pounds per 1,000 square feet. These carbohydrates provide the energy food that the beneficials need to flourish. Does the sugar attract ants? No, not when it's broadcast. As a final reminder, most seasoned organic gardeners don't need to worry about grubs. The natural populations of fungi, bacteria, parasitic nematodes, and other soil biology will control these pests.

If you see some extremely large grubs, from half-dollar to silver-dollar size, chances are good that you have the larva of the rhinoceros or ox beetle. It's an eater of organic matter and a helpful friend.

A Malcolm Story: Light Trap

Here's a very effective way to catch moths of all types and also adult June beetles, which are the parents of grubworms.

I use a 60-watt common light bulb. I've tried all colors, wattages, and types, but the common 60-watt seems to catch the most bugs. Hang the light over a bucket a little below the rim, and fill the bucket one-third full of soapy water. Put it out about the end of March and keep it on each night. Place it high enough so a child or pet can't get to it. You will catch hundreds of moths and June beetles each night. Empty it at least every other night because the bugs will start to decay and stink. Dead insects are good compost ingredients, so don't waste them. When it starts attracting and trapping beneficials such as green lacewings and praying mantids, discontinue use of the light trap.

JUNE BUG—see June Beetle

KATYDID

COMMON NAME: Katydid

SCIENTIFIC NAME: Order Orthoptera, family Tettigoniidae, several species

SIZE: Adult—1½"

IDENTIFICATION: Adults are green with large angular wings and hind legs modified for jumping. They are very noisy. Eggs are gray-brown, flat, and laid in double rows on twigs of plants.

BIOLOGY AND LIFE CYCLE: One generation a year. Winter hibernation in the egg stage. Incomplete metamorphosis. Usually five or six nymphal (instars) stages.

HABITAT: Many orchard plants, landscape gardens, shade trees. Deciduous woods and open fields.

FEEDING HABITS: Adults feed on garden and landscape plant foliage but don't do much damage.

ECONOMIC IMPORTANCE: Very little. More than anything, they are noisy.

NATURAL CONTROL: Good biodiversity, birds, and praying mantids.

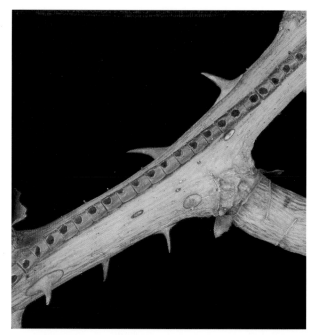

Katydid egg chain on plant stem (B)

Katydid nymph (B)

Katydid adult (H)

ORGANIC CONTROL: Garlic-pepper tea spray as a repellent. Garden-Ville Fire Ant control formula.
INSIGHT: Katydids show up bright and shiny with a flashlight at night. They sing only at night with their distinctive "katy-did, katy-didn't"—and they are very loud. Normally only the males sing.

KISSING BUG

COMMON NAMES: Big Bed Bug, Bloodsucking Cone Nose, Cone Nose Bug, Kissing Bug, Mexican Bed Bug, Bloodsucker
SCIENTIFIC NAME: Order Heteroptera, family Reduviidae, *Cimex lectularius*
BODY LENGTH: Adult—¾" to 1"
IDENTIFICATION: Dark brown, almost black. Broad, flat abdomen with yellow markings along edges. The head is long and conical. The thorax is narrow in front.
BIOLOGY AND LIFE CYCLE: Eggs are laid in sheltered places. Nymphs hatch and grow slowly into adults. They may feed on insects. Usually one generation per year. Incomplete metamorphosis.
HABITAT: Found in poultry houses and horse stalls.
FEEDING HABITS: The normal diet of the kissing bug is bed bugs. They also suck blood from poultry and other animals and humans as a last resort.
ECONOMIC IMPORTANCE: Spread Chagas disease.
NATURAL CONTROL: Good screens on windows and doors of homes. Caulk and seal cracks and crevices.
ORGANIC CONTROL: Diatomaceous earth and pyrethrum. Citrus oil spray.
INSIGHT: The outlaw of the assassin bug family. Some species of the kissing bug are known to inflict a very painful bite with a considerable number of ill effects that may last weeks. This is not the true bed bug.

The normal diet of the bloodsuckers is bed bugs (*Cimex lectularius*), small bugs that suck blood from poultry or people at night and then hide during the day. If the bloodsucker gets in your house and finds no bed bugs, then you become the target.

If you wake up some morning and have a big welt that is about the size of a quarter or larger and that doesn't hurt but itches like the devil, you probably donated a little blood to this demon. Start taking apart the bedding and drapes because it's hiding there somewhere; if you don't find it, you will wake up the next morning with another itchy welt. Do not scratch. Wash the swelling and surrounding area thoroughly with soap and water—then it will be okay to scratch. This bug carries a deadly sleeping sickness called Chagas disease. It doesn't inject the disease organisms while sucking your blood; they are carried in the bug's feces. If you scratch without first washing, you may infect yourself. In the South, the bug deposits feces near the bite. But the farther north the bug goes, the farther it deposits its feces from the bite, making infection less likely with scratching.

When the bloodsucker decides to have dinner on you, it is usually at night. It doesn't want to be disturbed, so it carefully walks lightly over your body, so lightly you can't feel it. When it finds the location for its banquet, it uses a strong anesthetic on the spot. Then it will sit there and pig out until it's full as a balloon and you won't feel a thing.

The bloodsucker can also use its sucking snout to sting when it feels a need for defense. The sting is extremely intense, and the effects may last for weeks or months.

The kissing bug got its name from its habit of biting people when it accidentally flew against their face.

Kissing bug (B)

LACE BUG

COMMON NAME: Lace Bug
SCIENTIFIC NAME: Order Heteroptera, family Tingidae, *Corythucha* spp.
SIZE: Adult—about ⅛"
IDENTIFICATION: Lace bug adults are flat and lacy-looking. The wings of most lace bugs are transparent. Wings are much wider than abdomen. The nymphs are flat and oval-shaped. Both have piercing-sucking mouthparts.
BIOLOGY AND LIFE CYCLE: Incomplete life cycle. Female lays tiny eggs on underside of leaves and then covers them with a little cone of dark, sticky excrement. Wingless nymphs often have long body spines. All stages are found in groups under leaves. Most species overwin-

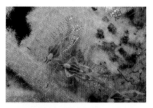

Lace bugs (BP)

Lace bugs on bur oak (H)

ter as adults. They hang out in plant bark and have several generations a year.
HABITAT: Broadleafed evergreens such as azaleas, pyracanthas, and rhododendrons and some deciduous plants such as oaks, hawthorns, elms, walnuts, fruit trees, sycamores, and cotton plants.
FEEDING HABITS: Suck sap from underside of leaves using piercing-sucking mouthparts. Damage appears on leaf surfaces as pale brown or yellow specks.
ECONOMIC IMPORTANCE: Damage to foliage can make nursery plants unmarketable. The mottling of the leaf surface can severely reduce photosynthesis.
NATURAL CONTROL: Provide proper irrigation and other care to maintain plant health. Encourage beneficial insects and microbial activity.
ORGANIC CONTROL: Horticultural oil, citrus oil, and molasses. Neem and biological products containing beneficial fungi. Garden-Ville Fire Ant Control formula.
INSIGHT: Pesticides do not restore damaged foliage. Lace bugs are beautiful when viewed under a microscope, and it has been said that they look as if they were cut out of fine gauze.

LACEWING

COMMON NAMES: Brown Lacewing, Green Lacewing, Lacewing, Aphid Lion
SCIENTIFIC NAME: Order Neuroptera. Green Lacewing—family Chrysopidae; Brown Lacewing—family Hemerobiidae, many species
SIZE: Adult—½" to ¾"
IDENTIFICATION: Adults are light green or brown; they have lustrous eyes, long antennae, and veined wings. Larvae look like tiny alligators with sickle-shaped jaws. Adults hold wings in tentlike fashion while at rest. Some

Lacewing eggs hatching (B)

Green Lacewing eggs (B)

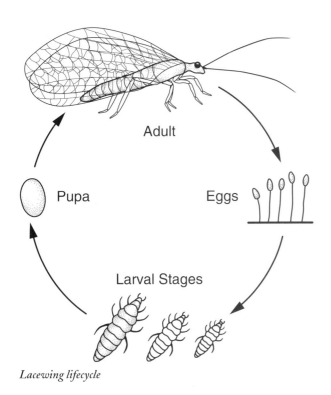

Lacewing lifecycle

species have prominent golden eyes. Brown lacewings are smaller and their eggs are not stalked.

BIOLOGY AND LIFE CYCLE: Complete metamorphosis—eggs, larvae, pupae, and adults. Adults feed on nectar and honeydew or possibly take no food. Larvae are ferocious predators of many insect pests. Adults are active fliers at night. Females lay several hundred eggs in spring and summer. Eggs of the green lacewing are connected to the end of long silk stalks, singly or in clusters, on limbs, twigs, leaves, or even inorganic objects. Brown lacewing eggs are not on the silken stalks. Larvae are pinkish brown and very mobile, progressing through three instars in two to three weeks. They pupate in silken cocoons attached to underside of leaves and emerge in about five days by cutting a hole in the cocoon. Overwinter as adults or cocoons. Three or more generations a year.

HABITAT: All gardens and naturally maintained areas. Vegetable and ornamental crops are host plants.

FEEDING HABITS: Larvae or "aphid lions" feed on aphids, thrips, mites, mealybugs, scale, whiteflies, eggs of leafhoppers, moths, cabbage loopers, corn earworms, Colorado potato beetles, asparagus beetles, leaf miners, and several other small caterpillars and beetle larvae. Developing larvae eat from 100 to 600 aphids a day.

ECONOMIC IMPORTANCE: Control of many troublesome insects. One of the most important beneficial insects.

Green lacewing adult (B)

Lacewing larva attacking an aphid (BP)

Brown lacewing adult (H)

NATURAL CONTROL: None needed.

ORGANIC CONTROL: None needed; should always be encouraged.

INSIGHT: Green lacewings are one of the most effective beneficial insects. They are fragile-looking flies that fly around, look pretty, and mate. Nice life! The lacewing's larvae are the hard workers. They are voracious eaters of aphids, red spider mites, thrips, mealybugs, cottony-cushion scale, and many species of worms. The larvae are called aphid lions or ant lions. Larva and eggs can be purchased commercially. Use at least 500 to 1,000 eggs per release in the average garden.

To store lacewings prior to release, refrigerate the eggs or larvae for a few days at 38–45 degrees Fahrenheit, which will delay development but not hurt the eggs. Do not freeze.

Green lacewing adults, eggs, and larvae can be hand-sprinkled wherever harmful insects exist or are suspected. Larvae and eggs are the most practical to use. Even put in the wrong place, they will travel 100 feet if necessary for their first meal. A pill bottle with a quarter-inch hole in the cap is a good device for distributing the eggs. A salt shaker will work if the size of the holes is slightly increased. Lacewing eggs are very small. A thimble will hold about 10,000 eggs. Watch out for fire ants; they will eat the eggs like jelly beans. Biweekly releases of 2,000 to 4,000 eggs per residential lot or per acre is ideal.

LADY BEETLE

COMMON NAMES: Lady Beetle, Lady Bird Beetle, Ladybird, Ladybug

SCIENTIFIC NAME: Order Coleoptera, family Coccinellidae. Twospotted Lady Beetle—*Adalia bipunctata*. Ninespotted Lady Beetle—*Coccinella novemnotata*. Twicestabbed Lady Beetle—*Chilocorus stigma*. Convergent Lady Beetle—*Hippodamia convergens*. Ashygray Lady Beetle—*Olla abdominalis*. Asian Lady Beetle—*Harmonia axyridis*.

SIZE: Adult—1/16" to 3/8", larva—1/2"

IDENTIFICATION: Adults are shiny round beetles with short legs and antennae. Heads are hidden beneath the front of the thorax. Adult beetles come in many colors— black, red, orange, yellow, or gray. Larvae are dark gray or black with yellow, orange, or white side markings. They look like small alligators with three pair of distinct legs.

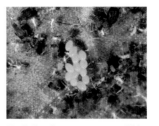

Lady beetle eggs among aphids (B)

Lady beetle larva (B)

Convergent lady beetle larva (B)

Lady beetle larva, commonly called "rag mop" (B)

Harmonia lady beetle larva (B)

Short spines on each segment. Eggs are yellow ovals laid in clusters.

BIOLOGY AND LIFE CYCLE: Development from egg to adult may take only two or three weeks. Adults can live from several weeks to months. Adults overwinter and lay eggs on tree bark, foliage, or stems in the early spring. Females lay from 200 to 1,000 eggs over a three-month period. Typically four larvae instars over a twenty-day period; travel as far as 40 feet in search of prey. Last instar attaches to leaf and forms a pupa that is yellow-orange to black. Pupal stage lasts three to twelve days.

HABITAT: Hedgerows, under leaf litter, under rocks, and in other protected places. Many vegetable and ornamental crops. Field crops and forests.

FEEDING HABITS: Feed on aphids, mites, and other soft-bodied insect pests. Unfortunately, the imported Asian or harmonia lady beetles like the taste of ripe plums and peaches and will eat the fruit if something else provides an opening.

ECONOMIC IMPORTANCE: Great control of aphids and other small troublesome insect pests. Can be stored in refrigerator for several weeks. Release about 1,500 beetles per 1,000 square feet in the home garden.

NATURAL CONTROL: Very few enemies. They don't taste good. You don't believe it? Try one.

ORGANIC CONTROL: None needed; should be encouraged.

Convergent lady beetle pupa (B)

Harmonia lady beetle pupa (B)

Twicestabbed lady beetle pupa (H)

Twicestabbed lady beetle adult (B)

INSIGHT: Ladybugs are the most popular and most universally known of all the beneficial insects. There are several hundred species in North America, and all are beneficial. The most common native varieties are orange with black spots, gray with black spots, and black with two red spots. The black and gray varieties are arboreal and usually seen in trees. All ladybugs should be protected. The *Hippodamia convergens*—orange with black spots and converging white lines on the pronotum (shield behind the head)—is the most available commercially.

For ladybugs to thrive and reproduce, they need flowering plants for a nectar and pollen source. Legumes such as peas, beans, clover, and alfalfa are especially good, but all flowering plants can help. Temporary artificial food can be made by diluting a little honey with a small amount of water and mixing in a little brewer's yeast or bee pollen. Smear small amounts of this mixture on small pieces of waxed paper and fasten these to plants. Replace these every five or six days or when they become moldy. Keep any extra food refrigerated between feedings. Discontinue when a ladybug population is established. Aphids are the ladybug's favorite real food. When using ladybugs indoors or in a greenhouse, screen off any openings to prevent their escape.

If you have noticed a very colorful ladybug on your roses or goldenrod or even on the walls inside you house, congratulations—the Asian lady beetle has found you. *Harmonia axyridis* looks a lot like our native convergent lady beetle but has large white splotches on the sides of its pronotum instead of the converging white lines of our native. They will range in color from yellow or tan to orange and deep red. Some have many black spots, others have none. They also seem to be shinier than our natives. They are aggressive, do a great job of cleaning up troublesome pests, and have naturalized across Texas. If you find a large cluster of these pretty friends on the wall of your bedroom next winter, scoop 'em up and remove them to the garden.

See also Lindorus Lady Beetle, p. 89.

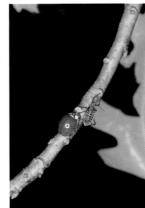

Harmonia lady beetle in peach hole pecked by bird (H)

Harmonia attacking giant bark aphid (H)

Harmonia lady beetles mating (H)

Ashygray lady beetle feeding on worm (B)

Convergent lady beetle on rosemary (H)

A Malcolm Story: A Welcome Visitor

One evening many years ago while resting on the porch thumbing through a farm magazine, I ran across an article about the Colorado potato beetle and all the loss it was causing. The article told of the poison being used to control the beetle and described the range of that troublemaker, which included Texas.

After reading the article, out of curiosity I went to inspect my potato patch. Sure enough, even though there were no holes in the leaves and the plants looked healthy, there were beetles crawling all over them. Early the next day I bought the recommended poison and was out dusting when a friend walked up and said, "Beck, stop! You're killing the ladybugs." He was too late. I had already dusted the whole patch. My friend described the difference between lady beetles and potato beetles. I thought, "So I poisoned a few good bugs. So what?"

A week or so went by. I was out looking over the field again and saw no potato bugs—also no ladybugs. The plants, however, didn't look so good; they looked sick. The leaves were cupped and curled and weren't that healthful green they had been before. On closer inspection, I discovered why. Plant lice (aphids) were all over the stems and undersides of the leaves. The plants looked terrible. I began thinking, "What do I do now? Maybe I better call my friend who said to stop killing the ladybugs."

My friend informed me, "Sure, Beck, I knew this would happen. The ladybugs were there feeding on the aphids and keeping them in check. The poison killed potato bugs, aphids, and ladybugs alike. The aphids, however, reproduce extremely fast, a generation a week, while lady beetles are much slower. It will take the lady beetles awhile to come back in numbers large enough to get the aphid population back in control. Now you will probably need to use more poison because you upset the balance of nature."

Then I began to feel upset, not only because I killed the good bugs and the bad bugs were destroying my garden but because I, a country boy, was being told something by a city boy that I should have known.

I asked my friend how he knew all about good and bad bugs. He had been reading a magazine called *Organic Farming and Gardening*. He gave me some back issues, which I read. All through the magazines the editor was trying to sell the idea that adapted plants, in their proper environment, in a soil balanced in minerals, rich in organic matter, with an abundant, balanced soil life of earthworms and microorganisms, would be strong and healthy. Destructive insects are not attracted to healthy plants. Then I read more in my farming magazine. All through it the idea was being promoted that we need poison and chemicals of all kinds to grow our food and be profitable farmers.

I thought for a while about this chemical philosophy and then about the organic philosophy. Which idea was the best? The question kept coming back: why should we need toxic materials to grow the food we eat? Was nature designed that way? After more thought, I decided gardening and farming could be more fun, more successful, and more profitable if we followed the natural laws. The food we ate would be more healthful, too.

I really became a student of that organic magazine, and in it I noticed an ad for ladybugs. Since I had killed some, I felt that maybe I should order some. Soon the mailman dropped off the ladybugs at the mailbox and blew his horn to let me know of the perishable delivery. All excited, I picked up the container, ran out to the garden, took out my pocket knife, and cut the package open. The ladybugs crawled out by the thousands—all over me. Then they flew up in the air about 15 feet and headed west, right back to California. Then I read the instructions! "Be gentle when handling the insects and first release only a few late in the evening. If they crawl about searching as if hungry, release the rest. If they only want to fly away, close the container and put it in the refrigerator for a few days, then try releasing again later."

It's important to release ladybugs and other beneficial insects during the cool parts of the day and after wetting the foliage because they will be thirsty when first released.

LADY BIRD BEETLE—see Lady Beetle

LADYBUG—see Lady Beetle

LAUREL BUG—see Scarlet Laurel Bug

LEAFCUTTING ANT—see Texas Leafcutting Ant

LEAFCUTTING BEE

COMMON NAMES: Leafcutter Bee, Leafcutting Bee, Plug Bug
SCIENTIFIC NAME: Order Hymenoptera, family Megachilidae, several species
SIZE: Adult—¼" to ¾"
IDENTIFICATION: Adults are stout-bodied and dark brown to black, sometimes with yellow or beige markings. Wings are clear or smoky. They range in size from about as large as honey bees to about half as large. Large heads and highly polished black or metallic blue or green bodies. Sometimes bands of white hairs across the abdomen.
BIOLOGY AND LIFE CYCLE: Solitary insect that uses pieces of leaves to line its nests in cavities in the ground, dead wood, hollow stems, snail shells, pipes, and other

Leafcutting bee adult (L. Wayne Clark, FWNC)

Leafcutting bee larva eating grasshopper (B)

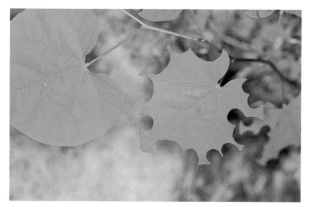

Leafcutting bee damage to redbud leaves (H)

openings. Leafcutters use their mandibles to cut neat circles or partial circles out of the edges of leaves to obtain material for their nests. You've probably seen this damage on your rose foliage.

HABITAT: Many plants, but especially roses, hollies, and fruit trees. They are common everywhere.

FEEDING HABITS: Pollen and nectar from many flowers.

ECONOMIC IMPORTANCE: Important plant pollinators and should not be killed. Troublesome around machine shops because they will plug up any exposed pipes. Mechanics have learned to tape over the ends of pipes, fuel lines, and other openings.

NATURAL CONTROL: Good biodiversity will keep them from being too abundant. Birds, praying mantids, and lizards.

ORGANIC CONTROL: None needed in most cases—their damage is only cosmetic.

INSIGHT: Mason bees are very closely kin. They are metallic blue or green in color. *Osmia* spp. are short metallic-colored pollinators that nest in the ground or in natural cavities. Mason bees will also seek a cavity in wood, soil, masonry, pithy stems of plants, keyholes, and snail shells. They line the holes with cement made of clay, sand, and a sticky secretion from their mouths instead of using leaves, as the leafcutting bee does. In either case, eggs are placed in each cell with a mass of pollen, nectar, or honey.

Mason bee house (H)

Leaffooted bugs mating (B)

LEAFFOOTED BUG

COMMON NAMES: Leaffooted Bug, Leaffooted Plant Bug
SCIENTIFIC NAME: Order Heteroptera, family Coreidae, *Leptoglossus phyllopus*
SIZE: Adult—¾"
IDENTIFICATION: Dark brown bug that looks like an elongated stink bug. Antennae are four-segmented. Hind legs flattened like a leaf. Eggs are white and key-shaped and are laid on the underside of leaves.
BIOLOGY AND LIFE CYCLE: Adults pass the winter in sheltered spots. One brood a year. Incomplete metamorphosis—eggs, nymphs, and adults.
HABITAT: Most gardens and natural areas. Many food crops and some ornamentals. Beans, citrus, peas, pecans, potatoes, tomatoes, and wild areas.
FEEDING HABITS: Adults and nymphs like to suck the juice from leaves, shoots, fruits, buds, and seeds.
ECONOMIC IMPORTANCE: Attack and damage crops of several species such as asparagus, tomatoes, cotton, peaches, potatoes, oranges, and many other crops.
NATURAL CONTROL: Birds, snakes, lizards. Good biodiversity. Parasitic flies such as the tachinid fly. Assassin bugs, birds, wolf spiders, and frogs.
ORGANIC CONTROL: None usually needed. Citrus oil products will eliminate a heavy infestation.
INSIGHT: Kin to squash bugs.

LEAFFOOTED PLANT BUG—see Leaffooted Bug

LEAFHOPPER

COMMON NAME: Leafhopper, planthopper
SCIENTIFIC NAME: Order Homoptera, family Cicadellidae, many species
SIZE: Adult—¹⁄₁₀" to ½"
IDENTIFICATION: Adults are distinctive wedge-shaped insects with triangular heads. Most are brown or green, but some are brightly decorated. All have well-developed hind legs for jumping. Nymphs are very similar to adults, but paler in color and wingless.
BIOLOGY AND LIFE CYCLE: Incomplete metamorphosis. Adults overwinter and lay eggs in rows or clusters when leaves emerge. Eggs hatch in ten to fourteen days, nymphs develop for one to four weeks. Two to five generations a year.
HABITAT: Fruits, vegetables, and ornamental plants.
FEEDING HABITS: Adults and nymphs suck juices from stems and undersides of leaves, causing a mottled look.
ECONOMIC IMPORTANCE: Toxic saliva can cause stunty leaf growth or warty, crinkled, or rolled edges. Some are vectors of plant disease.
NATURAL CONTROL: Maintain healthy plants. Protect natural enemies such as parasitic wasps and flies, damsel

Leafhopper or planthopper (H)

Leafhopper (B)

Leafhopper resembling mealybug (H)

bugs, minute pirate bugs, lady beetles, lacewings, and spiders. Birds, frogs, lizards, and insectivorous insects.

ORGANIC CONTROL: Strong blasts of water and citrus oil products. Horticultural oil for heavy infestations.

INSIGHT: Entomologists say that leafhoppers are responsible for spreading more than 150 plant disorders.

LEAFMINER

COMMON NAMES: Leafminer, Leafminer Fly, Serpentine Leafminer

SCIENTIFIC NAME: Order Diptera, family Agromyzidae

SIZE: Adult—1⁄10"

IDENTIFICATION: Adults are black and yellow flies that are rarely seen. Larvae are short, pale-green, translucent maggots. Eggs are white and cylindrical.

BIOLOGY AND LIFE CYCLE: Adults emerge from overwintering cocoons in the soil in early spring and lay

eggs in clusters under leaves. Tiny yellow larvae mine tunnels through leaves for one to three weeks, then pupate for two to four weeks in the leaf before dropping to the

Leafminer adult (BP)

Leafminer larva (BP)

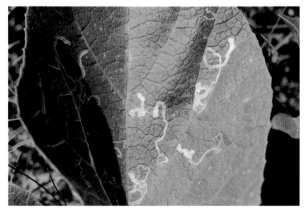

Leafminer damage (B)

soil. Two to three generations a year, more in greenhouses.

HABITAT: Yaupon holly, mums, nasturtiums, and other ornamentals. Beans, beets, cabbage, chard, lettuce, peppers, tomatoes, and other vegetables. They especially like dark vegetables and lamb's-quarter.

FEEDING HABITS: Larvae tunnel through leaf tissue, leaving unsightly trails.

ECONOMIC IMPORTANCE: Can destroy seedlings but causes only a cosmetic problem on mature plants.

NATURAL CONTROL: Leafminers have many natural enemies such as hummingbirds. *Dacnusa sibirica* is a parasitic wasp specific to some leafminers. Beneficial nematodes will attack the pupae in the soil.

ORGANIC CONTROL: Floating row cover on vegetable crops. Neem products or citrus oil products.

INSIGHT: Spraying regularly with fish, seaweed, molasses, vinegar, and garlic works well to repel these pests. With organic practices the leafminer never becomes a problem because of its many natural enemies. Where beneficial insects are destroyed by massive spraying to vegetable, cut flower, and greenhouse crops, the leafminers have become almost uncontrollable. A large pecan grove operator told us that the more they sprayed with chemicals, the worse the leafminers got. When they stopped spraying chemical poisons, the leafminers disappeared.

LEAFROLLER

COMMON NAME: Canna Leafroller, Leafroller

SCIENTIFIC NAME: Order Lepidoptera, family Torticidae, several species

SIZE: Adult wing span—1⁄2" to 1¼"

IDENTIFICATION: Adults are small, dull-colored, brown or yellow. Larvae are small worms that conceal themselves in rolled-up plant foliage. The canna leafroller is larger and is a semi-transparent green color.

BIOLOGY AND LIFE CYCLE: The larvae roll up the leaves

Leafroller on canna leaves (H)

Leafroller damage on canna leaf (H)

of plants and feed within the nest. A number of larvae will often work together to make large ugly nests.

HABITAT: Fruit trees, shade trees, and ornamentals such as roses and cannas.

FEEDING HABITS: Feed on the foliage of ornamentals, fruit and shade trees.

ECONOMIC IMPORTANCE: Disfigurement of plant foliage and reduction of photosynthesis.

NATURAL CONTROL: Predatory wasps and flies.

ORGANIC CONTROL: *Bacillus thuringiensis* sprays, beneficial nematodes.

INSIGHT: Little has been written about these pests.

A Malcolm Story

The leafroller has been troublesome on only one plant on my farm, a concord grape. By late season it has almost every leaf on the vines pulled together. Vines that get early evening shade are bothered very little. The concord is not considered adapted to the San Antonio area. The leafroller pulls the leaves together for protection, but I have noticed a big black wasp that has a bright yellow strip across its back cut a square 5/16-inch hole in the leaf and reach in and get the leaf roller. This beneficial is rare. I have yet to get a photo or identification.

LESSER MEALWORM—see Guano Beetle

LESSER PEACH TREE BORER—see Peach Tree Borer

LIGHTNING BUG—see Firefly

LINDORUS LADY BEETLE

COMMON NAMES: Singular Lady Beetle, Scale Destroyer

SCIENTIFIC NAME: Order Coleoptera, family Coccinellidae, *Lindorus lopanthea*

SIZE: Adult—3/32", larva—5/32"

IDENTIFICATION: Much smaller than convergent ladybugs, with velvety black wing covers and a deep reddish-orange head, thorax, and abdomen. The larvae are dark gray and shaped like other lady beetle larvae and have light-colored bands running lengthwise along the abdomen.

BIOLOGY AND LIFE CYCLE: The life cycle is thirty-five to sixty days, depending on the temperature. The beetles do not hibernate in cold temperatures or low light as other insects do. Adults are active down to 40 degrees F.

HABITAT: Citrus trees or wherever hard scale can be found in high densities.

FEEDING HABITS: Larvae and adults feed on hard scale.

ECONOMIC IMPORTANCE: Help to control purple scale and red scale in citrus crops as well as other armored scale with relatively thin scale covers.

NATURAL CONTROL: Other than humans with poisons, none known.

ORGANIC CONTROL: None needed.

INSIGHT: These insects were first imported to the United States from Australia in 1892 and again from South Africa to Texas in 1959. They are an excellent insect for scale control, although they don't survive the winter very well and need to be reintroduced annually. Lindorus beetles are so voracious that it is difficult to ensure a food supply for sustaining mass production in insectaries. One California insectary, Rincon-Vitova, has now worked out a system for feeding them so we can have a year-round supply to release in greenhouses.

Lindorus lady beetle adult and larvae eating scale (B)

LOCUST BORER

COMMON NAMES: Chevron Bug, Locust Borer
SCIENTIFIC NAME: Order Coleoptera, family Cerambycidae, *Megacyllene robiniae*
SIZE: Adult—up to ¾"
IDENTIFICATION: Velvety black with golden yellow chevron bars over whole body.
BIOLOGY AND LIFE CYCLE: Females cut pits deep into bark and deposit one egg in each pit. Larvae hatch, feed, and pupate under the bark. One generation per year; adults emerge in late summer.
HABITAT: Black locust trees and other locust and soft-wooded trees.
FEEDING HABITS: Adults feed on pollen and nectar of goldenrod flowers and a few other similar plants. Larvae feed on both sapwood and heartwood of locust trees.
ECONOMIC IMPORTANCE: Damaging to locust trees in pure stands.
NATURAL CONTROL: Ichneumon wasps parasitize the larvae.
ORGANIC CONTROL: Healthy, fast-growing trees are bothered less. Heavy mulch over tree root zone has proven to be an effective repellent. These pests seem to be less damaging when locust trees are interplanted with other trees.
INSIGHT: Adults are very visible and attractive because of their stripe design.

LONGHORNED BORER—see Cottonwood Borer

LONGLEGGED FLY

COMMON NAME: Longlegged Fly
SCIENTIFIC NAME: Order Diptera, family Dolichopodidae, several species
SIZE: Adult—⅜"
IDENTIFICATION: Small flies with metallic, shiny, often green and bristly bodies. Male's genitalia are large and held curved under the body. Female's abdomen ends in a point. Wings are much longer than the body. These are the pretty little green flies you see often in your garden.

BIOLOGY AND LIFE CYCLE: Adults are mostly predaceous on soft-bodied insects. Some feed on flower nectar. Larvae are round white predators and live in wet soil, rotten wood, bark, and plant stems.
HABITAT: Ornamental and vegetable gardens.
FEEDING HABITS: Adults capture and eat many small soft-bodied troublesome insects.
ECONOMIC IMPORTANCE: Adults are effective predators of mosquito larvae and many other soft-bodied insects.
NATURAL CONTROL: Lizards and birds.
ORGANIC CONTROL: None needed.
INSIGHT: We see lots of 'em around the vegetable garden. These are helpful flies—don't hurt 'em!

LOOPER—see Cabbage Looper

LOVE BUG

COMMON NAMES: Love Bug, March Fly
SCIENTIFIC NAME: Order Diptera, family Bibionidae, *Plecia nearctica*
SIZE: Adult—⅞" to 1"
IDENTIFICATION: Wetland flies that are called love bugs because the male and female are usually seen together in the act of copulation.
BIOLOGY AND LIFE CYCLE: These bugs emerge twice a year. Their mating flights are in May and September, which is when they smash themselves en masse on the front of your car and windshield. They lay their eggs in rotting organic matter. Flights last four or five days; each adult lives only two to three days. Pupal stage lasts seven to ten days. Females lay 100 to 300 eggs, which are deposited beneath decaying vegetation. Flights are usually restricted to daylight hours and temperatures over 68 degrees. At night love bugs rest on low-growing vegetation.
HABITAT: Old rotting grass and other organic matter in low damp areas. They become active in the air around ten o'clock in the morning.
FEEDING HABITS: Adult lovebugs are harmless and do not sting or bite. They feed on nectar, especially that of sweet clover, goldenrod, and other wildflowers.

Locust borer (B)

Longlegged fly (B)

Love bugs in one of their common resting places (B)

Luna moth (RB)

ECONOMIC IMPORTANCE: Good for the car wash business. Larvae feed on decaying plant material and help break it down.

NATURAL CONTROL: Birds such as robins and quail. Armadillos eat the larvae. Earwigs, beetles, and centipedes.

ORGANIC CONTROL: None needed.

INSIGHT: Phil Callahan explains in his wonderful book *Tuning into Nature* that mating love bugs actually do you a favor by smashing into the windshield as you drive at night. They make you stop, clean the windshield, and get a cup of coffee. Callahan's humorous comment aside, love bugs are a nuisance to motorists. Besides messing up the windshield and paint, they clog radiator fins and can cause overheating. They can also cause truck refrigeration to malfunction. Beekeepers report that the bugs repel bees from flowers.

LUNA MOTH

COMMON NAMES: Luna Moth, Moon Moth

SCIENTIFIC NAME: Order Lepidoptera, family Saturniidae, *Actias luna*

SIZE: Adult wing span—5", larva—2½" to 3"

IDENTIFICATION: Large, night-flying, startlingly beautiful moth with translucent green wings and long tail. The color of the wings' edges vary from purple to yellow. The large green larvae are translucent light green, with a light yellow line along the side and red or orange knobs.

Luna moth larva (RB)

BIOLOGY AND LIFE CYCLE: Large brown eggs are laid in irregular groups. The larvae are large caterpillars that eat lots of foliage; cocoons are made from leaves and loosely cover the pupae. Usually two to three generations a year. Cocoons are found in the leaves on the ground.

HABITAT: They like many trees such as hickory, pecan, willow, maple, persimmon, birch, oak, and sweetgum.

FEEDING HABITS: Larvae eat the foliage of deciduous trees.

ECONOMIC IMPORTANCE: Not highly destructive. Their beauty is certainly worth a little damage.

NATURAL CONTROL: Predatory wasps and bats.

ORGANIC CONTROL: None needed.

INSIGHT: The luna moth is unrelated to the swallowtail butterfly even though they look similar. In Texas look for luna moths on sweetgum trees.

MANTID—see Praying Mantis

MARCH FLY—see Love Bug

MASON BEE—see Leafcutting Bee

MAY BEETLE—see June Beetle

MAY BUG—see June Beetle

MEALWORM

COMMON NAMES: Mealworm, Yellow Mealworm
SCIENTIFIC NAME: Order Coleoptera, family Tenebrionidae, *Tenebrio molitor*
SIZE: Adult—½" to 1", larva—1" to 1½"
IDENTIFICATION: Male and female mealworms look alike. Adults are flattened black beetles. Larvae are white when hatched but become yellow and resemble wireworms.
BIOLOGY AND LIFE CYCLE: Female beetles deposit whitish oval eggs from 1 to 1,000 in food materials. Eggs hatch in four to eighteen days. Larvae live for six to nine months and usually overwinter in this stage. Pupal stage is white and is passed without any cocoon or protective covering.
HABITAT: Damp grains, especially grains that have been undisturbed for some time.
FEEDING HABITS: Feed in and around grain bins, especially in dark places where the grain has not been disturbed in a long time. Mealworms like meal, bran, meat scraps, feathers, and dead insects.
ECONOMIC IMPORTANCE: Destruction of food products.
NATURAL CONTROL: Moving and disturbing the grain from time to time.
ORGANIC CONTROL: Diatomaceous earth in grain.
INSIGHT: Mealworms are sold as a food source for insectivorous pets such as hedgehogs and reptiles.

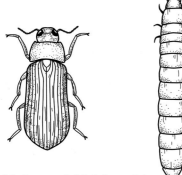

Mealworm, adult left, larva right

MEALYBUG

COMMON NAME: Mealybug
SCIENTIFIC NAME: Order Homoptera, family Pseudococcidae, several species
SIZE: Adult—⅒"
IDENTIFICATION: Female adults have soft, oval, segmented pink bodies covered by white waxy material. The rarely seen males have two wings and look like tiny flies.
BIOLOGY AND LIFE CYCLE: Female adults lay eggs in a cottony white mass that hatches in ten days. Active yellow nymphs called crawlers feed for one or two months or more. Several generations a year. Some mealybugs bear live young. Females molt twice; males form a thin cocoon before becoming adults. Winter is passed in all stages.
HABITAT: Most fruit trees, grape, potatoes, and many ornamental and indoor foliage plants. They especially like citrus, grapes, and tropical plants. Common pest on interior plants and outdoor landscaping plants that are in stress.
FEEDING HABITS: Female adults and nymphs suck juice from primarily the new growth of plants. Leaves turn yellow, and fruit drops prematurely. Honeydew from these insects supports growth of sooty mold and other diseases. Males don't have mouth parts (all they do is mate).

Mealybug (B)

Mealybug infestation on Aralia (H)

ECONOMIC IMPORTANCE: Can damage plant foliage and reduce fruit production.

NATURAL CONTROL: Birds and lizards. Healthy, stress-free plants are immune to this pest.

ORGANIC CONTROL: Attract and release parasitic wasps. Release mealybug destroyer *Cryptolaemus montrouzieri* (indoors only), lady beetles, lacewings. Strong water spray, seaweed, and garlic tea or garlic/pepper tea.

INSIGHT: This is one of the most common insect pests on indoor plants, but it will attack landscape and garden plants as well. It is quick to show up on stressed plants.

A Malcolm Story

My old farm at one time had more than a hundred pecan trees, but neglect and the drought of the early 1950s had taken their toll. Only about twenty of the large trees were in fair condition; the rest were dead or near death when we bought the place in 1957. On the north side of the house, which was also the front, stood one of the oldest trees. It was probably put there to provide summer shade. The trunk was straight and about thirty inches in diameter; other than its size, it was in very poor condition. From the tips of the limbs to where the wood was five or six inches in diameter, it was already dead. Down near the trunk there were a few yellowish, sick-looking leaves, and there was a thick infestation of mealybugs feeding under the live bark.

The soil under the tree was packed hard. On one side was the driveway to the garage, and on the opposite side, a school bus was parked every day between routes, leaving a large oil soak.

Knowing it would take up to fifty years to grow another that size, we sure did not want to lose this tree. We talked to the experts. Most said the tree was past the point of no return, but one old nurseryman, Mr. Fanick, said a lot of tender love and care might bring it back. He said it would need feeding and watering, the leaves should be sprayed with zinc, and the trunk with a chemical poison.

Since our finances were extremely low and because the tree might not survive anyway, we decided not to spend any money on it. When winter came, I cut it back since we heated with wood and needed it anyway. When I got through, there were only a few large branches left on the trunk. We didn't do any spraying because of cost—besides, the products weren't organic.

A neighboring farmer had a wire cage out in the middle of his feedlot into which he put all the animal droppings, wasted hay, corn cobs, and such, so I asked the old farmer if I could have some. He looked at me, thought for a moment, then said, "If you clean it all up you can have it." It amounted to about six cubic yards. We hauled it all and spread it as a mulch under the tree, starting about four feet from the trunk and extending out to about six feet beyond the original drip line.

Realizing the hard-packed condition of the soil, I knew the roots couldn't get air, and it would be a long time before the nutrients from the compost could get down into the soil, so I decided to help. I took a three-foot-long piece of half-inch pipe and cut off one end at an angle; I fitted the other end into a water hose. I turned up the pressure on our well pump, then used the pipe to make holes in the soil under the tree about four feet apart and eighteen inches deep over the whole mulch area. The holes were made with more of a washing than drilling action, which aerated really well without damaging the tree roots. I was washing subsoil out, and the return water was carrying compost tea down into the holes.

Winter passed, spring came, and the tree came out with lots of lush growth. By the third year, it had started producing nuts. The neighbors who knew the farm said the nuts were more than twice the original size. But at harvest time, we had the biggest surprise. Instead of nuts with two kernels of meat in each, a big percentage were triplets—three kernels of meat in each nut. The tree produced good crops of nuts every year, but the number of triplets got fewer and fewer each year.

When the tree came out at first, the new branches were real thick, just a few inches apart; everyone said I would have to prune or thin, but I didn't do anything. I just let nature take its course. The dominant branches shaded out the weaker limbs and developed a beautiful canopy.

Within two years after the mulching, the bark of the trunk cleared up. No mealybugs. The health of the tree— its own immunity—somehow prevented the infestation from continuing. The tree has had only that one compost mulch, along with aeration treatment, and has never even had the recommended zinc spray. To this day—over forty years later—the tree is beautiful, healthy, and giving lots of cool shade in the summer and delicious nuts in winter.

MEALYBUG DESTROYER

COMMON NAME: Mealybug Destroyer

SCIENTIFIC NAME: Order Coleoptera, family Coccinellidae, *Cryptolaemus montrouzieri*

SIZE: ⅓"

IDENTIFICATION: Adults are dark brown or black lady beetles with orange head, thorax, abdomen, and wing tips. Larvae look like white rag mops and closely resemble their prey, the mealybug. Eggs are yellow ovals.

BIOLOGY AND LIFE CYCLE: Complete metamorphosis, with four larval stages. Females mate soon after hatching and start laying eggs about five days later. Eggs are deposited in the fluff of mealybugs. Eggs hatch in eight to ten days. Most active in sunlight and warm weather.

Mealybug destroyer (BP)

Mealybug destroyer larva (BP)

Mexican bean beetle larva (B)

Mexican bean beetle adult with damaged wing (B)

Larvae are active for about three weeks; pupate on plants; adults emerge two or three weeks later. Adults will overwinter in mild climates. Several generations a year.

HABITAT: Citrus, grapes, greenhouse plants, and house plants.

FEEDING HABITS: Adults and young larvae catch prey and gobble it up. They prefer eggs and other young larvae. Older larvae will eat anything nearby. Mealybugs are their favorite food, but they will also eat aphids and other small insects.

ECONOMIC IMPORTANCE: Control of mealybugs and aphids, especially in greenhouses.

NATURAL CONTROL: Insectivorous animals.

ORGANIC CONTROL: None needed.

INSIGHT: Release two to five per infested plant in greenhouses, ten to twenty per house plant; cover with sheer curtain or floating row cover to hold beetles in place. Will freeze outdoors—for greenhouse use only.

MEASURING WORM—see Cankerworm

MEXICAN BEAN BEETLE

COMMON NAME: Mexican Bean Beetle
SCIENTIFIC NAME: Order Coleoptera, family Coccinellidae, *Epilachna varivestis*, also *Cerotama* spp.
SIZE: ¼"
IDENTIFICATION: Adult beetles are oval, yellowish brown or copper-colored, with sixteen black spots arranged in rows across the wing covers. They look just like fat lady beetles. Larvae are fat yellow grubs with no legs but spines from each segment. Eggs are yellow ovals.
BIOLOGY AND LIFE CYCLE: Adults overwinter in organic matter. They emerge in spring to feed for a while; females lay eggs on end in clusters of forty to sixty on the underside of bean leaves. Eggs hatch in five to fourteen days, larvae feed for two to five weeks, pupae attach to lower sides of leaves, adults emerge in a week. New adults are solid yellow at first, later darken and become spotted. Several generations a year.
HABITAT: Most abundant in weedless fields and in the bean garden.
FEEDING HABITS: Adults and larvae feed on the undersides of leaves, causing a skeletonizing effect.
ECONOMIC IMPORTANCE: Will destroy bean crops.
NATURAL CONTROL: Plant a biodiverse garden and use

lots of flowers. Release spined soldier bugs, parasitic wasps, and assassin bugs.

ORGANIC CONTROL: Plant cover crops or mulch bare soil. Cover young plants with floating row cover. Soybeans can be planted as a trap crop to be destroyed when infested. Crush egg masses daily. Spray citrus oil, garlic-pepper tea, or neem (Garden-Ville Fire Ant Control formula).

INSIGHT: Neither of us has ever seen a serious infestation of this insect in Texas. This beetle is troublesome in the Northeast, skips Texas for some reason, then goes on down into Mexico and causes more trouble. Because most insect books mention it and its romantic name is easy to remember, people falsely identify other beetles as the Mexican bean beetle and end up unnecessarily using pesticides.

MILLIPEDE

COMMON NAMES: Millipede, Thousand-Legged Worm
SCIENTIFIC NAME: Rusty Millipede—order Spirobolida, Garden Millipede—order Polydesmida
SIZE: Adult—½" to 3"
IDENTIFICATION: Wormlike soil dwellers with two pair of legs per segment. When being handled, will leave an odor on your hands. Slower-moving than centipedes, body is rounded instead of flat like the centipede's. Short antennae. Many species have an offensive odor.
BIOLOGY AND LIFE CYCLE: Not poisonous but can cause allergic reactions. Fluid can damage eyes. Lay eggs in the soil. Nymphs are shorter and have fewer segments. Incomplete metamorphosis.

Millipede (B)

HABITAT: Protected moist areas, under logs and stones, and in greenhouses.

FEEDING HABITS: Feed mostly on decaying organic matter. Will sometimes damage seedlings, especially in damp soils. Some millipedes are predators and eat small insects. Some millipedes will eat plant roots, but for the most part they are beneficial breaking down organic matter.

ECONOMIC IMPORTANCE: Beneficial in breaking down organic matter, but will eat fruit that rests on the ground—such as strawberries and tomatoes.

NATURAL CONTROL: Mulch bare soil to keep low-growing fruit off the soil. Maintain biodiversity.

ORGANIC CONTROL: Dry soil out with wood ashes or diatomaceous earth. Drench soil with citrus tea if millipedes become a problem.

INSIGHT: Millipedes are sometimes mistaken for the pest wireworms.

MINUTE PIRATE BUG

COMMON NAMES: Flower Bug, Insidious Flower Bug, Minute Pirate Bug

SCIENTIFIC NAME: Order Heteroptera, family Anthocoridae, *Orius* spp.

SIZE: ¼"

IDENTIFICATION: Adults are small, quick-moving, black and white bugs. Nymphs are shiny ovals that change from yellow to orange to mahogany brown. Some have red eyes.

BIOLOGY AND LIFE CYCLE: Adult females insert tiny white or clear eggs into plant stems or leaves. Eggs hatch in three to five days, nymphs feed on small insects for two or three weeks before molting into the adult stage. Mated females overwinter in bark, weeds, and mulch, but the males die before winter. Two to four generations a year.

HABITAT: Pollen and nectar plants like goldenrod, daisies, yarrow, and alfalfa. Prefer mixed plantings. Flowering plants, corn, and other field crops. Also found in the wild.

FEEDING HABITS: Feed on insect eggs, small caterpillars, thrips, mites, and aphids. Nymphs and adults are predatory. Will attack almost any pest insect. Very good at finding prey deep inside flowers. Adults also feed on pollen.

ECONOMIC IMPORTANCE: Excellent for control of thrips as well as aphids, spider mites, corn borer, corn

earworm, and potato leafhopper. Collect minute pirate bugs from goldenrod in fall and move to the garden. Release one adult per plant.

NATURAL CONTROL: Biodiversity.

ORGANIC CONTROL: None needed.

INSIGHT: There is evidence that populations increase in corn plantings with broadleaf and grassy weeds. *Orius tristicolor* and *Orius insidiosus* are available commercially, shipped as nymphs. They are "thrill killers"—they kill more insects than they require for food.

MITE—see Predatory Mite, Spider Mite

MOLE CRICKET

COMMON NAME: Mole Cricket, Southern Mole Cricket

SCIENTIFIC NAME: Order Orthoptera, family Gryllatalpidae, *Scapteriscus acletus*

SIZE: 1" to 1¼"

IDENTIFICATION: Adults have large eyes. Grayish with mottled white spots on top of the area behind the head. Velvety bodies; broad, spadelike front legs adapted for digging.

BIOLOGY AND LIFE CYCLE: Incomplete metamorphosis. Adults have wings.

HABITAT: Loose sandy soils such as golf course greens and vegetable gardens.

FEEDING HABITS: Feed on soil insects.

ECONOMIC IMPORTANCE: Their tunneling damages bermudagrasses, ornamentals, and vegetables. In some case the damage is enough to cause the grass to die.

NATURAL CONTROL: Insectivorous animals and beneficial nematodes.

ORGANIC CONTROL: Beneficial nematodes. Frequent thin applications of compost or sprayings of compost tea.

INSIGHT: There are other species of mole crickets that are grass feeders. The southern mole cricket is the only one known to be causing problems in Texas. These problems are caused while the cricket is actually doing some good in feeding on troublesome soil insects.

Mole cricket (B)

Minute pirate bug (BP)

MONARCH BUTTERFLY—see Butterfly

MOSQUITO

COMMON NAME: Mosquito
SCIENTIFIC NAME: Order Diptera, family Culicidae
SIZE: ⅛" to ⅜"
IDENTIFICATION: Adults are slender delicate flies with small heads and long, slender, sucking mouthparts. Clear wings. Antennae are feathery on males, hairy on females. Some fly with a high-pitched whine.
BIOLOGY AND LIFE CYCLE: The females are the bloodsuckers, feeding on many vertebrate hosts. Males don't bite but feed on nectar and honeydew. Eggs are laid singly or in floating groups of fifty to three hundred. Larvae are called wigglers.
HABITAT: Any aquatic area.
FEEDING HABITS: Females suck blood of animals. Males occasionally eat nectar and honeydew.
ECONOMIC IMPORTANCE: Serious disease vectors.
NATURAL CONTROL: Mosquito-eating fish; predators such as bats, purple martins, hummingbirds, damselflies, aquatic beetles, spiders, predatory mites, and dragonflies.
ORGANIC CONTROL: Habitat drainage. Treatment of stagnant water with *Bacillus thuringiensis* 'Israelensis'. Spray for adult infestations with garlic-pepper tea, Garrett Juice plus citrus oil, and Garden-Ville Fire Ant Control (see Appendix C). To avoid being bitten by mosquitoes, use essential oil of lavender to mask the human odors that attract mosquitoes. Avon Skin-So-Soft and other herbal repellents also work.
INSIGHT: Mosquitoes are pests—in fact, they're a menace. Not only can they easily spoil a fancy garden party, but they can cause malaria, encephalitis, and other serious diseases. Control to eliminate the pest from spreading serious diseases is important, but it's also important to note that more home repellents are used in futile attempts to control mosquitoes than any other home insect pest. The problem with most insecticides is that they don't work. They kill as many or more beneficial insects as pests.

Mosquito (ARM)

A Howard Story

About fifty years ago my grandfather appeared before the Pittsburg, Texas, city council and told them a big insect problem was about to happen. The weather had been unusually wet, and Granddad knew that the mosquitoes would soon take over.

The council didn't listen to his idea about spraying a light coating of oil over the surface of all the ponds and lakes, so he decided to take matters into his own hands. He stopped at several local gas stations and filled pop bottles with used oil. Even though the mosquitoes had already started to emerge from the ponds and attack people, Granddad ended the problem by simply throwing the oil-filled pop bottles in every pond he could find in Camp County. The mosquito problem had been eliminated.

Now, I don't recommend that you all run down to the corner gas station and start dumping motor oil in lakes and streams; we don't need a mini-version of the Alaska oil spill. But the lesson is good. The way to control mosquitoes is not to spray poisonous chemicals into the air and onto your skin to try to eliminate the adults. Proper mosquito control is done by killing the larvae of the insects in the water where they breed and grow. The cleanest oils for use in lightly coating the surface of standing water include the horticultural oils. Restraint is the key—don't use too much.

Cities should seriously consider the mosquito problem resulting from heavy spring rains every year. Like the medfly-concerned cities in California, they are thinking about spraying a chemical poison. Spraying anything toxic is a bad idea because you don't control mosquitoes by spraying the air. You might as well run around your neighborhood swinging a fly swatter. What's more, toxic chemical insecticides such as malathion, Dursban, or diazinon not only kill the target insect pests but also a large percentage of beneficial insects such as fireflies, dragonflies, honeybees, ladybugs, and green lacewings.

The proper way to control mosquitoes is to treat the breeding areas—ponds, lakes, creeks, trapped water, and other wet places where the eggs are laid, hatch into larvae, and then turn into adults.

Malathion, a chemical pesticide often used for mosquitoes, is said to be safe for people and for the environment because the product breaks down relatively quickly. Relatively quickly compared to what? I have serious doubts about the safety of a product that will damage the paint on cars. It seems that as malathion and other chemical insecticides break down, the resulting compounds, metabolites, may actually be more toxic and dangerous than the original compounds. It's a bad idea—simple as that. There are safer and more effective ways of controlling mosquito outbreaks.

In most years the breeding places can be reduced by providing good drainage and eliminating swampy areas where practical and dumping the water out of vessels such as pots, old tires, and other containers that hold stagnant water. During wet years the standing water is immense.

Airplanes may be needed for large-scale control, but

homeowners can kill mosquitoes in breeding places by applying organic controls to the water surface. Safe products include garlic tea, instant coffee, mineral oil, or *Bacillus thuringiensis* 'Israelensis'. Garlic tea can be made by grinding garlic bulbs and pouring the slurry into the standing water. For this purpose, straining the solids out isn't necessary. Instant coffee crystals can be put into stagnant water at about 2 tablespoons per 100 square feet of water surface. Mineral oil can be used by itself or mixed with one of the other materials to make an effective mosquito control.

The best product for controlling these miserable pests is *Bacillus thuringienses*, which is sold as Dipel or Thuricide to biologically control caterpillars and loopers. The strain 'Israelensis' is specifically targeted at mosquito larvae. Sold under the names Bactimos, Teknar, Vectobac, and Mosquito Attack, it can be bought in granular form or floating briquettes, which last longest and are easiest to use. It is an organic product and will not harm fish or aquatic plants. Another low-toxicity product is called Altosid. It is also available in briquettes and is a growth regulator to prevent the adult mosquito from emerging from the larval stage. One briquette per 100 square feet is needed. Deep, flowing water should not be treated. Mosquitoes breed and reproduce in shallow, stagnant water.

Wildlife can help a lot with mosquito control. Night hawks, barn swallows, whippoorwills, bats, purple martins, dragonflies, water fowl, frogs, and fish find mosquitoes a favorite evening treat. Fish such as the tiny and very common Gambusia provide terrific mosquito control. This is another reason I don't use or recommend harsh chemical pesticides that are sprayed in a general application.

To rid your garden of adult flying and biting mosquitoes, try to use something a little safer than the chemical insecticides. A few solutions worth trying are citronella candles or lamps, pennyroyal mint crushed and spread around the party area, or tansy and pennyroyal mint planted near doorways and gathering places. Electrocuting lamps are said to kill large numbers of mosquitoes, but the crackling bug-zappers are more annoying than the mosquitoes. Furthermore, the percentage of kill is exaggerated, and lots of beneficial insects also get killed. They should not be used.

For the quick fix, if you have a big party with lots of people who don't eat enough garlic to repel mosquitoes, spray the foliage of trees and shrubs with citrus oil, garlic tea, or hot pepper spray. These products will kill the adult mosquitoes that rest on the cool underside of leaves during the heat of the day. This organic method solve an immediate insect problem, and your yard won't smell like the inside of a chemical plant. No matter which organic method you choose, they are all better than the chemical alternatives.

Mosquito Blues

Why do mosquitoes feast on one individual and avoid the next? In *Sugar Blues*, Bill Dufty claims that mosquitoes like sugar. USDA's Phil Callahan says mosquitoes hone in on the ketone in the human breath. We can, of course, speculate that sugar affects the ketone, and over-sugared people are simply more attractive to mosquitoes. Ditto for animals.

Dufty gave up sugar as part of a health recovery program and now religiously avoids sugar-containing foods. As a consequence, he can lay [*sic*] stripped to his bathing trunks in an area where mosquitoes literally fly off with victims sunbathing a few feet away.

From *Acres U.S.A.*

MOTHS—Moths are part of one of the largest orders of insects, Lepidoptera, which contains more than 100,000 described species and includes moths, millers, butterflies, and skippers. The name means "scaly winged." Moths are often considered to be the ugly members of this group. Many are dull gray or brown, but others are quite beautiful. See Armyworm, Bagworm, Cabbage Looper, Cankerworm, Codling Moth, Corn Earworm, Cutworm, Grain Pests, Leafroller, Luna Moth, Mealworm, Peach Tree Borer, Pecan Gall Worm, Pecan Nut Casebearer, Puss Caterpillar, Sod Webworm, Sphinx Moth, Squash Vine Borer, Tent Caterpillar, Tobacco Hornworm, Tomato Hornworm, Webworm, Woolly Bear.

MUD DAUBER

COMMON NAMES: Mud Dauber, Sphecid Wasp, Thread-Waisted Wasp
SCIENTIFIC NAME: Order Hymenoptera, family Sphecidae, many species
SIZE: 1" to 1½"
IDENTIFICATION: Solitary, shiny blue-black wasp that builds mud nests on the sides of buildings. Their heads are wide, and their waists are thread-thin.
BIOLOGY AND LIFE CYCLE: Adult female wasps

paralyze insects and other wasp prey by stinging. They then lay an egg on them and store them in a cell of the mud nest. The larvae feed on the living tissue of the stored insects.
HABITAT: Most flowering plants and food crops.
FEEDING HABITS: Female adults hunt and paralyze spiders, crickets,

Mud dauber (H)

cicadas, flies, and leafhoppers. Before sealing each egg cell, she drops a spider in to feed the larva later. Adults like flowers and feed on nectar and pollen.

ECONOMIC IMPORTANCE: Control of spiders, especially black widows.

NATURAL CONTROL: Birds and spiders.

ORGANIC CONTROL: None needed.

INSIGHT: Extremely beneficial insects. Their favorite food is the black widow spider. When the mud dauber catches spiders, she doesn't kill them. The sting paralyzes the leg muscles so the spider can't move. She then carries them to a mud chamber, lays an egg with the spider, and seals the chamber. Her egg hatches into a wasp larva; the larva crawls among the spiders, eating their leg muscles first. The larva doesn't feed on the spider bodies until last, so the spider remains alive longer.

The cicada killer (another beneficial wasp) is a close relative of the mud dauber. It's OK to destroy mud dauber nests if holes are present. The holes indicate that the new adults have emerged. The mud nests are not reused.

Mud dauber dragging spider (B)

Mud dauber nest broken open and full of black widow spiders (B)

Mud dauber nest with holes from which adults have emerged (B)

NEMATODE

COMMON NAMES: Nematode, Root Knot Nematode, Roundworm, predatory nematodes, beneficial nematodes
SCIENTIFIC NAME: Root Knot Nematode—*Meloidogyne* spp. Steiner Nematode—*Steinernema carpocapsae* (the most commonly available beneficial nematode). There are many other species of both troublesome and beneficial nematodes. *Hederohabditis* is the genus available for use on fire ants and grubworms.
SIZE: Adult—⅟₅₀" or less
IDENTIFICATION: Most nematodes are slender, translucent, unsegmented round worms.
BIOLOGY AND LIFE CYCLE: Eggs are laid by the female in masses or can stay inside the female to hatch when she dies. Larvae are mobile in the soil. Adults result after several molts. Life cycle can take three or four weeks. Beneficial nematodes kill by unleashing bacteria that grow, feed on, and liquefy the body tissues of the pests.
HABITAT: Soil, soil animals, and plant roots. Many ornamental and food crops.
FEEDING HABITS: Troublesome nematodes feed on many vegetable and ornamental plants. Feeding causes lesions and galls on roots and stimulates excessive branching. Beneficial nematodes feed on grubs, roaches, termites.
ECONOMIC IMPORTANCE: Plant-attacking nematodes reduce plant vigor, stunt growth, and cause death. Beneficial nematodes give important control of grubs, roaches, termites, fleas, ticks, and other troublesome pests.
NATURAL CONTROL: Harmful nematodes are controlled primarily through healthy biodiverse soil containing beneficial fungi.
ORGANIC CONTROL: Citrus peelings ground and mixed into the soil prior to planting. Liquid biostimulants to help encourage beneficial soil life. Drenching soil with neem or sugar water. Humates and small amounts of sulfur stimulate beneficial microbes in the soil. Stop using high-nitrogen artificial fertilizers and toxic pesticides. The dynamic, natural condition of the soil will control most harmful nematode infestations.
INSIGHT: Yes, we realize these aren't insects. Some nematodes are harmful to plants. Others are free-living and feed on organic debris, microorganisms, and other nematodes. Beneficial

Predatory nematodes attacking a roach (BS)

Predatory or beneficial nematodes attacking a grubworm (BS)

Root knot nematode damage to tomato plant roots (H)

nematodes can be purchased and used to control armyworms, cabbage loopers, Colorado potato beetles, corn rootworms, cutworms, grubs, and other soil pests. Nematodes control insect pests by entering through the mouth or body openings; once inside the host, they feed and reproduce until the pest is dead. New nematodes emerge in search of new victims. The most commonly available beneficial nematodes include *Steinernema carpocapsae* and *Hederohabditis* spp., which uses a single sharp tooth to gnaw through the outer covering of pests. Early applications prior to heavy pest infestations, followed by monthly followup applications, is the ideal schedule when pest infestations are present. Once balance is reached, no more releases are necessary. Beneficial nematodes can be purchased in dry or wet formulations. They can be stored for short periods of time at 42°F.

The problem nematodes you have probably heard about the most are called root knot nematodes. As they feed on plant roots, they cause cancerous-looking knots to form. Other destructive nematodes live in and eat roots but do not form the knots. They are sometimes more destructive since they are harder to detect. Symptoms include a lack of plant vigor and poor growth. When a plant's root system is eaten away, it can't pull the proper amount of water and nutrients from the soil.

When nematodes are a problem, it's a signal that the soil is not in balance and is lacking sufficient beneficial life. When soil health is poor, the balance of good and bad microbes is out of kilter. Poor plant selection is the other possible cause of nematode infestation. Unadapted plants are usually in stress and thus susceptible.

How do we rid the soil of these pests? You don't—but you can encourage a naturally controlled population. Remember that insects, worms, and other pests are not a problem unless the populations are out of balance and therefore out of control. We can help restore balance by changing our methods of pest control and fertilization. Use spray products and fertilizers that stimulate microbial and beneficial nematodes that will attack and destroy plant-eating nematodes. If given the chance, the good guys will win out.

A Malcolm Story: Nematodes and Cedar Chips

A railroad co-worker of mine grew greenhouse tomatoes for extra income. His greenhouse was 6,000 square feet, and he allowed me to mulch a double row of tomatoes in the center of the building as part of our cedar flake research. His tomatoes were already planted and standing about eighteen inches tall when I put a one-inch layer of cedar mulch around the plants. The rest of the house was left without mulch. I saw this co-worker often, and each time he told me that the cedar-mulched tomatoes were no different from the rest. One day late in the season, however, he said he had tomato plants beginning to droop all over the house because of root-knot nematodes—except in the mulched row. He told me that it was his fourth year to grow tomatoes in the same spot and that the experts had said that by the sixth to seventh year, it would be impossible to continue growing them because of the nematodes, even if he fumigated with a toxic chemical each year to sterilize the soil.

Nematodes are very small round worms, sometimes called eel-worms, that move around in the soil and feed on and lay eggs in plant roots causing knots to form which causes the plant to lose nourishment and become stunted. Not all nematode species are harmful. Some are even beneficial. There are predator types that destroy other harmful insects, including the troublesome nematode. Even the troublesome nematodes in very small numbers can be beneficial. They seem to stimulate extra production in plants. Several times I have seen a plant grow bigger than its neighbor, and on inspecting its roots, I noticed a few nematode knots where the neighboring smaller plants had none. Throughout nature,

researchers have found that a small amount of damage from any pest seems to increase plant growth. The secret is balance.

In the greenhouse, I thought maybe the mulching effect just helped the plants with their moisture needs, so we cut off the irrigation line to the mulched row to test my theory. The plants still didn't droop. This seemed strange, so when the season was over, I helped clean out all the old plants from the greenhouse. We inspected the roots of each plant and found the mulched row had about 90 percent less nematode damage than any other row in the house. This was a very exciting discovery, so I called the tomato greenhouse Ph.D. at A&M to discuss it with him. He had no explanation, but he did invite me to a greenhouse growers conference at College Station.

During the conference, I struck up a conversation with the person having breakfast across the table from me and told him about my mulching experience. Immediately he brightened up and introduced himself as a Ph.D. from Mississippi. He said he would be giving a talk at two o'clock that afternoon on that very subject. He said he always suggested that growers put wood chips on the floor of the greenhouses to walk on. The chips kept the soil from packing when walked on, and their feet wouldn't get muddy. As the chips decayed, they gave off carbon dioxide to feed the plants. He noticed that in the mulched houses the nematodes were much less of a problem, and in some houses the nematode population was almost eliminated within seven years.

After his talk, he asked me to elaborate on my experience in the tomato greenhouse. Everyone in the audience wondered, "How do wood chips deter nematodes?" The Mississippian didn't know, but he suspected it must be a phenol or aromatic in the wood. I thought it was some biological action because I had read of a beneficial fungi that destroyed nematodes. There were lots of experts there, but none had heard of a nematode-destroying fungus. One grower at the meeting who was having big nematode problems decided he would grow in pure cedar flakes. He put down plastic sheeting film to separate the infested soil from the cedar, then planted his tomatoes. I visited him about the time the tomatoes started ripening. He said, "Malcolm, something is wrong. I have the worst nematode infestation I've ever had, and I don't understand it."

This grower didn't realize it, but he proved that the nematode deterrent wasn't chemical; it had to be biological. All of his tools and watering equipment probably had nematodes or their eggs on them, and he accidentally reintroduced the nematodes into a sterile environment. The cedar flakes are sterile from the steam cooking and void of any beneficial fungi or other competing soil life. The nematodes had nothing to hold them in check.

Now, years later, you can go to Texas A&M and they will show you pictures of two different fungi attacking nematodes. One loops around a nematode and pops its head off; another grows into the nematode and devours it. In order for these beneficial fungi to flourish, they need a fertile, aerated, balanced soil with a supply of carbon to use as energy, and cedar flakes are a good energy source.

There are many types of microorganisms that aid in decomposition. They each take a turn feeding on and decomposing carbon products such as cedar flakes. Bacteria usually start the process, and their populations explode to high numbers and then subside. Other populations of microorganisms, such as actinomycetes, algae, and fungi, explode and then subside. Each species takes its turn at dominating. The nematode-destroying fungi are probably late in the dominating cycle, and since cedar flakes are slow to decompose, there is still energy left for the nematode-destroying fungi. This is one explanation of how the cedar flakes help control destructive nematodes. The mulching effect was also helpful in the nematode control. Nature has been mulching the soil to feed and keep it healthy since the very beginning. Mulching is the best and often the only nematode control needed for perennials.

There are other methods of controlling nematodes, one of the easiest of which is rotating susceptible with nonsusceptible plants when growing annuals. Elbon (cereal) rye is an excellent plant to rotate. It is a trap crop. Nematodes get in rye roots but can't reproduce.

Chitin-type products such as shrimp, crab shells, and bat guano used as fertilizer are good nematode destroyers. Nematode eggs have a chitin shell, and the beneficial microbes stimulated by the addition of chitin soon go on to destroy the nematode eggs.

NITIDULID BEETLE

COMMON NAMES: Nitidulid Beetle, Oak Wilt Beetle, Sap Feeding Beetle
SCIENTIFIC NAME: Order Coleoptera, family Nitidulidae, several species
SIZE: Adult—¼"
IDENTIFICATION: Adults look like tiny June bugs.
BIOLOGY AND LIFE CYCLE: Nitidulids inhabit fungal mats beneath the bark of diseased red oaks (*Quercus texana* and *Quercus shumardii*). Infectious beetles emerge from the fungal mats and deposit oak wilt spores in wounds on healthy trees by feeding in sap.
HABITAT: Texas live oaks, red oaks, and blackjack oaks.
FEEDING HABITS: Sap from cuts or wounds on oak and other trees. Also feed on rotting fruit in the orchard.
ECONOMIC IMPORTANCE: This beetle spreads the devastating oak disease called oak wilt (*Ceratocystis*

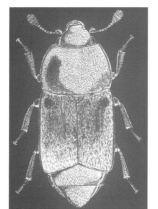

Nitidulid beetle (TFS)

Crack over oak wilt mat on red oak (TFS)

Oak wilt in live oak (TFS)

Oak wilt in red oak (TFS)

Oak wilt fungal mat on red oak (TFS)

fagacearum), which has killed thousands of live oaks and red oaks in Texas.

NATURAL CONTROL: Keep trees in healthy condition so they can resist the beetle and disease. Mulch or maintain the natural habitat under trees.

ORGANIC CONTROL: The Texas Forest Service recommendation is to trench to separate the roots of infected trees from those of healthy trees and inject chemical fungicide into the trees. We do not recommend that approach. There's only anecdotal evidence so far, but we've seen excellent results from the following organic program.

1. Aerate the root zone heavily. Go far out beyond the dripline.

2. While the holes are open, apply all the following for each 1,000 square feet: 80 pounds Texas greensand, 80 pounds lava sand, and 20 pounds cornmeal. Volcanite plus the cornmeal can also be used.

3. Apply a 1-inch layer of compost followed by a 3- to 5-inch layer of shredded native tree trimmings.

4. Spray the foliage monthly or more often if possible with Garrett Juice plus garlic tea (see Appendix C).

INSIGHT: Infestations cause fungal mats to form on red oaks only, not on live oaks. For that reason, live oak wood can be used for firewood without any worry. Red oak wood needs to be stacked in a sunny location and covered with clear plastic to form a greenhouse effect to kill the beetles and fungal mats. When oaks are ground into mulch, the aeration kills the pathogens and eliminates the possibility of disease spread.

OAK LEAF SAWFLY—see Sawfly

OAK WILT BEETLE—see Nitidulid Beetle

ORANGE TORTRIX

COMMON NAMES: Grape Leafroller, Orange Tortrix
SCIENTIFIC NAME: Order Lepidoptera, family Tortricidae, *Argyrotaenia citrana*
SIZE: ¾" to 1"
IDENTIFICATION: Caterpillars are greenish yellow to pale straw color. They fold the leaves together for protection while they feed inside. When the leaves are pulled apart, they wiggle fast and drop from sight. Adults are orangish to gray moths. The caterpillars wriggle vigorously when touched.
BIOLOGY AND LIFE CYCLE: Cream-colored eggs are laid in groups that overlap like fish scales. And they have overlapping generations. The first damage is in early summer.
HABITAT: Orchards and vineyards.
FEEDING HABITS: Attacks grapes, citrus, stonefruit, bougainvillea, apples, and strawberries. Besides webbing leaves together, they also build webs in and feed on bunches of grapes. Their web can easily be mistaken for a spider web.

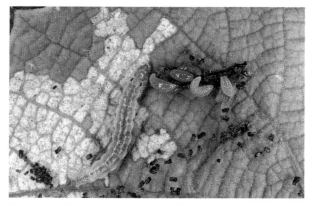

Orange tortrix larvae, one parasitized (B)

ECONOMIC IMPORTANCE: The caterpillars fold the leaves together in perfect halves and hold them tightly together with webbing while feeding on a thin outer layer; they avoid eating holes all the way through the leaves and exposing themselves. If no measure of control is used, they will soon fold every leaf on the grapevine.
NATURAL CONTROL: Wasps, tachinid flies, and general predators that feed on their eggs.
ORGANIC CONTROL: Healthy, adapted varieties of grapes. Pheromone traps, and Garden-Ville Fire Ant Control.
INSIGHT: This is a very interesting but troublesome insect that is difficult to photograph.

A Malcolm Story

Many times I have watched a big shiny black wasp that has one bright yellow strip across its body cut holes about ⅜-inch square in the folded grape leaves, reach in and pull out the orange tortrix larvae, and carry them away. Unfortunately I have never been able to catch it on film. I have also found a small black wasp that parasitizes them.

I grew twelve concord grapevines in five-gallon containers in a row with about five feet of space between each. The first two vines were in a shaded area that got about six hours of morning sun, the next two got eight hours of sun, the next two got ten hours of sun, and the rest got sun all day. The vines were in that location for four years. For some strange reason the more sun the vines got, the more the orange tortrix attacked them. The vines in the most shade got very little damage, but damage increased as the vines got more sun. I planted four of the vines in my orchard among the fruit trees and had the same experience.

ORIUS—see Minute Pirate Bug

OX BEETLE—see Rhinoceros Beetle

PALMETTO BUG — see Cockroach

PAPER WASP

COMMON NAMES: Paper Wasp, Yellowjacket
SCIENTIFIC NAME: Order Hymenoptera, family Vespidae, *Polistes* spp.
SIZE: Adult — ¾" to 1"
IDENTIFICATION: Yellow and black wasps that are usually called yellowjackets. When wings are at rest, they are folded and held out to the side rather than folded over the back like other wasps. Nests are papery, slightly rounded, 4 inches or greater in diameter; they hang upside down.
BIOLOGY AND LIFE CYCLE: Social insects living with queens, males, and sterile female workers. Overwintered and mated females start nests in the spring in a sheltered place. Cells of a paperlike substance are built from a single connection to a structure or plant in a shady location. Several females may work together. One egg is laid in each cell. Larvae hatch and are fed chewed-up

Paper wasps (B)

insects and spiders. When ready to pupate, they spin silk caps to close off the cells. Queens lay fertilized eggs that become females. Fertilized female larvae (new queens) are fed a special diet and are the only ones to survive the winter. They are the last batch of females to hatch in the fall. All others, males and females, die. Surviving queens hibernate in dense foliage such as dead palm leaves or in rubbish or old squirrel nests.
HABITAT: Sheltered spots under the eaves and overhangs of buildings. Also in barns, chicken houses, and other outbuildings. Adults feed on flower nectar or fruit that has been bird-pecked.
FEEDING HABITS: Wasp larvae are carnivorous and are fed moth and butterfly larvae that are chewed up by the adult wasp workers.
ECONOMIC IMPORTANCE: Control of several troublesome caterpillars of moths and butterflies.
NATURAL CONTROL: Spiders. Splash water on nest to knock wasps off, then move nest to higher but similar location in the shade. Don't try this if you're allergic to wasp stings or if you are chicken!
ORGANIC CONTROL: Soapy water or citrus oil products if the nest is in a problem area. Do this only as a last resort — these insects are very beneficial.
INSIGHT: Texas yellowjackets are similar but live in nests in the ground and are more aggressive. The wasp's most serious enemies are humans with aerosol spray cans.

A Malcolm Story

Most wasps are beneficial — probably all of them, even the stinging kind. A favorite food of wasps is the tent caterpillar and fall webworm, which often disfigures pecan, fruit, and shade trees. Wasps like all caterpillars. The tiny trichogramma wasp can be easily purchased and is very effective for controlling cutworms, moths, and the

Paper wasp taking care of larvae in the nest (B)

pecan casebearer. It lays its eggs in the eggs of the pest. When the wasp's eggs hatch, the larvae feed on the pest's eggs. For best results, trichogramma wasps should be released every two weeks after bud break in the spring.

Even the stinging wasps like yellowjackets sting only if you threaten them, and the mud dauber only if you try to catch it! Trichogramma wasps and most of the smaller wasps don't sting at all. The mud dauber's favorite food is the black widow spider. Unless a wasp nest is located where a child might bump into it, it should be left in place. If the nest is in a dangerous location, spray the wasps with water. While they are on the ground unable to fly, move the nest to a higher, safer place and reattach with a nail. The wasps will go right back to it as if nothing has happened. You might get stung, so don't try this procedure if you are highly allergic to wasp stings.

Wasp stings are very painful and can be dangerous because of allergic reactions. I have been stung, but only when I bumped a nest and moved too fast; the wasps took my action as a threat against them. Through studying, observing, and actually playing with wasps, I have learned that they only sting when they sense their nest is being threatened. Don't threaten them, not even mentally; they can sense your feelings.

One day a neighbor came over to borrow a cyclone seeder that was stored in a shed. When I reached down to pick up the seeder, I turned and bumped a very large wasp nest. There must have been at least sixty wasps on the nest. As soon as I realized what I had done, I froze. It took all the nerve I had, but I stood very still as the wasps flew around me and bumped into my face and bare arms. Still, I didn't get a single sting. I waited a couple of minutes until they were all settled back on the nest and then I slowly moved on.

Another time, the wasps decided to build their nest above our back door. That door is used dozens of times each day by the children, grandchildren, and my wife and me. Because we are pretty tall people, the nest was only a few inches away every time we went in or out the door. Still, they never bothered us. They kept enlarging their nest until a wasp or two was knocked off every time the door was opened. My wife kept warning me that sooner or later someone would get stung. Sure enough, they got her first, but she said it didn't hurt very much.

I did plan on moving the nest, but I kept putting it off. One day I let the screen door slam and knocked several wasps off the nest. One wasp came and gave me a warning shot on the hand. It didn't hurt much either—not as much as I knew it could have. It seemed like a warning to me, and I finally took heed. I promptly got a bucket of water and splashed it on them; it knocked all the wasps to the ground and with their wings wet they couldn't fly. That gave me plenty of time to break the nest loose and fasten it with a thumbtack about a foot

higher. In a few minutes, the wasps dried out, flew back to the nest, and went about housekeeping as if they had never been moved. Over the years I have moved many wasp nests without being stung, and the wasps have always gone back to the nest. The only time that didn't happen was when I moved one from the shade to the sun. They don't like direct sun on their nests and refused to move back to it.

Around our place of business we always have lots of wasp nests. If the nests are low or positioned so a customer or employee can accidentally bump into them, I move them. The porch across the front of our office usually has a wasp nest in all four corners. One day a lady came into the office and said she got stung by a wasp out by the coke machine near the corner. She said it didn't hurt as much as stings usually do. I asked her if she had threatened the wasp in any way; she said she hadn't even noticed the nest. Her tone of voice let me know that I was acting more concerned about the wasps that my customers.

About a week later, an employee also got stung while at the coke machine, and he too said it didn't hurt much. But I wondered why those wasps were being so aggressive. I got a stool and sat out on the porch and just watched the wasps for a while. It didn't take long until to discover the reason for their aggression. A spider had built its web across the corner of the porch. A wasp came flying in toward the nest and momentarily got entangled in the web. While fighting to get loose, it must have sent some kind of distress signal because all the rest of the wasps left the nest in search of the possible enemy. I moved the spider web, and no one has been stung since.

Realizing how beneficial wasps are, I have been protecting them for more than twenty-five years. They seem to have gotten friendly toward us. Even when someone does accidentally bump a nest, they usually don't sting; and when they do, it is very light.

A young landscaper was loading some material from a storage shed one day when he raised his head directly into a wasp nest. Five wasps stung him in the face. He came running to the office scared, but not half as scared as I was after I found out what had happened. I offered to take him to the hospital. He said that it had scared him but didn't hurt. I made him rest in the office for a few minutes to make sure there wouldn't be an allergic reaction. After just a few minutes there wasn't any pain, swelling, or any sign that he had been stung. I wonder. Are the wasps getting less poisonous or can they actually govern how badly they want to hurt us? Do they recognize us as not being a threat to them?

We now have 270 pecan trees here on the farm and the wasps keep the trees almost completely clean of webworms. Our neighbors have more webworms in one tree than we have on the whole farm. When the wasps catch a webworm or other troublesome worm, they rip the worm open and dig out balls of meat to feed their young larva. The adult wasp is a vegetarian and eats very little, usually nectar from flowers. In the process, they do a little pollinating as well. They often get blamed for damaging fruit such as peaches and plums, but in fact they are only drinking juice at a hole in the fruit that a bird pecked.

PARASITOID — see Braconid Wasp, Ichneumon Wasp, Tachinid Fly, Trichogramma Wasp

PARASOL ANT — see Texas Leafcutting Ant

PEACH TREE BORER

COMMON NAMES: Lesser Peach Tree Borer, Peach Tree Borer, Tree Borer, Twig Borer
SCIENTIFIC NAME: Order Lepidoptera, family Sesiidae, *Synanthedon* spp.
SIZE: Adult — ¾", larva — 1"
IDENTIFICATION: Adults are clear-winged, narrow, blue-black wasplike moths with yellow marks. Eggs are brown or gray and laid in bark or in the soil near the base of fruit trees. Larvae (borers) are white or pale yellow caterpillars with brown heads. They burrow into the tree trunk near the ground line.
BIOLOGY AND LIFE CYCLE: One generation a year. Larvae hibernate in tree burrows or in soil. They pupate in burrows or in brown cocoons in the soil.
HABITAT: Peach, plum, apricot, cherry, and other fruit trees.
FEEDING HABITS: Borers chew inner bark of lower tree trunk. Mass of gummy sawdust appears at base of trees.
ECONOMIC IMPORTANCE: Damage to tree trunks. Vectors of wilt fungi and other diseases.
NATURAL CONTROL: Healthy soil, compost, thick mulch over root system. Ichneumon and other predatory wasps.
ORGANIC CONTROL: Tobacco dust (snuff) or sticky tape around base of tree. Squirt beneficial nematodes into holes. Treat soil with beneficial nematodes. Paint tree trunks with Tree Trunk Goop (see below).

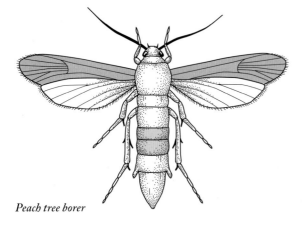

Peach tree borer

INSIGHT: This insect is easy to control by keeping plants healthy, but it has become the poster insect for the wrong approach to pest control. In forty years and three separate orchards, Malcolm has never seen a peach tree borer in any of his organically grown trees.

A Howard Story

In August every year the organiphobes still recommend the brain-dead advice of spraying every peach, plum, and nectarine in Texas with a toxic chemical borer preventative. These people should be sued for serious environmental pollution. Their recommendation wastes money, contaminates the land, kills off many beneficial insects and natural enemies of the borers, and does not control the targeted pest.

Even organic gardeners have plants in stress from time to time. For example, many of the vegetables we try to grow and all the fruit trees we plant are not well adapted to the soils and climate of North Texas. In other words, these plants are at a disadvantage from the beginning. When we start out with plants that aren't too happy about their plight, it's critical to provide excellent drainage, even moisture, mulch or cover crops, and regular releases of beneficial insects. Organic products used as preventatives are also important — materials like garlic tea, seaweed, and neem.

Since there are no perfectly adapted peach trees for North Texas, there is often a need to kill pests. Borers are high on the list of pests that sometimes need a specific control. Now, you can use the toxic pesticides such as lindane and chorpyrifos, but I wouldn't. You might kill more than the targeted pest. Victims may include beneficial microorganisms, beneficial insects, and even larger animals. What would I use instead? Tree Trunk Goop (see Appendix C).

The first time I used Tree Trunk Goop, a rain washed it off just a day after I applied it. That made me wonder about its effectiveness, but several gardeners have reported great results — borers gone. And even if the material washes off the trunk, it feeds the soil and the tree roots. In most cases the stuff slowly wears off as the trunk grows. There's an additional benefit. Tree Trunk Goop feeds the tree through the trunk. Yes, plants can take in nutrients through the trunks and stems just as they do through the leaves and roots. Tree Trunk Goop is a disgusting-looking mess, but you'll get over it as soon as you see how well it works.

PECAN GALL WORM

COMMON NAME: Pecan Gall Worm
SCIENTIFIC NAME: Order Coleoptera, family Curculionidae, *Anthornomus* spp.
SIZE: Adult — ⅛", larva — ³⁄₁₆"

BIOLOGY AND LIFE CYCLE: Complete metamorphosis. Adults fly at night and hide during the day. Larvae are snow white and pointed on both ends. Adults look like miniature boll weevils (they're in the same family).

HABITAT: Pecan and hickory trees.

FEEDING HABITS: Feeds in galls formed by phylloxera, which are small aphidlike insects.

ECONOMIC IMPORTANCE: None as far as we can figure.

NATURAL CONTROL: None needed.

ORGANIC CONTROL: None needed.

INSIGHT: A very interesting little weevil that looks like a miniature black boll weevil. The larva is very active when disturbed. Larvae are found on pecan leaves in galls formed by pecan phylloxera usually after the phylloxera are gone. Most people think the white worm caused the gall. In some years 90 percent of the galls will have worms in them. Besides these weevil larvae, other species of insects, such as the hickory shuckworm moth larvae, find the galls a cozy home to inhabit. The galls offer good protection and plenty to eat (the larvae feed on the gall walls).

Pecan gall worm adult (B)

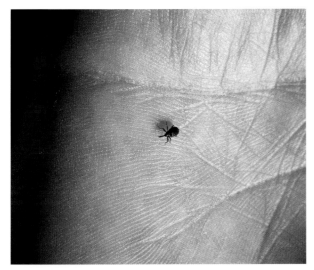

Pecan gall worm larva in phylloxera gall (B)

Pecan nut casebearer (B)

Pecan nut casebearer larva (B)

PECAN NUT CASEBEARER

COMMON NAMES: Casebearer, Pecan Casebearer, Pecan Nut Casebearer

SCIENTIFIC NAME: Order Lepidoptera, family Pyralidae, *Acrobasis nuxvorella*

SIZE: Adult—⅓" to ½"

IDENTIFICATION: Adults are light gray moths that fly at night and hide in daylight. Holes and weblike material will be seen in the buds of pecans. Terminal shoots will wither and die. Larvae are white to pink at first, later olive gray to green.

BIOLOGY AND LIFE CYCLE: Casebearers overwinter as small cocoons. The larvae become active about the time of bud break. They first feed on buds and then tunnel into the rapidly growing shoots. The larvae's entrance is marked with weblike material. Larvae of succeeding generations feed on nuts during the late spring and summer.

HABITAT: Pecan trees.

FEEDING HABITS: Damage is done in early spring, just after pollination.

ECONOMIC IMPORTANCE: Damage to pecan crops can range from a very light thinning, 10 percent or so, to a loss of 80 or 90 percent of the entire crop.

NATURAL CONTROL: Trichogramma wasps and other beneficial insects.

ORGANIC CONTROL: *Bacillus thuringiensis* sprays.

INSIGHT: See Trichogramma Wasp.

PECAN WEEVIL

COMMON NAME: Pecan Weevil

SCIENTIFIC NAME: Order Coleoptera, family Curculionidae, *Curculio caryae*

SIZE: Adult—⅜", larva—⅗"

IDENTIFICATION: Brownish weevils covered with yellow hairs. The female's snout is as long as the body. Larvae are creamy white grubs that overwinter in earthen cells 1 to 2 inches in the ground.

BIOLOGY AND LIFE CYCLE: The larvae stay in the soil for one to two years, pupate in the fall, hatch three weeks later, stay in the soil for another year, and emerge in the fall to mate. The females deposit two to four eggs in as many as twenty five pecans.

HABITAT: Pecan and hickory. Only certain pecan groves.

FEEDING HABITS: Late-season pest. Adults feed on nuts in the water stage. Eggs are deposited when kernels are young and starting to mature.

ECONOMIC IMPORTANCE: Infestations can destroy a large portion of pecan crops.

NATURAL CONTROL: Beneficial nematodes and other soil microorganisms.

ORGANIC CONTROL: Establish healthy, resistant trees by building soil health so beneficial microbes in the soil can attack grubs, especially since the weevil larvae spend so much time in the soil. Jarring infested trees has been used to catch "possum-playing" adults.

PHARAOH ANT—see Sugar Ant

PHYLLOXERA

COMMON NAME: Phylloxera

SCIENTIFIC NAME: Order Homoptera, family Phylloxeridae, several species

SIZE: Adult—1/50"

IDENTIFICATION: Yellowish, aphidlike insects but smaller; identified by the pea-size galls they form to live and reproduce in.

BIOLOGY AND LIFE CYCLE: Incomplete metamorphosis. Male and female adults are wingless until the fall of the year, then appear with wings. They mate and deposit eggs to overwinter. Like aphids, they also give birth early in the season.

HABITAT: Grape leaves and roots, pecan and other tree leaves.

FEEDING HABITS: Inject an agent into leaves to form galls to live in while they feed on the gall walls.

FEEDING HABITS: In the West very damaging to

Phylloxera galls on pecan leaf (B)

European variety of grapes. We have had no complaints of them on grapes in Texas. They do get on pecan leaves and are known to bother native varieties, but we are now beginning to find a few on some improved varieties.

NATURAL CONTROL: Casebearer moth larvae and a weevil larvae are often found living in the galls. They feed on the gall wall, which may disturb the very small phylloxera enough to upset their life cycles. We can't pinpoint any specific insects as predators, but every insect has something to keep it in balance. Ladybugs and green lacewings probably help.

ORGANIC CONTROL: Horticultural oil and citrus oil products could help, but we really don't recommend any treatment because of damage to beneficial insects.

INSIGHT: Some growers try to control phylloxera with horticultural oil. We don't think it does much good and we know that it kills beneficials, so it's probably a waste of money.

PHYTOSEIID MITE—see Predatory Mite

PILLBUG AND SOWBUG

COMMON NAMES: Pillbug, Roly-Poly Bug, Sowbug

SCIENTIFIC NAME: Order Isopoda, Subclass Crustacea. Pillbug—*Armadillidium vulgare*, Sowbug—*Porcellio laevis*

SIZE: Adult—¼" to ⅝"

IDENTIFICATION: Adults are gray and sometimes brown crustaceans with a segmented armor covering. Seven pair of barely visible short legs. Pillbugs curl up into a ball when disturbed. Nymphs look like small light-colored adults. Sowbugs are larger, flatter, and faster; they have a tail and can't roll up as tight as pillbugs.

BIOLOGY AND LIFE CYCLE: Females carry eggs and nymphs in a pouch for several weeks. Nymphs and adults prefer moist conditions and cannot live long in dry conditions. They often explode in populations during the warm spring rains. Snails like the same conditions. Young take a year to reach maturity. Live up to eight years.

HABITAT: Moist beds, compost piles.

Sowbug (B)

Pine beetle larvae (RB)

FEEDING HABITS: Feed mostly on decaying organic matter but can be severe plant pests, especially on young seedlings.

ECONOMIC IMPORTANCE: Beneficial to the breakdown of natural organic matter, but they obviously get tired of eating dead brown stuff sometimes and attack plants.

NATURAL CONTROL: Let beds dry out between waterings.

ORGANIC CONTROL: Dust hot red pepper powder around plants. Dilute with diatomaceous earth for economy; sprinkle it around young seedlings. Put an apple core or some brewer's yeast in a glass (plastic is safer) countersunk into the soil. Cover it with a dish or pot. Spray with concentrated citrus oil. Add molasses and manure tea for even better results. Coffee grounds on top of mulch also help.

INSIGHT: Both pillbugs and sowbugs are beneficial in helping to break down organic matter.

PINE BEETLE

COMMON NAMES: Pine Beetle, Southern Pine Beetle
SCIENTIFIC NAME: Order Coleoptera, family Scolytidae, *Dendroctonus frontalis*
SIZE: Adult—⅟₂₅" to ⅓"
IDENTIFICATION: Small brown bark beetles that eat "galleries" of tunnels and form S-shaped trails just inside the bark. Single insect attacks are very hard to detect. Severe infestations cause the natural dark green color foliage to fade to a light green.

Pine beetle tunnels under bark (RB)

Pillbug (B)

Pine beetle (RB)

BIOLOGY AND LIFE CYCLE: Overwinter as both larvae and adults in the galleries in trees. Infestations enlarge rapidly in the late spring as beetles outside the area are attracted by pheromones (potent odors that the beetles alone can detect) given off by attacking females.

HABITAT: Pine forests and individual trees.

FEEDING HABITS: Outbreaks can kill many acres or attack individual trees.

ECONOMIC IMPORTANCE: Most common damaging insect on pines.

NATURAL CONTROL: Ichneumon wasps and woodpeckers; trees free of stress.

ORGANIC CONTROL: Soil improvement, mulch of trees' root systems. Avoid monoculture plantations. Remove infested trees. Use pheromones to override the females' communication with other beetles.

INSIGHT: This pest is primarily a problem in plantations of monocultures planted after clear cutting.

PINE TIP MOTH

COMMON NAME: Pine Tip Moth
SCIENTIFIC NAME: Order Lepidoptera, family Tortricidae, *Rhyacionia* spp.
SIZE: Adult—½", larva—¼" to ⅜"
IDENTIFICATION: Adult is reddish brown with silver-gray markings. Larva is light brown to orange with dark head.
BIOLOGY AND LIFE CYCLE: Overwinter in pupa. Emerge to deposit eggs late February in South Texas and April in North Texas, depending on weather. Two to five generations per year; varies according to cool weather.
HABITAT: Pine forest, Christmas tree plantations.
FEEDING HABITS: The hatching larva construct a small silken web in the axil formed by the needles and stem, then bore into the stem at the tip of the bud. Larva feed for two to four weeks before pupation.
ECONOMIC IMPORTANCE: Most damaging to Christmas tree plantations; damage to the buds causes deformed young trees.
NATURAL CONTROL: Egg parasites such as trichogramma wasps, spiders on adults, bats and birds.
ORGANIC CONTROL: Fast-growing, healthy trees show resistance. Seemingly not a problem on large trees.
INSIGHT: With a good organic program, we could be growing all our Christmas trees economically here in Texas instead of importing them down from the North.

A Howard Story

I got a call one winter from a Christmas tree grower who said he had been listening to my radio show and wanted to try to manage his tree farm with organic techniques. In the past he had been spraying with various pesticides to try to control pine tip moth and other pests. I recommended changing over to an insect release program. He released green lacewings and trichogramma wasps the next spring and had good results. In fact, he had such good results he eventually cut back to releasing only the wasps continued to have excellent pest control.

More tree growers will convert to organic programs soon, and it will be for economic reasons. As the Christmas tree grower observed, it takes much less time to release beneficial insects than it does to spray pesticides.

PLANT BUG—see Fourlined Plant Bug, Tarnished Plant Bug

PLANT LOUSE—see Aphid

PLUG BUG—see Leafcutting Bee

PLUM CURCULIO

COMMON NAME: Plum Curculio
SCIENTIFIC NAME: Order Coleoptera, family Curculionidae, *Conotrachelus nenuphar*
SIZE: Adult—⅕"
IDENTIFICATION: Adults are brownish gray weevils with warty wing covers and white hairs on the body. Short, thick, curved snout. Eggs white to gray, elliptical, laid in crescent-shaped slits in the skin of fruits. Larvae are white worms with light brown heads. Damage in fruit appears as crescent or half-circle wounds.
BIOLOGY AND LIFE CYCLE: Two or three generations a year. Adults hibernate in the soil. Larvae hatch in the fruit and tunnel within before leaving to pupate in the soil. Brown rot often follows, causing deformed fruit and premature fruit drop. Adults emerge from late July to October. Feed on ripe or fallen fruit until fall.
HABITAT: Most fruit trees and blueberry orchards.

Pine tip moth damage (B)

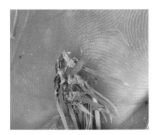

Pine tip moth larva (B)

Pine tip moth pupa (B)

Plum curculio

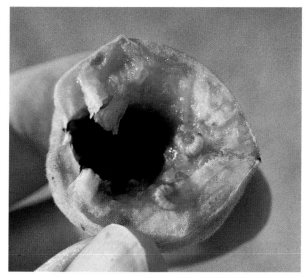

Plum curculio larvae (B)

Potter wasp (B)

Potter wasp pot (B)

Potter wasp pot, sealed (H)

Potter wasp pot, hatched (H)

FEEDING HABITS: Adults and larvae feed on fruit, especially cherries, plums, peaches, apricots, apples, and pears.
ECONOMIC IMPORTANCE: Damage and loss of fruit production. Wounds to fruit and premature drop.
NATURAL CONTROL: Improve soil, mulch all bare soil, and plant adapted trees. Let chickens or other grazing foul eat the dropped fruit. Mulch heavily with compost. Birds and beneficial nematodes.
ORGANIC CONTROL: Spray with Garrett Juice plus citrus and garlic. First spray should be just before bud break in the spring, second spray after blossoms have fallen, third spray in mid-season. See appendix.
INSIGHT: A common pest problem in chemically grown fruit crops. Incredibly heavy chemical spray programs have been used for this pest and still haven't achieved good control. The overall organic program including the use of pheromones will control this pest quite well.

POTATO BEETLE—see Colorado Potato Beetle

POTATO BUG—see Colorado Potato Beetle

POTTER WASP

COMMON NAME: Potter Wasp
SCIENTIFIC NAME: Order Hymenoptera, family Eumenidae, many species
SIZE: Adult—¾"
IDENTIFICATION: Solitary black wasp with yellow stripes.
BIOLOGY AND LIFE CYCLE: Complete metamorphosis. We once watched a potter wasp build its nest at Howard's house; it took three days.
HABITAT: Around buildings and protected areas where it can find moist clay to build the clay brood pot, nectar to snack on, and caterpillars to seal in with its eggs.

FEEDING HABITS: Adults sip nectar; the larvae feed on paralyzed caterpillars.
ECONOMIC IMPORTANCE: Like all wasps, beneficial in helping to control troublesome plant-eating worms.
NATURAL CONTROL: None needed—beneficial.
ORGANIC CONTROL: None needed.
INSIGHT: Skilled at working clay into pretty little pots; they don't seem to mind people watching or photographing them at work.

POWDER POST BEETLE

COMMON NAME: Powder Post Beetle
SCIENTIFIC NAME: Order Coleoptera, family Lyctidae
SIZE: Adult—¹⁄₁₂" to ⅕", larva—⅛" to ⅓"
IDENTIFICATION: Adults are small brown beetles; not often seen. Larvae look like small white grubs with large heads. Holes in wood are ¹⁄₁₆" to ¼".
BIOLOGY AND LIFE CYCLE: Larvae overwinter and pupate in the spring. Adults emerge in the spring or early summer. Eggs are laid in the pores of wood. Larvae eat wood and pack burrows with fine flourlike frass. Several generations a year.
HABITAT: Dry wood (does not have to be in contact with the soil). Timbers of buildings, log cabins, lumber, furniture, tool handles, wheel spokes, oars, barrels, and flooring.
FEEDING HABITS: Larvae eat hard dry wood.

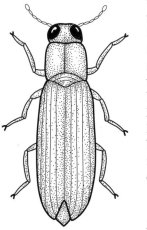

Powder post beetle

Powder post beetle damage (H)

ECONOMIC IMPORTANCE: Second only to termites as destroyers of seasoned wood.
NATURAL CONTROL: Ichneumon wasps.
ORGANIC CONTROL: Boric acid products. Use of kiln-dried wood.
INSIGHT: These are destructive little guys that are hard to control after they have started their tunneling. The little critters must be heat or light sensitive.

A Malcolm Story

I once cut some green mesquite posts, shaved all the bark off, gave them a good coat of creosote, and used them as support under a building. The powder post beetles still ate hundreds of holes right through the creosote. The eggs must have already been in the wood, waiting for the right drying conditions. After a few months I saw no more larvae activity. Because of the many holes, the posts quickly dried and soaked up another coat of creosote. The posts are still solid after thirty-five years, but I don't recommend creosote. With a little extra effort I could have poured concrete piers, which last forever—far longer than toxic creosote-treated posts.

PRAYING MANTID—see Praying Mantis

PRAYING MANTIS

COMMON NAMES: Devil's Horse, Mantid, Praying Mantid
SCIENTIFIC NAME: Order Mantodea, family Mantidae, *Mantis* spp.
SIZE: Adult—2" to 3"
IDENTIFICATION: Adults are green, gray, or brown with long bodies, papery wings, and enlarged front legs designed to grasp prey. Eggs are light brown or tan and are usually attached to stems and twigs. Native egg case is thin and hard like papier-mâché. (Be careful not to confuse the egg case with that of the puss caterpillar, a soft hairy insect larva with a powerful sting.)
BIOLOGY AND LIFE CYCLE: One generation a year. Hibernate in the egg stage. Adult females glue fifty or more eggs together to form an egg case. Wingless nymphs emerge from slits in the side of the egg casing in the spring and feed on larger and larger insects as they grow.
HABITAT: Most food and ornamental plants.
FEEDING HABITS: Nymphs and adults feed on aphids, beetles, bugs, leafhoppers, flies, bees, caterpillars, wasps, butterflies, and anything else that ventures by, including small animals like lizards and snakes—also each other.
ECONOMIC IMPORTANCE: Questionable. They are interesting insects but undependable for control of problem insects.
NATURAL CONTROL: Various insect parasites.
ORGANIC CONTROL: None needed.
INSIGHT: These insects are friendly to people and even make good pets. But they will eat any insect, including their own kind. They like caterpillars, grasshoppers, beetles, and other critters. They are not discriminating and eat beneficial as well as pest insects. However, Malcolm says he has never seen a praying mantis eat a beneficial insect other than old worn-out bees. So they are pretty good pest control helpers. They can even be used indoors.

Egg case of native praying mantis (B)

Puss caterpillar, not to be confused (B)

Egg case of imported praying mantis (H)

Green praying mantis (B)

Brown praying mantis (H)

PREDACEOUS STINK BUG

COMMON NAMES: Twospotted Stink Bug, Stink Bug
SCIENTIFIC NAME: Order Heteroptera, family
Pentatomidae, *Perillus bioculatus*
SIZE: Adult—⅜" to ½"
IDENTIFICATION: Shieldlike body of adults ranges from
red and black to yellow and black. Black spots on the
underside. Antennae are black. Red and black nymphs.
BIOLOGY AND LIFE CYCLE: Females lay several hundred
gray, barrel-shaped eggs in tight clusters of fifteen to
thirty, usually on foliage. Nymphs cluster after hatching,
then disperse to feed. Two to three generations a year.

Predaceous stink bug eating potato beetle larva (B)

Predaceous stink bug eating moth (H)

HABITAT: Potatoes, eggplants, tomatoes, beans, cole
crops, asparagus.
FEEDING HABITS: Predator of Colorado potato beetle,
bean beetle, corn earworm and moth, asparagus beetle,
and cabbage looper. Nymph will devour Colorado potato
beetle eggs. Larger nymphs and larvae eat the larvae.
ECONOMIC IMPORTANCE: Beneficial predator.
NATURAL CONTROL: Birds, snakes, and lizards.
ORGANIC CONTROL: None needed.
INSIGHT: These insects are very beneficial. Check out
the photo of nymphs sucking the guts out of a cockroach.
See also Stink Bug.

PREDATORY FLY—see Tachinid Fly

PREDATORY MITE

COMMON NAMES: Phytoseiid Mite, Predaceous Mite
SCIENTIFIC NAME: Order Araci, family Phytoseiidae,
Phyoseiulus persimilis, Galandromus occidentalis
SIZE: Adult—1/15"
IDENTIFICATION: Look like pest mites but move faster
and have fewer hairs. They are red and about half the size
of a pinhead. Adults are very small, nymphs are smaller
and lighter in color. Mites are not insects; they are related
to spiders. Adults have four pair of legs and two body
regions.

BIOLOGY AND LIFE CYCLE: Females emerge from overwintering in tree bark or soil litter to lay eggs on leaves among prey. Eggs hatch in three or four days. Nymphs molt several times and become adults in five to ten days.

HABITAT: Plants infested by spider mites, thrips, and fungus gnats. Strawberries, blackberries, raspberries, tomatoes, orchard crops, onions.

FEEDING HABITS: Effective predators of troublesome spider mites, especially the twospotted mite, European red mite, and citrus red mite. Some feed on pollen, thrips, and fungus gnats.

ECONOMIC IMPORTANCE: One of the most successful commercially available biological control agents. Used to control plant-eating mites. Release two mites per square foot or two for each small plant. In the field use 1,000 to 10,000 per acre.

NATURAL CONTROL: None needed.

ORGANIC CONTROL: None needed.

INSIGHT: The predatory mite is orange in the adult stage and pale salmon in its immature stage. Unlike the two-spotted spider mite (which is red), it does not have spots. Predatory mites have pear-shaped bodies, and their front legs are longer than those of pest mites. Beneficial mites move about quickly when disturbed or exposed to bright light and multiply much faster than pest mites.

Females lay about fifty eggs a day; each mite eats from five to twenty eggs or mites per day. Release predatory mites at the first sign of spider mite damage. If there is more than one spider mite per leaf, you will probably need to reduce the populations of pest mites with seaweed spray.

Predatory mites (BP)

Psyllids on persimmon leaf (B)

PSYLLID

COMMON NAME: Psyllid

SCIENTIFIC NAME: Order Hymenoptera, family Psyllidae, many species

SIZE: Adult—1⁄32" to 3⁄16"

IDENTIFICATION: The large, easily visible ones have black bodies with clear wings, which they hold over their bodies like a gabled roof. Nymphs are flat and oval and don't look like the adults.

BIOLOGY AND LIFE CYCLE: Egg, nymph, and winged adult. Most are free-living, although some species make the galls on hackberry leaves.

HABITAT: Trees and garden plants.

FEEDING HABITS: Sucking, causing curled, deformed stems and leaves.

ECONOMIC IMPORTANCE: Damaging to new leaves. Some species carry a disease known as "psyllid yellows." There is a small psyllid that causes the stems of potato plants to swell up and turn purplish, which really hurts production of farm crops.

NATURAL CONTROL: The egg-eating and predator insects such as lady beetles and green lacewings. Birds and other insectivorous animals.

ORGANIC CONTROL: Garlic or citrus sprays, biodiversity, and healthy plants.

INSIGHT: The potato psyllid is so small that it isn't detected until the damage is done. Prevention through an organic program is the best control.

A Malcolm Story

On the farm, we are troubled by the potato psyllid at one location, while 300 feet away in a different soil texture they haven't yet been a problem. I haven't figured out why. We also get the large psyllids on the new growth on our persimmon trees some years. Blasting them off with Garden-Ville Fire Ant Control formula contains them.

PUSS CATERPILLAR

COMMON NAMES: Asp, Flannel Moth, Puss Caterpillar

SCIENTIFIC NAME: Order Lepidoptera, family Megalopygidae, *Megalopyge opercularis*

SIZE: Adult—1", mature larva—1"

IDENTIFICATION: Adults are moths that lay eggs that hatch into a dangerous larva. They are worms with pretty hairdos but will sting severely. The sting comes from hollow spines hidden by the soft fur in several colors ranging from blond to dark brown.

BIOLOGY AND LIFE CYCLE: One generation per year. Winter passed in cocoons attached to twigs. The moth emerges from an overwintering cocoon in late spring or late summer to deposit its eggs on trees and shrubs. In a few days the eggs hatch into tiny, fuzzy, whitish larvae

Puss caterpillar larva (H)

that look like small tufts of cotton. Puss caterpillars become darker as they mature.

HABITAT: Oaks and other tree trunks primarily.

FEEDING HABITS: Larvae feed mainly on deciduous trees and shrubs. They usually don't do a lot of damage.

ECONOMIC IMPORTANCE: Dangerous stings, especially for youngsters.

NATURAL CONTROL: Predatory flies and wasps.

ORGANIC CONTROL: *Bacillus thuringiensis* products.

INSIGHT: Contact on tender skin is extremely painful. Put scotch tape over the sting and then remove it to pull out the irritating spines; then wash the area well to remove any remaining poison. Juice from the stems of comfrey plants may help relieve the pain. There is no really good home first-aid for the stings, so the best thing to do is consult a physician. Sensitive people may become very ill.

A Malcolm Story

The asp is easy to identify, despite their different colors. Some may be brunettes, some are gray, most that I have seen are blondes. My mother reached around a post to unlatch a gate and accidentally rubbed the inside of her wrist on one; it put her in bed for two days.

This moth is not very prolific. For protection, nature gave them hair that secretes poison. This helps ensure the survival of their species. Usually, there are never enough asps to warrant insecticidal control, but if necessary use Bt. I consider the asp the biggest enemy to the praying mantis, not because it attacks the mantis in any way but because ignorant humans often mistake the mantis egg case for that of the poisonous asp and mistakenly destroy every mantis egg case they come across.

RED ANT—see Harvester Ant

REDBUG—see Chigger

RED DYE BUG—see Cochineal

RED SPIDER MITE—see Spider Mite

RHINOCEROS BEETLE

COMMON NAMES: Giant Beetle, Hercules Beetle, Ox Beetle, Rhino Beetle, Rhinoceros Beetle, Unicorn Beetle
SCIENTIFIC NAME: Order Coleoptera, family Scarabaeidae, several species
SIZE: Adult—up to 2", larva—up to 3"
IDENTIFICATION: Very large beetles with horns; males have more prominent horns than the females. Many different sizes and colors.
BIOLOGY AND LIFE CYCLE: Complete metamorphosis.
HABITAT: Larvae found in sawdust, rotting stumps, and compost piles. Adults are found around lights at night.
FEEDING HABITS: We have never found adults feeding. The books say they may feed some on plants, mostly nectar. Larvae feed on and help break down organic matter.
ECONOMIC IMPORTANCE: Good catfish bait, add fascination to nature, help in the decay of high-carbon organics.
NATURAL CONTROL: None needed. Insectivorous animals such as opossums and armadillos love them, especially the giant larvae.
ORGANIC CONTROL: None needed.
INSIGHT: Ferocious-looking but harmless. Collectors prize the adults, fishermen prize the larvae. Often found in the compost pile, where they are totally beneficial. In Japan they are kept as pets and sold in stores. Perfect specimens are sold for as much as $3,000. Kept in cages and fed a special diet, they will live up to two years. Ounce for ounce, these giant beetles are among the world's strongest animals. One bug scientist glued weights on a rhinoceros beetle's back and found it could carry up to one hundred times its own weight, although it did get tired. With only thirty times its own weight, the beetle showed no sign of fatigue, often walking for half an hour. This is comparable to a fifty-year-old man walking a mile with a Cadillac on his back.

ROACH—see Cockroach

ROBBER FLY

COMMON NAME: Robber Fly
SCIENTIFIC NAME: Order Diptera, family Asilidae, many species
SIZE: Adult—½" to ¾"
IDENTIFICATION: Adults have a large head, prominent eyes, a bristly humped thorax, long legs, and a thin tapering abdomen. Slender bodies, but some resemble bumblebees. Most are gray, brown, or black.
BIOLOGY AND LIFE CYCLE: Adult females lay small cream-colored eggs on plants, on rotten wood, or in the soil. Small, clean, segmented, cylindrical larvae have a distinctive head. Pupae are spiny and not enclosed in a puparium. They pupate in the soil. Larvae overwinter in the soil. One generation a year. They are encouraged by flowering plants.
HABITAT: Many vegetable and ornamental crops. Biodiverse gardens and wooded areas. Larvae are found mostly in decaying organic matter under litter.

Rhinoceros beetle (B)

Rhinoceros beetle grubs (B)

Rhinoceros beetle adult and larva (B)

Rhinoceros beetle larva and June beetle larva (B)

Robber fly (B)

FEEDING HABITS: Adults prey on small to medium insects. Larvae feed on small soil-borne insects, including grubs, root maggots, beetle pupae, and grasshopper eggs—basically anything they can catch. Attack and eat butterflies, wasps, bees, horseflies, winged ants, grasshoppers, leafhoppers, beetles, and other flies. They will eat beneficials, although rarely. The troublesome plant feeders are slower and easier to catch. They suck their prey dry with hypodermiclike mouthparts.

ECONOMIC IMPORTANCE: Help to control troublesome insects, especially flies, beetle grubs, and mosquitoes.

NATURAL CONTROL: Birds.

ORGANIC CONTROL: None needed.

INSIGHT: The common name of this ferocious insect comes from its habit of pouncing on prey. The larvae of robber flies are also predaceous. They live in decaying organic matter and attack other insect larvae, especially beetle grubs.

ROLY-POLY BUG—see Pillbug, Sowbug

ROOT APHID—see Aphid

ROOT KNOT NEMATODE—see Nematode

ROOTWORM—see Cucumber Beetle

ROUNDWORM—see Nematode

ROUGH STINK BUG—see Brochymena

ROVE BEETLE

COMMON NAME: Rove Beetle
SCIENTIFIC NAME: Order Coleoptera, family Staphylinidae, several species
SIZE: Adult—⅛" to 1"
IDENTIFICATION: Fast-moving brownish or black beetles with very short front wings that leave much of the

Rove beetle (ENT)

abdomen uncovered. Full-length hind wings are folded and concealed beneath the stubby front wings. When disturbed, they turn up the tip of their abdomen and assume a stinging pose. Larvae look like adults without wings.

BIOLOGY AND LIFE CYCLE: Rove beetles are scavengers or predators on insects found in filth. Most species overwinter as adults, laying eggs in the soil in the spring. Larvae have three molts, then pupate in the soil.

HABITAT: Decaying animal and vegetable matter in the soil. They can be found in corn tassels, root and cabbage crops, compost, and other organic matter.

FEEDING HABITS: Active at night. Predators of aphids, springtails, mites, nematodes, slugs, fly eggs, and maggots. They are scavengers and predators.

ECONOMIC IMPORTANCE: Control of several troublesome insects.

NATURAL CONTROL: None needed—beneficial.

ORGANIC CONTROL: None needed.

INSIGHT: We haven't seen many of these insects, but we know they're around.

SAP FEEDING BEETLE—see Nitidulid Beetle

SAWFLY

COMMON NAMES: Oak Leaf Sawfly, Sawfly, Tenthredinid Sawfly
SCIENTIFIC NAME: Order Hymenoptera, family Tenthredinidae, many species
SIZE: Adult—½", larva—about ¼"
IDENTIFICATION: Adults are small wasps that cannot sting. The name comes from the sawlike structure at the end of the female's abdomen, used to cut into leaves to lay eggs. Larvae look like translucent slugs, usually yellowish green and shiny with black heads. Some are covered with a slimy material.
BIOLOGY AND LIFE CYCLE: Females lay eggs on the back side of leaves. Larvae hatch and feed on the tissue between the veins, causing a skeletonized effect. Larvae overwinter in cocoons.
HABITAT: Red oaks and white oaks primarily.
ECONOMIC IMPORTANCE: Damage is usually spotty on trees and not significant.

Sawfly grubs on red oak (H)

Sawfly grub damage (H)

NATURAL CONTROL: Enemy insects. Biodiversity.
ORGANIC CONTROL: Microbial disease products, horticultural oil, and citrus oil products.
INSIGHT: You see some of this damage every year, but it never seems to be anything other than cosmetic and temporary. Some sawflies attack and damage fruit trees, elms, roses, and pines.

SCALE

COMMON NAME: Scale
SCIENTIFIC NAME: Order Homoptera. Soft Scale—family Coccidae, Armored Scale—family Diaspididae
SIZE: Adult—¹⁄₁₀" to ⅕"
IDENTIFICATION: Adult scales attach themselves to bark, shoots, or foliage. If they are hollow and flake off easily, they are dead. Live ones range in color from white to dark brown.
BIOLOGY AND LIFE CYCLE: Soft scales like garden and ornamental plants. Armored scales prefer orchard crops. All have incomplete metamorphosis. Soft scales are covered with a secreted waxy or cottony material. Males may have a single pair of wings. Females can give birth to live scales as crawlers. Nymphs have legs and brown antennae. Armored scales secrete and build a stronger coating. Young are born alive or hatch from eggs and are active until after the first molt. Males have wings, well-developed antennae, and simple eyes—females don't.
HABITAT: Garden, farm, and landscape plants.
FEEDING HABITS: Scales suck plant sap through piercing, sucking mouthparts. Will attack many ornamental and food crops.
ECONOMIC IMPORTANCE: Can do severe damage by reducing vigor and stressing plants. Serious citrus pest.
NATURAL CONTROL: Twicestabbed, lindorus, and

Scale (ARM)

Scale on red oak trunk (B)

vedalia lady beetles; parasitic aphids; parasitic wasps. Healthy plants.

ORGANIC CONTROL: Dormant oil in winter, horticultural oil year round, and citrus oil products in the growing season.

INSIGHT: Mealybugs are closely related to scale and controlled with the same methods. San Jose scale, a tiny species of scale related to the fruit tree pest, is used to make shellac.

SCARAB BEETLE—see Dung Beetle

SEED BUG—see Bigeyed Bug

SCARLET LAUREL BUG

COMMON NAMES: Laurel Bug, Scarlet Laurel Bug
SCIENTIFIC NAME: Order Hemiptera, family Miridae, *Lopidea* spp.
SIZE: Adult—⅜"
IDENTIFICATION: Scarlet red with black tail.
BIOLOGY AND LIFE CYCLE: Incomplete metamorphosis. Females insert eggs into plant tissue using a bladelike ovipositor.
HABITAT: Overwatered flower beds and lawns. Stressed Texas mountain laurels in nurseries.
FEEDING HABITS: Feeds on young growth, blooms, and seed pods.
ECONOMIC IMPORTANCE: Indicates that laurels are stressed—due to overwatering, poor drainage, compacted soil, and other problems.
NATURAL CONTROL: Biodiversity.
ORGANIC CONTROL: Usually does not cause enough damage to worry about. Citrus oil products for heavy infestations.
INSIGHT: Seem to be very serious some years but normally not.

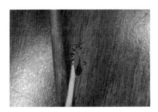

Scarlet laurel bug on mountain laurel (B)

SCORPION

COMMON NAME: Scorpion
SCIENTIFIC NAME: Order Scorpiones, family Buthidae
SIZE: Adult—2" to 4"
IDENTIFICATION: Scary-looking creatures having upturned and very dangerous tails with powerful stingers on the end.
BIOLOGY AND LIFE CYCLE: Scorpions are not insects. They are arachnids and kin to spiders. All species are nocturnal and usually hide out during the day.
HABITAT: Humid, protected spots in dry climates.
FEEDING HABITS: Scorpions will sit in the same spot for days, waiting for the right prey to venture by. The

Scorpion (B)

stinger is used to immobilize the prey while being held by the pinchers. They feed on insects like crickets and roaches.

ECONOMIC IMPORTANCE: Painful sting; but beneficial in that they are predaceous and eat roaches.
NATURAL CONTROL: Snakes. Remove wood piles and rock piles near the home; control the food source, such as crickets and roaches.
ORGANIC CONTROL: Pyrethrum and diatomaceous earth products. Citrus-based sprays like Garden-Ville Fire Ant Control.
INSIGHT: Malcolm admits that as a youth he would cut their stingers off and take them to school to scare girls.

SHARPSHOOTER

COMMON NAME: Sharpshooter
SCIENTIFIC NAME: Order Homoptera, family Cicadellidae, many species
SIZE: Adult—up to ½"
IDENTIFICATION: Tubular leafhoppers that range in color from dark brown to green. Wings are almost parallel to the body when at rest. They "spit" honeydew and have the curious habit of playing hide and seek by scooting around to the other side of stems when you try to touch them. They will also spring off the plant like a bullet when disturbed.

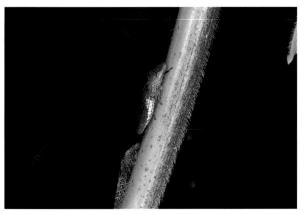

Sharpshooter (B)

LIFE CYCLE: Female adults lay eggs into the soft tissue of stems. Nymphs hatch and disperse quickly to feed. Incomplete metamorphosis; one or more generations a year.

HABITAT: From meadows and undeveloped land to cultivated gardens. They love crape myrtles.

FEEDING HABITS: Nymphs and adults suck juices from various plants with their piercing, sucking mouthparts.

ECONOMIC IMPORTANCE: None.

NATURAL CONTROL: Biodiversity. Birds, lizards, and beneficial microorganisms.

ORGANIC CONTROL: Rarely abundant enough to warrant control, but the citrus oil products will get 'em.

INSIGHT: There are two theories on the origin of the name sharpshooter: their method of expelling honeydew with force and their habit of leaping out of danger with the speed of a bullet. Your choice.

SHOT HOLE BORER

COMMON NAMES: Bark Beetle, Shot Hole Borer

SCIENTIFIC NAME: Order Coleoptera, family Scolytidae, *Scolytus rugulosus*

SIZE: Adult—¹⁄₁₀"

IDENTIFICATION: Adult beetles are dark brown to black and blunt on each end. They have well-developed wings. They drill small holes in tree trunks about the size of pencil lead. Larvae are snow white.

BIOLOGY AND LIFE CYCLE: Adult beetles appear from April through June. Mated females seek out trees that are in somewhat unhealthy or stressed condition. They enter the cambium layer, excavate a gallery, and deposit white

eggs. The female usually dies with the tip of her body blocking the entrance to the egg gallery. Young grubs (larvae) hatch and burrow into the inner bark. Their tunnels are full of frass, unlike the clean parent gallery. When fully grown after six to eight weeks, the larvae change into pupae and later into adult beetles. One to three generations a year.

HABITAT: Apple, peach, pear, plum, cherry, quince, serviceberry, chokeberry, and many other stressed trees.

FEEDING HABITS: Eat small holes in the twigs, branches, and trunks of stressed trees.

ECONOMIC IMPORTANCE: Not much. This is not a serious pest if the soil and trees are managed properly.

NATURAL CONTROL: Keep trees healthy by improving the soil.

ORGANIC CONTROL: Tree Trunk Goop (see Appendix C).

INSIGHT: Native to Europe but has naturalized across the United States.

SILVERFISH

COMMON NAMES: Firebrat, Silverfish

SCIENTIFIC NAME: Order Thysanura, family Lepismatidae. Silverfish—*Lepisma saccharina*, Firebrat—*Thermobia domestica*

SIZE: Adult—¼" to ¾"

IDENTIFICATION: Slender, flattened, wingless, segmented, silver-gray and black, covered with scales. End of abdomen has three taillike filaments. Firebrats are very similar but much darker.

BIOLOGY AND LIFE CYCLE: Very primitive insects. Nocturnal and fast-moving. Can go long periods of time without food. Incomplete metamorphosis. Immature stages are similar to the adults. A segment is added with each molt. Nymphs take up to two years to reach maturity.

HABITAT: Silverfish like cool places or warm, damp ones. Firebrats like warm, humid places. Both live indoors and outdoors under stones, in caves, in debris, and in ant nests.

Silverfish (BP)

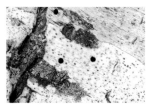

Shot hole borer larvae damage in peach bark (B)

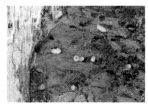

Shot hole larva under peach bark (B)

FEEDING HABITS: Feed on starchy materials like glue, flour, damp textiles, book bindings, and wallpaper paste. Also dry meat, oats, paper products, waste materials, and decaying plant and animal matter.

ECONOMIC IMPORTANCE: Common pest in homes and libraries. Book and document damage. Beneficial in the wild.

NATURAL CONTROL: Spiders.

ORGANIC CONTROL: Indoor control is all that is ever needed. Diatomaceous earth, boric acid, and pyrethrum products.

INSIGHT: Considered living fossils, silverfish are older than dinosaurs—at least, that's what we read.

SIXSPOTTED SPHINX—see Tobacco Hornworm

SLUG, SNAIL

COMMON NAMES: Slug, Snail

SCIENTIFIC NAME: Order Stylommatophora, several families and species

SIZE: Snail—1½", slug—⅛" to 3"

IDENTIFICATION: Slugs have green blood and are covered by a layer of slime or mucus. Most are gray, tan, or black. Some are green and some have distinctive dot patterns. They leave a slimy trail wherever they go. Eggs are clear ovals laid in jellylike masses. Decollate snail looks like its small end has been broken off. Snail shells are made up of calcium.

BIOLOGY AND LIFE CYCLE: Adults lay eggs in moist soil. Eggs hatch in two to four weeks, take two years to reach maturity. Life span is one to six years, depending on the species. Eggs are usually less than a quarter inch and often have a thick outer shell of calcium carbonate. They are normally laid in clutches of three to fifty.

HABITAT: Moist gardens.

FEEDING HABITS: Slugs and snails feed primarily on decaying organic matter, but they also have a taste for your best ornamental and vegetable plants. They feed at night (although on damp drizzly days they will stay out all day). Will climb trees or eat on the ground. They like to eat fungi, lichens, green foliage, worms, centipedes, insects, animal feces, carrion, and other slugs.

ECONOMIC IMPORTANCE: Very destructive to many garden plants and food crops. The decollate snail is predatory and helps to control plant-eating snails, although there is some worry that it will destroy the balance of native snails—but we doubt it.

NATURAL CONTROL: Maintain permanent stands of clover and mulches to favor ground beetles and rove beetles (which eat slugs). Centipedes also eat slug eggs. Other predators include small mammals, snakes, frogs, toads, lizards, birds, and carnivorous beetles. In the insect world their biggest enemy is the larva of the lightning bug.

Slug (B)

Decollate snail (B)

Snail (B)

ORGANIC CONTROL: Copper bands are supposed to work, but they sound like too much work to us. Dust dry hot pepper in problem areas—it works great. Mix with diatomaceous earth for economy. Coarse-textured, crushed hot pepper like as that used on pizza is best. Citrus oil spray works well, and coffee grounds sprinkled on top of the mulch also helps.

INSIGHT: Trapping can be done with banana peels, eaten grapefruit halves, apple cores, and beer or yeast water traps. Putting wood ashes or diatomaceous earth around plants helps repel snails and slugs. They all seem to be alcoholics—just one taste and they can't quit. Beer placed in a saucer or pan sunken to ground level will do them in.

Slugs and snails do have their good points. They help disperse seed and spores, break down organic matter, and keep down the population of other small pests. A big one called the decollate snail feeds on other snails.

The American Indians used them for food. Boiled or roasted snails were a staple in their diet.

A Malcolm Story

The predatory decollate snail, *Rumina decollata*, has naturalized in Texas. It is from North Africa, and populations are found in the Mediterranean region. It has naturalized in southern California, where it preys upon the brown garden snail. The brown garden snail is a European import that feeds on a variety of plants.

A University of California specialist in the biological control of snails conducted research in the early 1980s which demonstrated that the decollate snail is an effective natural enemy of the brown garden snail. Citrus farmers in southern California were anxious to colonize the decollate snail in their groves because chemical snail control practices were expensive, time-consuming, and not always effective. There was a real need to rear the predator to accelerate its distribution. At that time, Mike Rose, now research scientist and quarantine supervisor in biological control at Texas A&M University, was working on biological control of whitefly and scale insects in the southern California citrus groves. Mike organized a limited partnership for his wife Susan and children, fourteen-year-old Jake and twelve-year-old Anduin, to enter the business of raising snails for citrus growers.

The Rose family purchased old redwood boxes from Associates Insectary in Ventura County; the boxes had previously been used to rear mealybugs on potatoes for mass culture of the mealybug destroyer, *Cryptolaemus montrouzieri*. After rebuilding the boxes, clean soil was obtained from an organic avocado grove, and each of the 200 boxes was bottomed with about two inches of soil. The soil was needed for the snail to produce eggs and to maintain adequate humidity. The farm manager at Baker Ranch in Orange County then allowed the Roses to collect adult decollate snails to start a mother culture.

The mother culture was initiated from only 1,000 or so snails. The culture required care twice daily—feeding, misting with water to maintain humidity levels, transferring reproductive reproducing snails, and standardizing age and size classes of snails for sale.

The very first sale of snails was to Millard Beemer, a leading citrus farmer in San Diego's Pauma Valley. It was the first return after months of snail culture. The family dedicated an entire day and evening to preparation of snails for Mr. Beemer. After this first sale, the small

family business continued to grow and a mother culture of nearly a million snails was established.

The Rose family was preparing to move to Texas during the same period. The great potential for selling snails to citrus growers was recognized by several pest control advisor groups, which made offers to the Roses to buy their business. The sale was made, and in one day the Rose family decollate snail business was over.

The rewards from this endeavor were many. The family worked together and attained their goal of creating a thriving snail culture. The money from the sale of snails and the business was shared equally among the partners and provided the Rose children with their first computer and with savings that were later used to help pay for college and their first car. All in all, it was a wonderful learning experience—thanks to the decollate snail and its role in biological control of the imported brown garden snail.

This beautiful story tells how a family working together not only helped the citrus industry save their crops but also helped the industry avoid spreading poison. And they saved the money for good causes while at the same time experiencing the enjoyment of working with nature and operating a snail ranch.

Here on my own farm we have always seen lots of snails, and people were always asking what I did for snail control. My answer was, well, the snails must like me 'cause they never bother any of my plants. It wasn't until we enjoyed a visit from Mike Rose that I learned the truth: most of the snails we had were these good guys, keeping the troublemakers under control.

SNOUT BEETLE—see Weevil

SNOUT BUTTERFLY

COMMON NAMES: Miller, Snout Butterfly
SCIENTIFIC NAME: Order Lepidoptera, family Libytheidae. Two subspecies in Texas—*Libytheana bachmanii* and *larvata* (some books list three species in Texas).
SIZE: Adult wing span—1½" to 2"; larva—¾" to 1"
IDENTIFICATION: Larvae are green, the color of lush green hackberry leaves, with yellow stripes along the top and sides. The adult wings are patterned: blackish brown

Snout butterfly larva on silken thread (B)

Snout butterfly pupa (B)

Snout butterfly (B)

with creamy white and orange markings. The adult has elongated mouthparts up to ¼" long, forming the snout that gives them their name. We have noticed that the older butterflies usually lose the snout before they die.
BIOLOGY AND LIFE CYCLE: Complete metamorphosis. Believed to mate at night. In good weather conditions the period from egg to adult may take only fifteen days. Up to four generations a year. Books we consulted say they overwinter as adults. An entomologist we consulted said they overwinter in the pupa stage. We believe that in Texas, at least in the southern parts, they do both.
FEEDING HABITS: Larvae chew mostly hackberry tree leaves. Adults have a tube for siphoning liquids from flowers and damaged fruit.
ECONOMIC IMPORTANCE: Not considered damaging to crops. Adults and larvae are big in the food chain. After a big hatch, the adults are troublesome for drivers; they can quickly smear windshields and plug radiators.
NATURAL CONTROL: Birds.
ORGANIC CONTROL: None needed.
INSIGHT: They seem to have the heaviest flights (in the millions) after rains break a long drought. Sometimes they seem to be migrating north. A few days later they may go south. It sometimes seems they are just milling around in no general direction. That's why the old-timers

called them millers. Or maybe because of the flourlike powder on their wings.

The larvae are interesting. If you bump a branch or disturb the leaf they are feeding on, they quickly fall to the ground. If you look closely, they have kept a silken thread attached to the leaf they were feeding on. After they have fallen a couple of feet, they slow their fall to a halt. They are excellent bungee jumpers. If they are on a low branch they may hit the ground. It takes the larger larvae longer to slow their fall. Once they have stopped their fall, they hold still for a few moments; then with a winding action of their head they start back up the thread to their original leaf. They can do this with amazing speed. If they don't stop their fall before they hit the ground and can't start back up on time, the fire ants usually get them.

Cold conditions don't seem to hurt them. Malcolm kept some in a jar in the refrigerator for three hours, hoping to study them while they were inactive, but they quickly warmed up and flew away. Because of the variety of their heavy flights, they attract a lot of attention. Snout butterflies have been found in fossil shales in Colorado that are believed to be 35 million years old.

A Malcolm Story

A big flight of snout butterflies occurred in the San Antonio area and south about the time we were preparing this book. I could find very little information in books. I consulted three entomologists and all three were in disagreement. One said they always migrated north, another said south. I watched them go in every direction. One said they overwinter in the adult stage, the other two said in the pupa stage. One said the snout was the two forward legs held in that position. I inspected one and found there were still six legs besides the snout. The best information came from a fourteen-year-old boy. This little self-taught naturalist told me they lose their snout when they get old. I trapped a bunch in my big greenhouse and watched. In a few days, sure enough, they started losing their snouts. It's amazing how much a person, especially a child, can learn about nature by paying attention.

SOD WEBWORM

COMMON NAME: Sod Webworm
SCIENTIFIC NAME: Order Lepidoptera, family Pyralidae
SIZE: Larva—¼" to ¾"
IDENTIFICATION: Sod webworms are the larval form of lawn moths, which are small and range from white to gray in color. They are spotted and coarse-haired. The adults hold their wings close together at rest, are pale brown, and have a projection from the front of the head. Larvae are spotted and coarsely haired.

BIOLOGY AND LIFE CYCLE: Adults fly around and drop eggs into the turf. Larvae are light brown caterpillars with several rows of dark spots. They live on the soil surface in silken tunnels built in the thatch. They chew grass into closely cropped spots.

HABITAT: Unhealthy turf.

FEEDING HABITS: Feed at night on grass during the heat of summer; they like hot, dry turf. Shady areas are seldom invaded.

ECONOMIC IMPORTANCE: Lawn damage.

NATURAL CONTROL: Birds. Keep turf watered and healthy, mulch with compost.

ORGANIC CONTROL: *Bacillus thuringiensis* spray.

INSIGHT: More a problem on golf courses than on lawns. Blackbirds, robins, and other birds pecking holes in the turf is a sure sign of these pests.

SOLDIER BEETLE

COMMON NAME: Soldier Beetle

SCIENTIFIC NAME: Order Coleoptera, family Cantheridae, many species, *Chaubiognathus pennsylvanicus*

SIZE: ½ to ¾"

IDENTIFICATION: This is one of the ground beetles. Adults are long, narrow beetles, often orange or red with black or brown wings. Both larvae and adults are easily identified by their velvety covering.

HABITAT: Soldier beetles like to do their hunting in yarrow, daisies, and other flowering plants.

FEEDING HABITS: Aphids and other small insects pests.

ECONOMIC IMPORTANCE: Beneficial.

NATURAL CONTROL: None needed.

ORGANIC CONTROL: None needed.

INSIGHT: Colorful and highly beneficial insect that should be protected. Not seen that often but worth knowing about.

Soldier beetle (ENT)

Soldier fly (H)

Soldier fly larvae (H)

SOLDIER FLY

COMMON NAME: Soldier Fly

SCIENTIFIC NAME: Order Diptera, family Stratiomyidae, several species

SIZE: Adult—½"

IDENTIFICATION: Adult flies are bare of bristles and not strong fliers. Antennae have three segments, often carried in the form of a Y. Colors range from dark metallic to brightly banded with yellow and pale green. Wings are small and lie over each other. Unlike syrphid flies, they do not hover. Larvae are tough worms with small heads and pointed ends.

BIOLOGY AND LIFE CYCLE: Eggs are laid in decaying wood, mud, and dung. Larvae are maggotlike scavengers or predators. All are thick-skinned and somewhat flattened. Pupation happens in the last larval skin. Adults are dark, sometimes banded flies. All life forms are found in the same habitat.

HABITAT: Wet, low-lying areas, sappy wood, dung, and wet soil.

FEEDING HABITS: Adults feed on flower nectar; larvae feed on decaying organic matter.

ECONOMIC IMPORTANCE: Help with the breakdown of organic matter, especially dung. People raising earthworms find the manure-feeding larvae to be very helpful.

Spider web with morning dew (B)

NATURAL CONTROL: None needed.

ORGANIC CONTROL: None needed.

INSIGHT: Gardeners are sometimes concerned when they buy earthworm castings or other organic fertilizers and find these maggotlike worms. No reason for concern—they hurt nothing and are quite beneficial.

SORGHUM HEADWORM—see Corn Earworm

SOUTHERN CORNWORM—see Cucumber Beetle

SOUTHERN MOLE CRICKET—see Cricket

SOUTHERN PINE BEETLE—see Pine Beetle

SOWBUG—see Pillbug, Sowbug

SPHECID WASP—see Mud Dauber

SPHINX MOTH—see Tomato Hornworm

SPIDER

COMMON NAME: Spider
SCIENTIFIC NAME: Order Araneae, many families
SIZE: Varies
IDENTIFICATION: Spiders are not insects; they have eight segmented legs instead of six, as insects do. Many construct webs for capturing prey. Jumping spiders of the

family Salticidae are colorful and leap to capture prey on the leaves. Wolf spiders of the family Lycosidae run rapidly on the ground to catch prey at the base of plants. Garden spiders or orb-weavers of the family Araneidae string vertical webs to trap flying insects. Funnel-web spiders of the family Agelinidae create funnel webs and trap leafhoppers primarily.

BIOLOGY AND LIFE CYCLE: Males are often smaller than females. Not all spiders spin webs. Some live in

Spider and egg sac (B)

Spider dragging caterpillar to nest (B)

Argiope spider, one of the garden's most beautiful beneficials (H)

Wolf spider with captured squash bug (B)

Black jumping spider eating cucumber beetle (H)

tunnels. Most spiders lay eggs in silken sacs, which may be attached to the web or to twigs or leaves. Some carry the sac with them. Young are called spiderlings, look like adults, and are often cannibals.

HABITAT: Different spiders live in many different plants and habitats—beehives, wood scraps, fencerows, vegetable crops, and ornamental plantings.

FEEDING HABITS: Paralyze with venom and feed on insects and other small animals.

ECONOMIC IMPORTANCE: Spiders are highly beneficial because they feed on many troublesome insects. Black widows and brown recluses are the only poisonous spiders, and they are very dangerous ones.

NATURAL CONTROL: Mud daubers and other wasps. See Mud Dauber.

ORGANIC CONTROL: If a problem, knock the webs down with a broom. If they have to be killed, use soapy water or citrus. Vacuum thoroughly and often. Eliminate other insects—the spiders' food source. All but the black widows and brown recluses are totally beneficial.

INSIGHT: You'll probably never see a brown recluse because they're reclusive. They live in dark places and move about at night. The female black widow is easy to identify by the red hourglass on her abdomen. Beware of her venomous sting. It is very powerful and can cause illness or even death. The much smaller male isn't much

Spitting spider (H)

Garden spider (H)

trouble; in fact the female eats him alive after mating. Spiders are a great help in controlling moths whose larvae feed on apples, pecans, and other orchard crops. They also eat aphids in fruit trees and ornamental plants. See also Black Widow Spider, Brown Recluse Spider, Tarantula. See appendix for bites.

A Malcolm Story

It was spiders that fascinated me most during my childhood. There were so many different types, sizes, and colors, and they never ate our plants. Instead, they ate the bad bugs that were eating in our garden. They built all kinds of webs to snare their food. Some I saw flying through the air like kites, making their own string as they went. Others were black jumping spiders that hung around the windowsills in our house. They had big, green, friendly eyes that always looked right at you. They were welcome, and my parents wouldn't let anyone harm them. They were probably the spiders that gave me the biggest thrill because in the blink of an eye they could jump and catch a fly.

As a child I had very few toys, and they had to be shared with all my brothers and sisters. But I didn't care; the insects and spiders were more amusing anyway. There was one spider my mother taught me not to play with. But I don't believe I would have because of its deadly looks. This spider was shiny black with a bright red hourglass on its underside. The web was silky but ugly because it had no pretty pattern like other spider webs. My mother said this was the black widow spider and deadly poisonous. The black widow was so mean and hungry, she'd kill her husband after mating.

Later on in life I learned that the there are only two dangerous spiders in this country. The other one is called the brown recluse. They have an outline of a violin on their back. I have never seen one in nature; they must really live up to their name. The black widow is seen more often. During high school, I worked for a plumber for a couple of summers. Many homes then were built on piers, and the plumbing was underneath the house. If the house was fairly new, I always found numerous black widows. For some reason, I never saw them under old houses. They seemed to prefer new structures.

My wife, Delphine, loves nature as much as I do and at one time kept bees. One day she asked me to clean up a bee box that had been in storage. When I took off the top of the box, I realized I had torn open a mud dauber's nest. I knew mud daubers caught spiders, but I didn't know how many or what kind.

The first thing I did was get my camera and take pictures of the nest. Then I got a toothpick and started separating and counting the paralyzed spiders. When I got through identifying the spiders in this one nest, there were seventy-seven. Of those, all but eleven were black widows.

I'm sure nature gave us the black widow for a reason. One use we've already discovered is that her web is extremely strong for its thickness, and it makes good crosshairs in scopes. But we don't need a lot of black widows, so nature put the mud dauber here to keep that poisonous lady under control.

SPIDER MITE

COMMON NAMES: Spider Mite, Twospotted Spider Mite, Red Spider Mite
SCIENTIFIC NAME: Order Acari, family Tetranychidae, *Tetranychus urticae*
SIZE: Adult—1/150" to 1/50"
IDENTIFICATION: Adults are reddish brown and spiderlike with eight legs; no antennae, thorax, or wings. Eggs are laid at the base of plants or on the plants.
BIOLOGY AND LIFE CYCLE: Many generations a year; the life cycle lasts only a few days. Adults hibernate in winter in debris or in bark.
HABITAT: Many plants such as fruit trees, vegetables, ornamental plants, and house plants, especially stressed plants. Like dry climates. Spider mites like to overwinter in poke, Jerusalem oak, Jimson weed, and other weeds.
FEEDING HABITS: Both nymphs and adults pierce plant cells and suck juice. Feed on fruit, foliage, and roots. Infested leaves turn silvery or yellow, then curl and are covered with a fine web.
ECONOMIC IMPORTANCE: Serious damage to food crops and ornamentals.

Spider mites on tomato plant (H)   *Spider mite web between sticks* (H)

NATURAL CONTROL: Predatory spider mites, ladybugs, minute pirate bugs, thrips and lacewings, and lady beetles. Address the cause of the plant stress. Mites attack only sick plants.

ORGANIC CONTROL: Spraying just about anything every three days for nine days will get rid of them. Garlic-pepper tea and seaweed mix is one of the best sprays. Citrus oil sprays are also effective.

INSIGHT: Organic gardeners rarely have spider mite problems because of healthy soil, mulch, and adapted plants that have been planted properly. They are a problem only when soil is too wet or too dry.

A Malcolm Story

SEAWEED EXPERIMENT TO CONTROL RED SPIDER MITES

When Kelthane (a chlorinated hydrocarbon) was taken off the market, nonorganic growers complained that the government had taken away the only control for the two-spotted red spider mites. For years, however, organic growers had been keeping spider mites under control with their natural growing practices and in worst cases used soapy water sprays.

I had always used 1 tablespoon of liquid seaweed and 2 tablespoons of fish emulsion as a foliar feed; I had never had a spider mite problem and gave the slightly oily fish emulsion credit for the control until I heard of other gardeners using seaweed only and getting good control.

For the test I let two large tomato plants get dry and become heavily infested; the stems and leaves were crawling thick with millions of mites. I used 3 tablespoons of liquid seaweed per gallon of water and gave the plants a thorough misting. I checked the plants five days later using a magnifying glass and the low power of the microscope and found no red spider mites; but I did find numerous predator mites, *Phytoseiulus persimilis*, which are the natural enemy of the twospotted red spider mite. I checked again two weeks later and still could not find a single spider mite. There were still some of the predator mites but not as many as before since they weren't needed.

Liquid seaweed controls spider mites as well or even better than the toxic kelthane; at the same time, you're giving the plants a foliar feeding of probably the best micronutrient blend nature has to offer.

SPINED SOLDIER BUG

COMMON NAMES: Spined Soldier Bug
SCIENTIFIC NAME: Order Heteroptera, family Pentatomidae, *Podisus maculiventris*
SIZE: Adult—⅜" to ½" (about the size of stink bug but a little longer)

Spined soldier bug depositing eggs (B)

IDENTIFICATION: Adults are pale brown to tan and shield-shaped with prominent spines on the shoulders. Eggs are metallic bronze and barrel-shaped. Nymphs are round and quite colorful.

BIOLOGY AND LIFE CYCLE: Nymphs cluster at first and then disperse to feed. In the beginning they are red and black, then orange, white, and brown. Usually two to three generations a year. Females lay several hundred eggs in tight clusters of twenty to thirty on twigs and leaves.

HABITAT: Tomatoes, corn, beans, eggplant, cucurbits, asparagus, and onions.

FEEDING HABITS: Prey on hundreds of species, including corn borer, diamond-backed moth, corn earworm, armyworm, cabbage looper, imported cabbage worm, Colorado potato beetle, and Mexican bean beetle—a very beneficial insect.

ECONOMIC IMPORTANCE: Control of several troublesome insects.

NATURAL CONTROL: Birds.

ORGANIC CONTROL: None needed.

INSIGHT: A pheromone that attracts spined soldier bugs to your garden is available commercially.

SPITTLEBUG

COMMON NAMES: Frog Hopper, Meadow Spittlebug, Spittle Bug
SCIENTIFIC NAME: Order Homoptera, family Cercopidae, *Philaenus spumaris*
SIZE: Adult—up to ½"
IDENTIFICATION: Adults are oval, frog-faced, tan, brown, or black; similar to leafhoppers but fatter. They have sharp spines on the hind legs and jump when disturbed. Nymphs are similar to adults but wingless; they protect themselves inside a foamy mass of "spittle." Eggs are white.

BIOLOGY AND LIFE CYCLE: Incomplete metamorphosis. Overwinter in the egg stage, hatch in spring; nymphs develop for six to seven weeks in spittle masses on plants.

Spittlebug nymph (B)

Adults feed for the rest of the summer and start to lay eggs in early fall.

HABITAT: Alfalfa, clover, strawberry, grass, pecan, and other ornamental plants.

FEEDING HABITS: Adults and nymphs suck plant juices but are rarely a serious problem.

NATURAL CONTROL: No important predators have been discovered.

ORGANIC CONTROL: Rarely needed. Can be washed off with a strong blast of water.

INSIGHT: Spittlebugs can be found on almost any plant. Heavy infestations distort plant tissue and can slow plant growth. More damaging to herbaceous plants than woody plants.

SPOTTED ASPARAGUS BEETLE—see Asparagus Beetle

SPOTTED CUCUMBER BEETLE—see Cucumber Beetle

SPRINGTAIL

COMMON NAME: Springtail
SCIENTIFIC NAME: Order Collembola, several families and species
SIZE: Adult—¹⁄₁₆" to ¼"
IDENTIFICATION: Tiny, primitive, wingless beneficial insects. Prominent antennae and usually a forked structure under the abdomen, which allows them to spring into the air. Some have rounded bodies. Often deeply colored.
BIOLOGY AND LIFE CYCLE: Live in the soil. Incomplete metamorphosis. Very abundant in healthy soils.
HABITAT: In and on the surface of the soil, especially in decaying organic matter.

Springtail

FEEDING HABITS: Feed on and break down organic matter. Scavengers.
ECONOMIC IMPORTANCE: Very beneficial at breaking down leaf litter, compost, and fungi into soil components. Sometimes a pest in mushroom beds and on small seedlings.
NATURAL CONTROL: Gecko and other lizards.
ORGANIC CONTROL: Diatomaceous earth, baking soda, and citrus products.
INSIGHT: There are about 2,000 species worldwide.

SQUASH BUG

COMMON NAME: Squash Bug
SCIENTIFIC NAME: Order Heteroptera, family Coreidae, *Anasa tristis*
SIZE: Adult—⅝" or larger
IDENTIFICATION: Adults look like long stink bugs, are dark brown to black and covered with fine, dark hairs, and have a flat abdomen. Nymphs are pale green to light gray and have a reddish thorax and abdomen as they mature. Older nymphs are covered with a gray powder. Eggs are shiny metallic brown.
BIOLOGY AND LIFE CYCLE: Adults overwinter in protected spots. In the spring females lay eggs in groups on both sides of leaves. Eggs hatch in one to two weeks;

Squash bug eggs hatching (B)

Squash bug nymphs (H)

Squash bug adult (B)

nymphs develop in four to six weeks with five molts. Usually one generation a year.

HABITAT: Cucumber, squash, pumpkins, melons, and gourds. Foliage of cucurbits.

FEEDING HABITS: Adults and nymphs suck plant juices, causing foliage to wilt, blacken, and die.

ECONOMIC IMPORTANCE: Can destroy crops in the cucurbit family.

NATURAL CONTROL: Parasitic flies, spiders, assassin bugs, birds, and snakes.

ORGANIC CONTROL: Crush the copper-colored eggs when found on the backs of leaves. Hand-pick the first adults to appear in the spring. Plant lots of flowers for pollen and nectar to attract predatory flies. Cover seedlings with floating row cover and hand-pollinate. Spray compost tea, molasses, or citrus oil for serious infestations. Dust plants with whole wheat flour.

INSIGHT: One of Howard's listeners has this tip: plant pink petunias among squash plants. He did this and hasn't seen a squash bug since. It's worth a try.

A Malcolm Story

The first few years we planted squash on both farms, the squash bugs were troublesome. We couldn't find a single easy method to control them. They overwinter in the adult stage and if you hand-pick the first to appear before they deposit eggs, you can control them. But that's a very stinky job and highly impractical on large plantings. Other than wolf spiders, no other natural enemy seems to attack them. Maybe they taste bad.

Squash bugs are another sensor insect. Perfect growing conditions are the best control. This was proven to me when, on a challenge, I grew the big pumpkin.

While visiting with Sam Cotner and Robert Dewers at the agricultural extension office one day, I was invited to ride with them to visit Tom Keeter, the head horticulturist for the city of San Antonio. I had heard of Mr. Keeter in the past, and this visit was definitely no letdown. Lush plants of all types were growing everywhere in soil—in half barrels, buckets, and hanging

baskets. These ornamentals were beautiful, but they didn't excite me like his garden did. It was about an eighth of an acre filled with almost every vegetable that was in season. There were lima beans on tall trellises, tomatoes in cages, plus green beans, eggplants, and potatoes all beautifully mulched. What really caught my eye was a green pumpkin vine with some bright orange pumpkins bulging out from under the giant leaves. One of them was much larger than the rest. While I was standing there admiring it, Mr. Keeter walked up and asked, "How do you like my big pumpkin?"

Dr. Dewers had mentioned to me that Tom's garden was organic, and I guess it was the competitiveness in me that turned my admiration to a little bit of envy. I answered, "I can grow one that big!" Dr. Cotner and Dr. Dewers were standing nearby, and they jokingly sad, "Tom, why don't you give Malcolm some of those Big Mac pumpkin seeds and see what he can grow?" I love a challenge, and since I had popped off in earshot of three top agriculturists in the state, this was one challenge I would have to meet.

The following spring I chose a spot in the field close to the house and spread rotting stable bedding about two inches thick on top. Next I chiseled the soil with a sub-soiler in both directions, two feet deep, then irrigated with sprinklers to soak the soil to about that depth. After the soil dried to the correct moisture level (when a compressed handful readily breaks apart), I disk-harrowed to prepare the seedbed. Then I checked the Llewellyn moon-sign book for the best planting date, and on that date I raked up beds that were three feet in diameter and two inches high. The beds were twenty feet apart. I sprinkled about one-quarter pound of colloidal phosphate on each hill, then pressed ten pumpkin seeds tight to the phosphate-covered soil and covered the seeds and the rest of the hill with one inch of earthworm bedding. I watered each hill with a fine mist until they were well soaked. The mist works because large droplets of water tend to crust the soil, and I didn't want resistance when those seeds were ready to emerge.

After all the seeds were up, I thinned about once a week until the one best plant was left in each hill. After the soil was warm in mid-May, I mulched the whole area with another two inches of compost. Each time the plants needed watering, which wasn't very often, I sprinkled them until they got two inches of water, then foliar-fed with fish emulsion and liquid seaweed. I used two tablespoons of fish emulsion and one tablespoon of seaweed per gallon of water.

The pumpkin vines grew and grew, and after a number of fruits were set, I pinched off all except the biggest and best, leaving one to each plant. The pumpkins were really fun to watch. Each time we went to look at them, they were bigger than before. By mid-July, they were giants and still growing.

The Men's Garden Club had a flower and vegetable show at one of the shopping malls, and our organic garden club also had a show the same weekend. My pumpkins weren't mature yet. It had only been 99 days since planting, and the books say it takes 120 days to grow a pumpkin. I could see that one of my pumpkins was already bigger than Mr. Keeter's, and I couldn't wait to show it off. I cut it from the vine and weighed it. Tom's had weighed sixty-six pounds, and mine beat his by sixteen pounds. Had I left it on the vine to mature, I am sure it would have gone over a hundred pounds, as most of the rest weighed in the high nineties.

That season we had other pumpkins and squash planted in the same field. They were no more than 200 feet away, but they were not composted, and we were in our early years on our new (second) farm, so the soil was not yet built up to high fertility. You could certainly tell the difference between the two pumpkin patches. The uncomposted plants were being attacked by squash bugs, aphids, and powdery mildew, while my pet plants were completely untouched. Not a single insect or disease bothered them until after the pumpkins were ripe and the leaf surface was no longer needed.

Some experts still say you can't grow immunity to insects in plants. I wonder if these experts ever grew a really healthy plant? Besides these pest-free pumpkins, I have completely rid pecan trees of heavy infestations of mealy bugs under the bark by mulching heavily with compost. I have reversed gummosis on peach tree trunks with compost—completely cleared the symptoms in one year—and peach trees that looked healthy but had wormy fruit were made to grow fruit without worms as long as I kept them mulched with compost.

Over the years I have seen many times that healthy plants have immunity to diseases and insects. There were times when a seemingly healthy plant was attacked by diseases and insects, but there were other factors involved. Either the plant wasn't adapted to the environment it was being grown in, or it was being attacked by a new virus or insect that was imported without its natural checks. Even though the plant being attacked looked healthy, it didn't have the genes that could give it protection from the foreign intruder.

There is always a cause for every problem. Most important, we shouldn't blame nature for the things we perceive as problems. Troublesome insects and diseases are nature's police force with a message telling us that we are in some way bending the rules. Although nature is very forgiving, if we keep using toxins to kill the police force and ignoring its messages, we get ourselves into more and bigger problems.

Incidentally, for a squash that seems to be resistant to squash bugs and squash vine borers, try tatume squash, available from Lone Star Seed Company in San Antonio.

SQUASH VINE BORER

COMMON NAME: Squash Vine Borer
SCIENTIFIC NAME: Order Lepidoptera, family Sesiidae, *Melittia cucurbitae*
SIZE: Adult—1", larva—1" to 1½"
IDENTIFICATION: Adults are beautiful, narrow-winged black- and red-bodied moths that look like wasps. Eggs are brown, flat, oval, and singly laid on stems. Larvae are white caterpillars with brown heads.
BIOLOGY AND LIFE CYCLE: Larvae tunnel into the base of vine stems, feed for four to six weeks, and cause the entire plant to wilt and die. They hibernate as larvae or pupae in cocoons about an inch deep in the soil. One or two generations a year.
FEEDING HABITS: Larvae (borers) enter the base of the

Squash vine borer adult (B)

Squash vine borer larva (H)

Squash vine borer damage to plant stem (H)

Squash vine borer damage (H)

stem in early summer, causing a greenish frass, and leading to wilting, and death. They will also feed on fruit of cucumbers, gourds, melons, pumpkins, and squash.

ECONOMIC IMPORTANCE: Destruction of squash plants.

NATURAL CONTROL: Plant more than just a few plants. Plant early and promote vigorous growth. Plant cucurbits with more solid stems, such as butternut and winter squash. Beneficial nematodes.

ORGANIC CONTROL: Slit the stem and remove the borer. Pile soil over the damaged stalk. Some say injecting *Bacillus thuringiensis* or beneficial nematodes in the stalk with a syringe works. Both methods are a lot of trouble. Cover plants with floating row cover. Spray base of plants with pyrethrum or citrus oil products regularly. Spray plants with a Bt product when yellow flowers first bloom. Check the base of stems often to remove the reddish eggs before they hatch. Treat soil with beneficial nematodes.

INSIGHT: Squash vine borers tend to avoid big squash farms but destroy home gardens.

A Malcolm Story

The first year that the San Antonio Men's Garden Club had its picnic at our farm, we had a large planting of summer squash. The most common question was "How do you control the squash vine borer?" My answer was, "I'm not familiar with it." Several of the gardeners offered to show me one. They went into the patch with their pocket knives and slit open plant after plant but never found one. Some even accused me of using poison for control.

Sam Cotner, the agricultural extension vegetable specialist, was standing under a pecan tree watching and laughing; he bet them they couldn't find a single borer. He then explained that for some unknown reason the squash vine borer does not attack large or commercial plantings and then jokingly suggested that all you needed for protection was to put out a sign that read "SQUASH FOR SALE"—then the borers would think you were a large farmer and leave you alone.

Some home gardeners use a hypodermic needle to inject Bt into the hollow vines. Others keep a close watch and as soon as they see the worm frass that is evidence of a borer, they slit the vine with a sharp knife and destroy the worm. If they catch it in time before too much damage, the vine quickly heals.

One gardening friend of mine found what I think is the easiest control; he doesn't plant squash, but he eats just as well. He learned that pumpkins are seldom bothered by the borer, so he plants pumpkins and eats them while they are still small. He says they taste the same, maybe even better. As was suggested for squash bugs, try tatume squash for a resistant variety.

STINK BUG

COMMON NAMES: Stink Bug, Green Stink Bug

SCIENTIFIC NAME: Order Heteroptera, family Pentatomidae, *Acrosternum hilare*

SIZE: Adult—½" to ⅝"

IDENTIFICATION: Adult bugs are shield-shaped and brown, gray, or green. Some have brightly colored markings. Nymphs are similar, but smaller and wingless. Eggs are barrel-shaped.

BIOLOGY AND LIFE CYCLE: Adults overwinter in debris or weeds and emerge in the spring to lay 300 to 500 eggs in clusters on undersides of leaves. Eggs hatch in about a week, and nymphs develop into adults in five weeks. Usually two or more generations a year.

HABITAT: Beans, peas, cabbage, corn, okra, squash, tomatoes, peach, cotton, soybeans, alfalfa, peaches, citrus, ornamental plants, forage crops, and weeds.

FEEDING HABITS: Adults and nymphs suck juice from flowers, fruit, seed and leaves. Leaves wilt, turn brown, or have discolored spots. Fruit is scarred and sometimes "cat-faced." Pods sometimes drop, and seed can be deformed. Although most are sapsuckers, several species suck the blood of caterpillars, beetles, and other pests.

ECONOMIC IMPORTANCE: Cosmetic and sometimes serious damage to food crops and ornamental plants.

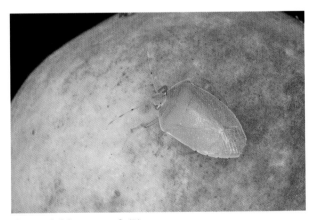

Green stink bug on peach (B)

Stink bugs hatching (B)

NATURAL CONTROL: Parasitic wasps and tachinid flies.

ORGANIC CONTROL: Hand-pick the bugs and crush the eggs; spray organic pesticides as a last resort. Use citrus oil sprays for heavy infestations.

INSIGHT: All Hemiptera insects have stink glands. The spined soldier bug *Podisus maculiventris* is an important natural enemy of the Mexican bean beetle. See also Predaceous Stink Bug.

STRIPED CUCUMBER BEETLE — see Cucumber Beetle

SUBTERRANEAN TERMITE — see Termite

SUGAR ANT

Sugar ant (BD)

COMMON NAMES: Sugar Ant, Pharaoh Ant

SCIENTIFIC NAME: Order Hymenoptera, family Formicidae, *Monomorium pharaonis*

SIZE: Adult — $\frac{1}{12}$" to $\frac{1}{10}$"

IDENTIFICATION: Very small ants, yellowish to golden to red. Most of their bodies are covered with minute pitted impressions.

BIOLOGY AND LIFE CYCLE: Complete metamorphosis.

HABITAT: Nests in any secluded spot. Frequent house invader; found in appliances, ductwork, light fixtures, and attics. Likes to be near heat and water source.

FEEDING HABITS: Sugar, grease, bread, toothpaste, food crumbs, and anything else that humans eat. They love proteins and sweet foods.

ECONOMIC IMPORTANCE: Beats us. Bound to be something — there's so many of them. Appear to just be an annoyance, causing no real damage. Difficult household pest to control.

NATURAL CONTROL: Remove food and water sources and keep house squeaky clean. Wipe cabinets and counters with mixture of one part water and one part vinegar. Lizards, frogs, toads, birds, and other insects.

ORGANIC CONTROL: Baking soda, boric acid, and diatomaceous earth. No ant will cross a DE barrier in dry-weather conditions. Use boric acid baits.

INSIGHT: Careless application of insecticides often make the sugar ant problem worse.

SWEAT BEE — see Hover Fly

SWEET POTATO BEETLE — see Tortoise Beetle

SWEET POTATO WHITEFLY — see Whitefly

SYRPHID FLY — see Hover Fly

TACHINID FLY

COMMON NAMES: Red-Tailed Tachina, Tachinid Fly
SCIENTIFIC NAME: Order Diptera, family Tachinidae, *Winthemia quadripustulata*
SIZE: Adult—⅜" to ½"
IDENTIFICATION: Adult flies are bristled or have fine hairs on the body. They look like big house flies. Larvae are thick-bodied maggots with tiny spines or plates. Caterpillar and beetle larvae get very agitated when trying to keep these flies from landing on them.
BIOLOGY AND LIFE CYCLE: Adults lay white oval eggs on host insect's body. Wings are slightly spread when at rest. Eggs hatch in a few days. Larvae enter the host after hatching and feed internally, then bore out of the host to pupate in the soil in a barrel-shaped pupal case. Tachinids overwinter as pupae or larvae in the host's body. Usually have more generations than their hosts. Sometimes eggs are laid on foliage near caterpillars so they will be eaten and hatch inside.
HABITAT: Many landscape and food crops, especially dill, parsley, sweet clover, yarrow, and other flowering herbs. They especially like buckwheat, alyssum, and daisies.
FEEDING HABITS: Larvae feed on caterpillars, beetles, fly larvae, true bugs, corn borers, corn earworms, imported cabbage worms, cabbage loopers, potato stem borers, cutworms, armyworms, Mexican bean beetles, Colorado potato beetles, stink bugs, squash bugs, tarnished plant bugs, cucumber beetles, sawflies, and grasshoppers. Adults feed on pollen, nectar, and honeydew or sometimes aphids and leafhoppers.
ECONOMIC IMPORTANCE: Help to control many troublesome insects. Tachinid larvae destroy the eggs of many pest insects, including caterpillars, beetles, true bugs, flies, crickets, grasshoppers, and katydids.
NATURAL CONTROL: Birds and lizards.
ORGANIC CONTROL: None needed—extremely beneficial insect.
INSIGHT: Looks like an ordinary house fly. Doesn't bite.

A Malcolm Story

The first time I met this insect was while inspecting our tomato field. Everything was calm and quiet except for one plant that had a large branch shaking vigorously. Curiosity drew me over for a look, and I found a big tomato hornworm on the branch with a common-looking fly that kept attempting to land on the worm. Finally she learned to land between vigorous wiggles, and each time she succeeded, she left behind a small white egg.

Right away I got out the bug books and learned that we call this bug a tachinid fly. The books also said there were more than 1,400 of this species described. They are considered an important parasite and are credited with saving the sugar cane industry in Hawaii.

The second time I met the fly was years later on our new farm. We were having a bad infestation of walnut caterpillars. They were doing more damage than I cared to stand for. That was before I found out about Bt, and I didn't know of a natural control for the caterpillars. The agricultural extension office offered me only toxic materials, which I was almost tempted to use, but I decided to wait a few more days. It was a good thing I did! While working under an old truck, I noticed a fly buzzing around near the ground. I saw it light on a walnut caterpillar, deposit an egg, fly off in a circle, then come back again. Over and over again, the fly deposited her egg on the caterpillar, then flew away only to return. I noticed she always deposited them close behind the head of the worm. Each time the worm would reach back and try to knock the egg off, but he couldn't bend his body enough to dislodge the eggs just behind his head.

I began inspecting and noticed all the walnut caterpillars—and there were plenty of them—had tachinid fly eggs deposited on them. I went and telephoned my friends at the agricultural extension office and told them I didn't think we would have to worry about the walnut caterpillar next year because their natural enemy had

Tachinid fly adult (H)

Tachinid fly eggs on walnut caterpillar (B)

Tachinid adult on dill flower (H)

Pet tarantula (B)

caught up with them. Sure enough, it has been almost twenty years since then and we haven't yet had the walnut caterpillar back in damaging numbers.

If I had been impatient and sprayed, I could have killed enough tachinid flies to widen the predator-to-prey gap. Some caterpillars would have escaped the toxic spray and would probably have come back in damaging numbers the next year. Sometimes the only help nature requires of us is patience.

TARANTULA

COMMON NAMES: Tarantula, Tarantula Spider
SCIENTIFIC NAME: Order Araneae, family Theraphosidae, *Aphonopelma* spp.
SIZE: Adult—2" to 4"
IDENTIFICATION: Large, hairy, light to dark brown spiders; distinctive and hard to confuse with other spiders.
BIOLOGY AND LIFE CYCLE: Males have longer legs and are more active than females. Males mature in ten or eleven years and don't molt after maturity. Females continue to molt and live twenty-five to thirty years. Neither males nor females are sexually mature until ten years old.
HABITAT: Protected areas in drier climates.
FEEDING HABITS: Nocturnal. Hide during the day, hunt

Tarantula and discarded skin (B)

by touch in the dark. Eat insects, lizards, and other small animals.
ECONOMIC IMPORTANCE: Control of troublesome insects. Not dangerous.
NATURAL CONTROL: General biodiversity. Tarantula hawk, which is a large wasp (also called pepsis wasp).
ORGANIC CONTROL: None needed. Tarantulas are beneficial and nonaggressive.
INSIGHT: The tarantula's bite is no worse than a wasp or bee sting—but they seldom bite. They make good pets. Tarantulas eat very little and don't bring fleas into the house. There are no vet bills, they don't bark or wet the floor or tear up furniture.

TARNISHED PLANT BUG

COMMON NAMES: Tarnish Bug, Tarnished Plant Bug
SCIENTIFIC NAME: Order Heteroptera, family Miridae, *Lygus linolaris*
SIZE: Adult—¼"
IDENTIFICATION: Adults are quick-moving, oval-shaped, light green to brown bugs. Forewings are black-tipped yellow triangles. Wings slope downward at the end. Nymphs are yellow-green and have five black dots. Eggs are long and curved.
BIOLOGY AND LIFE CYCLE: Adults emerge from debris in early spring to feed on fruit tree buds, then move to garden plants to lay eggs in stems and leaves. Eggs hatch in about ten days. Nymphs feed three to four weeks, then molt. Two to five generations a year.
HABITAT: Flowers, fruit trees, vegetables, and weeds.
FEEDING HABITS: Adults and nymphs suck sap from leaves, buds, and fruit, causing silvery brown spots, stunted growth, and dieback. Nymphs are the most damaging. Fruit becomes "cat-faced."
ECONOMIC IMPORTANCE: Damage to several ornamental and food crops.
NATURAL CONTROL: Bigeyed bugs, damsel bugs, and minute pirate bugs. Birds and lizards. Plant flowering plants and encourage biodiversity.
ORGANIC CONTROL: Citrus oil products on large infestations. Cover plants with floating row covers.
INSIGHT: Covering garden plants in the spring with floating row cover will help prevent these and other pests. The establishment of beneficial insect populations is the best long-term control.

Tarnished plant bug (ARM)

TATER BUG—see Colorado Potato Beetle

TENT CATERPILLAR

COMMON NAMES: Forest Armyworm, Forest Tent Caterpillar, Tent Caterpillar
SCIENTIFIC NAME: Order Lepidoptera, family Lasiocampidae, *Malacasoma spp.* Forest Tent Caterpillar (no tent)—*Malacasoma disstria*. Tent Caterpillar—*Malacasoma americanum*.
SIZE: Adult—2", larva—2"
IDENTIFICATION: Adults are heavy-bodied, hairy, yellow to brown moths. They have a short proboscis or none, short wings, and feathery antennae. Larvae are hairy with black heads and a white strip or row of

Tent caterpillar (H)

Eastern tent caterpillars (solid white line); forest tent caterpillar (keyhole-shaped white marks) (RB)

diamond-shaped marks along the back. Also brownish and blue or red markings along the side. Egg masses are covered with a hard foamy material.
BIOLOGY AND LIFE CYCLE: Adult moths do little or no feeding. Larvae live together in a silken tent. Cocoons are usually located in a protected place. Females lay eggs on twigs in summer, but eggs don't hatch until early spring. Larvae spin a silk tent in the protection of the nearest tree crotch. They feed for five to eight weeks, pupate in leaf litter, and emerge ten days later as moths. One generation a year.
HABITAT: Many deciduous trees and shrubs, especially apple, cherry, and plum. Field and vegetable crops during migrations.
FEEDING HABITS: Larvae feed on the foliage of trees and can completely defoliate the plants.
ECONOMIC IMPORTANCE: Will defoliate and stress deciduous trees.
NATURAL CONTROL: Birds; parasitic flies and wasps. Plant nectar and pollen plants to attract them.
ORGANIC CONTROL: Prune branches with tents and destroy. Spray caterpillars while young with Garden-Ville Fire Ant Control sprays or catch them in sticky tree bands. Release trichogramma wasps in the spring. Spray citrus oil products. Spray *Bacillus thuringiensis* product as a last resort.
INSIGHT: Do not kill caterpillars with white eggs or cocoons attached to their backs. These parasites will do the job for you. Texas has four species of tent caterpillars. The eastern tent caterpillar and western tent caterpillar both build large tents in the crotches of trees. The Sonoran tent caterpillars builds small tents, and the forest tent caterpillar doesn't build tents at all. The eastern has a solid white line down the back; the western has white dashes down the back. The Sonoran has yellow and blue markings. The forest has a row of keyhole-shaped white marks.

Termite tubes on wood fence (H)

Termite tubes around grass (B)   *Termites* (B)

TERMITE

COMMON NAMES: Subterranean Termite, Termite
SCIENTIFIC NAME: Order Isoptera, many families, genera, and species
SIZE: Adult—¼" to ⅜"
IDENTIFICATION: Winged adults are dark brown to black with compound eyes. Two pair of wings similar in size and shape. Workers are grayish white and eyeless. Short antennae. Termites have fatter waists than ants.
BIOLOGY AND LIFE CYCLE: Social insects. Females lay large eggs that hatch and small eggs for nymph food. Queen doubles in size and is unable to leave the colony. Workers appear first, then soldiers. Queens are long-lived.
HABITAT: Damp soil or damp timbers close to the ground. Wooded areas of soil and moist wood.
FEEDING HABITS: Feed on wood, paper, and other wood products; fungi; dried plant and animal products. Termites sometimes eat growing plants. They use intestinal protozoans to digest the chewed food.
ECONOMIC IMPORTANCE: Destroy wood structures.
NATURAL CONTROL: Beneficial nematodes.
ORGANIC CONTROL: Boric acid products, pyrethrum, beneficial fungi, and sand barriers (see below), especially in openings for plumbing in slabs.
INSIGHT: It isn't necessary to use toxic chemicals to treat your home or office for termites. Here's a safer and more effective approach.

The first step is to eliminate wet and moist wood from the house or other affected structures. Subterranean termites don't like dry wood. Check carefully for leaks of all kinds and have them fixed. Installing drainage systems around structures is sometimes necessary.

Sand will make an effective termite barrier. Not just any sand will work—you must use a 16-grit sand (also sold as 00 sandblasting sand) to create the barrier. The material can be sharp sand or washed silicon sand or ground basalt (which is lava rock). Termites can't get through it. Put the sand on each side of the foundation beam of the structure. The sand prevents the insects from building the earthen tubes up to the wooden parts of the

house. A trench or wedge of sand above the ground measuring 6 inches by 6 inches (or smaller) and filled with sand can be effective. The trench should run around the entire perimeter of the structure. Treat exposed wood with boric acid products. These materials soak into the wood and give long-lasting protection.

Physical barriers are important tools. Cracks in concrete beams and slabs provide access from the ground up into the structure. Fill the cracks with silicon caulking to prevent access.

If termite tubes are visible, break them and introduce beneficial nematodes or ants. Both are natural enemies and quite effective. One of the benefits of the damaging fire ants is that they like to eat termites. Beneficial nematodes can also be used in the soil around structures and are very effective if the soil is kept moist. Encouraging biodiversity is important—as always. When healthy populations of microorganisms and insects exists, the competition keeps heavy populations of bad bugs to a minimum.

Some pest control operators are starting to use these alternative techniques. Many others will soon follow. The public is demanding these least toxic approaches, partly because of their safety but also because they work! Ask your pest control company about these techniques and other low-impact controls, such as electronic guns and high- or low-temperature devices that fry or freeze the pests.

TEXAS LEAFCUTTING ANT

COMMON NAMES: Cut Ant, Cutter Ant, Fungus Ant, Parasol Ant, Texas Leafcutting Ant, Town Ant
SCIENTIFIC NAME: Order Hymenoptera, family Formicidae, *Atta texana*
SIZE: Adult—¹⁄₁₆" to ½"
IDENTIFICATION: Light to dark reddish brown ants. Antennae are long and elbowed without distinct club. Three or more pairs of sharp spines on the waist. Can be seen marching along well-worn trails. Those going back to the mound will have a large piece of leaf tissue.

Cut ants or town ants (Texas leafcutting ants) carrying grass blade (B)

Texas leafcutting ant mound (RB)

Cut ant damage (BD)

BIOLOGY AND LIFE CYCLE: Complete metamorphosis. Swarm from early April to early June. Workers travel on well-defined trails. They cut leaves and buds and take them back to the mound. They also gather some seed. Most active from May to September, foraging at night. Mounds are huge. They use the organic matter to build a compost pile underground. They feed on the fungus that grows from the compost. Queens can live ten years or longer.

HABITAT: Nests in well-drained soils. All vegetable and landscape plants.

FEEDING HABITS: Feed on fungus that grows on the compost pile made in the mound. The ants use all kinds of plant materials to make the compost piles. Howard's listeners report that these ants even use the berries and leaves of mistletoe.

ECONOMIC IMPORTANCE: Leafcutting ants will defoliate and kill food and ornamental plants. One of the most difficult ants to control.

NATURAL CONTROL: Lizards and birds love to eat 'em. Thick mulch around all plants helps. Beneficial nematodes help control all pests that live in the ground.

ORGANIC CONTROL: Treat the mounds with Garden-Ville Fire Ant Control. Citrus baits and beneficial nematodes are also effective.

INSIGHT: These ants are master compost makers and mushroom growers.

TEXAS YELLOWJACKET

COMMON NAMES: Hornet, Texas Yellowjacket, Yellowjacket

SCIENTIFIC NAME: Order Hymenoptera, family Vespidae. Texas Yellowjacket—*Vespula maculifrons*. Bald-Faced Hornet—*Vespa maculata*.

SIZE: Adult—¾"

IDENTIFICATION: Large wasplike flying insects. Hornets have shorter waists than wasps. Texas yellow-jackets build nests in hollow trees and in the ground. Bald-faced hornets have more dark coloring, and their large rounded paper nests are suspended fully exposed from tree branches.

BIOLOGY AND LIFE CYCLE: Complete metamorphosis. The last females to hatch each season mate and overwinter under bark or in the ground. They emerge in the spring to build paper cells in mouse burrows or holes in logs or trees.

HABITAT: Protected vertical or horizontal surfaces.

FEEDING HABITS: Adults eat nectar, fruit juices from holes pecked in fruit by birds. Some eat insects. The larvae are fed insect meat that has been chewed by adults. Most of this food consists of caterpillars, flies, and other troublesome insects. They are also attracted to soda pop and beer left in containers.

Texas yellowjackets (B)

ECONOMIC IMPORTANCE: Beneficial insects. Try to protect these insects if they aren't located in a dangerous place.

NATURAL CONTROL: Spiders, diseases, and parasites, but man is the biggest enemy.

ORGANIC CONTROL: Soapy water or citrus products if really necessary. Treat the underground nests at night. Put red cellophane over your flashlight because wasps and bees can't see red very well. Tip from Justin Schmidt, USDA biologist: use a soap or citrus oil drench and then cover the opening with a rock—and run like hell in case any of them escape.

INSIGHT: Texas yellowjackets make their nests underground with a small portion above ground level or in hollow trees or walls of buildings, with a small portion of the nest exposed to the outside.

The last females to hatch in a season mate and survive the winter in hiding places such as under bark of dead trees. In the spring each hornet starts a new colony. They work alone building a new nest of a few cells, hatching and feeding a few sterile females until they are mature and can take over the nest enlargement and other domestic duties.

The bald-faced hornet is similar in every way to the Texas yellowjacket except their bodies have more dark coloring and their large rounded paper nests are suspended from tree branches fully exposed. All wasps, hornets, and yellowjackets are very beneficial in helping to control destructive insects such as caterpillars. Some diseases or parasites may attack them, but we human beings are by far their most serious enemy. There is some indication that hornets help to control flies.

THOUSAND-LEGGED WORM—see Millipede

THREAD-WAISTED WASP—see Mud Dauber

THRIPS

COMMON NAME: Thrips

SCIENTIFIC NAME: Order Thysanoptera, family Thripidae. Onion thrips—*Thrips tabaci*. Western Flower Thrips—*Frankliniella occidentalis*.

SIZE: Adult—less than ⅟₂₅"

IDENTIFICATION: Barely visible, slender, fast-moving insects that range from pale yellow to black. Narrow, fringed wings. Nymphs are light green to yellow.

BIOLOGY AND LIFE CYCLE: Adults overwinter in plant debris or in bark. Females lay eggs in the spring that hatch in three to five days. Nymphs feed for one to three weeks, then molt to adult stage. Many generations a season.

HABITAT: Most gardens. Vegetables, flowers, fruit and shade trees. Causes leaves to crinkle, especially on beans.

FEEDING HABITS: Adults and nymphs rasp and suck the juice from plant cells and cause silvery speckles or streaks on leaves. Flowers turn brown on the edges and don't

Thrips (BP)

Thrips damage to roses (H)

open properly. Thrips will attack many different kinds of plants.

ECONOMIC IMPORTANCE: Causes reduced plant production and ruins flowers. A serious onion pest. Damage can cause decrease in bulb size. Spreads viruses.

NATURAL CONTROL: Bigeyed bugs are the most important natural control, along with minute pirate bugs, lacewings, and lady beetles. Heavy rainfall also helps. Nematodes applied in water drenches will control species that pupate in the soil.

ORGANIC CONTROL: Spray with horticultural oil or neem products when necessary or release predatory mites or pirate bugs. Garlic tea and seaweed sprays are very effective. Cover plants with row cover material.

INSIGHT: Will bite humans. Bite is similar to chigger bite and may cause a rash. Thrips do have one good point. Some species will eat spider mites.

Soft tick (B)

Hard tick (B)

TICK

COMMON NAME: Tick
SCIENTIFIC NAME: Order Acari, family Nuttalliellidae
SIZE: Adult—¹⁄₁₆" to ¼"
IDENTIFICATION: Ticks are not insects. They have eight legs and are related instead to mites, spiders, and scorpions. Two families—hard ticks and soft ticks. Tough, leathery, pitted skin and no apparent head. Only one body region. No antennae.
BIOLOGY AND LIFE CYCLE: Eggs, larvae, nymphs, adults. Ticks attach firmly to host and may go unnoticed for long periods. High reproductive rates. Ticks live up high—four or five feet above the ground in bushes, on trunks of trees, and on sides of buildings. Ticks mate on animals, then fall off and lay 1,000 to 6,000 eggs in the soil and in cracks and crevices. Eggs hatch in nineteen to sixty days, and the larval ticks attach themselves to a host animal, feed for three to six days, fall off, molt into the nymph stage, then go back to the host to engorge again. Some tick adults can live over 500 days without a meal.
HABITAT: Tall grass and weeds. Pastures and rangeland. Woodlands and shrubbery.
FEEDING HABITS: Suck blood of warm-blooded animals.
ECONOMIC IMPORTANCE: Vectors of several diseases.
NATURAL CONTROL: Cut brush and weeds. Wear protective clothing. Keep interiors well cleaned and vacuumed, fill cracks with steel wool or copper mesh. Ticks have few natural enemies other than fire ants.
ORGANIC CONTROL: Dust with diatomaceous earth and pyrethrum for severe infestations. Keep out mice. Stock firewood away from the house. Locate bird feeders away from the house. Spray with citrus oil or D-limonene products. Apply beneficial nematodes.
INSIGHT: Research has shown that beneficial nematodes are effective in controlling ticks. *Steinernema* nematodes wriggle into the body cavities of engorged female ticks. Another, Heterohabditis, uses a single sharp tooth to gnaw through the tick's outer covering. The nematodes release other microbes (fungi and bacteria) that actually do the killing.

Howard's Tick Control Program

The same basic program used for fleas works for ticks with a few exceptions.

1. Inspect cats and dogs regularly, carefully checking the ears and between the toes. Make close inspections when pets return from woods and other possible tick habitats. Comb to remove ticks, but be careful not to break off the mouthparts of any attached ticks. Remove embedded ticks by gently pulling with tweezers, not your fingers. Clean wounds made by ticks with soap and water and apply an antiseptic to prevent infection. Hydrogen

peroxide can be used not only to clean wounds but to also help remove ticks. Turn a bottle of hydrogen peroxide over on the attached tick and it will usually let go.

2. Confine the pets to specific sleeping areas to limit likely areas of infestation. Reduce hiding places by caulking cracks and crevices where ticks may hide between blood meals. Vacuum and use diatomaceous earth or baking soda in any remaining cracks.

3. Ticks like to climb, so treat tree trunks, caulk building cracks, and attend to areas on walls and around windows. Use a crevice tool on your vacuum cleaner to get into all small areas. The contents of the vacuum bag should be destroyed by burning or sealing in a plastic bag. See flea control for outdoor treatment.

4. Cleanliness is critical for the control of both fleas and ticks. Besides keeping the dust and dirt cleaned up, remove loose boards, trash, and debris that can harbor the various life forms of these pests. It sounds like a lot of work, but it's not if done on a consistent basis. This flea and tick program is affordable, has very low toxicity, and, most important, it works!

It goes without saying that all the above measures will work much better if your overall lawn and garden program is organic. With healthy biodiversity, the competition and predation of the microbes, insects, lizards, birds, and other animals provides powerful natural balance—as nature designed.

TIGER BEETLE

COMMON NAME: Tiger Beetle
SCIENTIFIC NAME: Order Coleoptera, family Cicindelidae, many species
SIZE: Adult—¼" to ¾"
IDENTIFICATION: Adults are shiny, dark blue-green or black, often with bright-colored markings, large eyes, and long legs. They are very fast runners and strong fliers; they make a buzzing sound. Larvae are segmented and S-shaped; a hump on their back has hooks for anchoring in burrows.
BIOLOGY AND LIFE CYCLE: Adults are attracted to light at night. Eggs are laid singly in the soil. Larvae develop there several years where they catch soil-borne prey. Adults also overwinter in the ground. One generation every two or three years. Larvae live in vertical burrows in sandy soil.
HABITAT: They like open areas, bare ground.
FEEDING HABITS: Adults and larvae eat many plant-eating insects. Adult beetles run their prey down. Larvae ambush them in their burrows. Ants are a favorite food.
NATURAL ENEMIES: Birds, snakes, and scorpions.
ECONOMIC IMPORTANCE: These guys are fierce

Tiger beetle (ENT)

predators, and although they eat some beneficials, they are considered very beneficial.
NATURAL CONTROL: None needed—very beneficial. Attract them by establishing permanent gardens. Don't leave lights on outdoors and don't use bug light traps.
ORGANIC CONTROL: None needed.
INSIGHT: Closely kin to ground beetles.

TIGER MOTH—see Woolly Bear

TOBACCO FLY—see Tobacco Hornworm

TOBACCO HORNWORM

COMMON NAMES: Carolina Sphinx, Hummingbird Moth, Sixspotted Sphinx, Tobacco Fly, Tobacco Hornworm
SCIENTIFIC NAME: Order Lepidoptera, family Sphingidae, *Manduca sexta*
SIZE: Adult—2½", larva—3" to 4"

Tobacco hornworm and damage (H)

IDENTIFICATION: Dark gray moths with six orange-yellow spots on each side of the abdomen. Caterpillars are large and green, with diagonal white lines and a red horn at the rear. Tomato hornworm has a black tail.

BIOLOGY AND LIFE CYCLE: Large green eggs, large green caterpillar larvae. Pupae have a tongue case resembling the handle of a pitcher. Adults are nectar-eating moths. This insect is almost identical to the tomato hornworm.

HABITAT: Tomatoes, potatoes, eggplant, green peppers, tobacco, and other plants in the nightshade family; various weeds.

FEEDING HABITS: Caterpillars eat foliage—mostly at night. Moths sip nectar from flowers at dusk.

ECONOMIC IMPORTANCE: Can defoliate plants overnight. These moths are important for the pollenation of deep-throated flowers and nightbloomers.

NATURAL CONTROL: Parasitic wasps and birds. Braconid wasps. Trichogramma wasps parasitize the eggs. Birds, skunks, and lizards.

ORGANIC CONTROL: Hand-picking. *Bacillus thuringiensis* products will kill them but spraying for these pests is a waste of time and money.

INSIGHT: Big beautiful caterpillar.

TOMATO HORNWORM

COMMON NAMES: Fivespotted Hawk Moth, Sphinx Moth, Tomato Hornworm

SCIENTIFIC NAME: Order Lepidoptera, family Sphingidae, *Manduca quinquemaculata*

SIZE: Adult—2½", larva—3" to 4"

IDENTIFICATION: Adults are narrow-winged gray moths with rows of orange dots along furry abdomens. They drink nectar from flowers at dusk. Torpedo-shaped body. Larvae are green caterpillars with a black horn on the tail (tobacco hornworm has a red tail) and white diagonal marks on the side. Eggs are round and green.

BIOLOGY AND LIFE CYCLE: Caterpillars are seen more often than the adult moths. They pupate in cells in the soil. Large brown pupae overwinter in soil and emerge in June and July. The pupa has a tongue case resembling a jug handle. Females lay eggs singly under leaves.

HABITAT: Tomatoes, potatoes, eggplant, green peppers, tobacco plants, and various weeds.

FEEDING HABITS: Caterpillars feed mostly at night on foliage of nightshade plants like tobacco and tomato. Moths sip nectar from flowers.

ECONOMIC IMPORTANCE: Can defoliate plants overnight. The adult with its long proboscis is necessary to pollinate deep-throated flowers and nightbloomers.

NATURAL CONTROL: Birds, parasitic wasps, and braconid wasps attack the worms. Trichogramma wasps attack the eggs. Skunks.

ORGANIC CONTROL: Hand-pick caterpillars. Spray

Various moth pupae; tobacco hornworm with the handle (B)

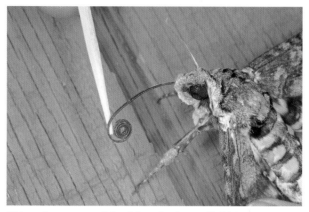

Tobacco hornworm adult with proboscis unrolled (B)

Sphinx moth tomato hornworm (B)

Bacillus thuringiensis products as a last resort only. Release lady beetles and lacewings to attack eggs.

INSIGHT: There are some 100 species of this moth in this country. They include the tomato hornworm, tobacco hornworm, hawk moth, and hummingbird moth.

A single worm can eat most of a tomato plant before pupating. Because of their large size and appetites, the adult females usually deposit only one egg per plant. The larvae of most species have a horn at the end of their body, which gives it some protection—at least from humans who are scared of being stung. However, the horn and the mouth of these caterpillars are harmless. In some species the developing moth's tongue or proboscis is so long that the pupa has a sheath curving out from the head and away from the body and then back, resembling a jug or pitcher handle.

They are easy to hand-pick but are often missed because they blend so well with the plant. Hungry skunks that nightly patrol fields love to eat tomato hornworm.

The adult moth could be considered beneficial. With that long proboscis, they are necessary pollinators, able to feed on the nectar of deep-throated flowers and—since they are active at night—of flowers that open only at night.

TOMATO FRUITWORM—see Corn Earworm

TOMATO PINWORM

COMMON NAME: Tomato Pinworm
SCIENTIFIC NAME: Order Lepidoptera, family Gelechiidae, *Keiferia lycopersicella*
SIZE: Adult—¼" to ½", larva—¼"
IDENTIFICATION: Adults are small gray moths. Larvae are yellowish gray or greenish, purple-spotted caterpillars.
BIOLOGY AND LIFE CYCLE: Complete metamorphosis. The larvae roll and tie leaf tips together and tunnel inside the leaves. The caterpillars then drop to the ground to pupate. Several generations a year.
HABITAT: Vegetable gardens, especially tomatoes but also eggplants, peppers, and potatoes.
FEEDING HABITS: Feed on tomato foliage and fruit. They cause leaf damage similar to that of leafminers and also damage stems and fruit. They will attack fruit at any stage of maturity. Favorite entry point is around the stems of the fruit under the calyx.
ECONOMIC IMPORTANCE: Can cause great damage to tomatoes, much greater than that of leafminers.
NATURAL CONTROL: Parasitic wasps and flies.
ORGANIC CONTROL: *Bacillus thuringiensis* sprays.
INSIGHT: This insect does not appear to be a significant pest in Texas, although it does pop up from time to time. Its damage seems to be the most severe on greenhouse plants. Severe infestations can result in fields sprayed with weed killers.

Tomato pinworm damage to fruit (BP)

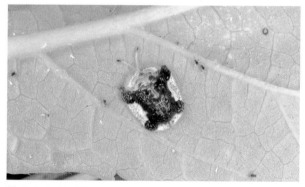
Tomato pinworm larva (BP)

Tortoise beetle (B)

TORTOISE BEETLE

COMMON NAMES: Gold Bug, Golden Tortoise Beetle, Sweet Potato Beetle, Tortoise Beetle
SCIENTIFIC NAME: Order Coleoptera, family Chrysomelidae, *Metriona bicolor*
SIZE: Adult—¼", larva—⅜"
IDENTIFICATION: Oval, flattened, squared at the shoulders, golden. Larvae are flat with a forked posterior appendage that curves forward over the body. Larvae have conspicuous thorny spines around the outside edge.
BIOLOGY AND LIFE CYCLE: Females lay eggs on foliage, and the spring larvae hang around on the underside of leaves in June and July.
HABITAT: Foliage of sweet potato, eggplant, and other morning glory and nightshade plants.

Treehopper nymph (B)

Buffalo treehopper (ENT)

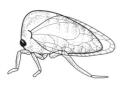

Side view

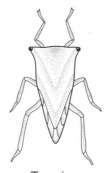

Top view

Treehopper

FEEDING HABITS: Adults and larvae eat the foliage of eggplant, sweet potato, and other nightshade plants. They eat holes and sometimes entire leaves.
ECONOMIC IMPORTANCE: Destruction of food crops.
NATURAL CONTROL: Insectivorous animals.
ORGANIC CONTROL: Beneficial fungi or citrus oil products.
INSIGHT: Larvae look like moving bits of dirt. The spiny dirt-laden larvae are found on the underside of leaves.

TOWN ANT — see Texas Leafcutting Ant

TREE BORER — see Peach Tree Borer

TREEHOPPER

COMMON NAME: Treehopper
SCIENTIFIC NAME: Order Homoptera, family Membracidae, many species
SIZE: Adult — ¼" to ⅓"
IDENTIFICATION: Treehoppers vary tremendously. Adults are green, brown, and black. Interesting hump-back shape, sometimes spinelike. Some are grotesquely shaped. Antennae are very small and hairlike. Hind legs are enlarged for jumping. Closely kin to leafhoppers. Both nymphs and adults hop vigorously when disturbed.
BIOLOGY AND LIFE CYCLE: All species are plant eaters.

Nymphs suck sap of grasses, shrub, trees, and other plants. Most have more than one generation a year. Overwinters as eggs laid on plants. Ants protect them for their honeydew. Females cut curved slits in inner bark where eggs are laid. Nymphs hatch in the late spring, drop to the ground, and feed on weeds and grasses until late summer.

HABITAT: Shrubs, trees, and other vegetation.

FEEDING HABITS: The adults do not suck sap like leafhoppers.

ECONOMIC IMPORTANCE: Relatively unimportant, although some diseases may enter through the egg-laying slits in the twigs of woody plants.

NATURAL CONTROL: Birds and predatory insects, nematodes.

ORGANIC CONTROL: None needed usually. Spray citrus oil products if heavy infestations occur. Horticultural oils are also effective as well as beneficial nematodes and dormant oil in winter for heavy infestations.

INSIGHT: Interesting little insects. Some have beautiful colorations. These insects are sometimes the source of the honeydew on trees. Buffalo treehoppers (*Stictocephala bisonia*) make many cuts in twigs and cause more severe damage than other treehoppers. They are particularly attracted to fruit trees. The adults are light green and triangle-shaped.

TRICHOGRAMMA WASP

COMMON NAME: Trichogramma Wasp

SCIENTIFIC NAME: Order Hymenoptera, family Trichogrammatidae, *Trichogramma* spp.

SIZE: Adult—1/50"

IDENTIFICATION: Adult wasps are yellow or yellow and black with bright red eyes, short antennae, and compact bodies. They look like gnats. A small hole in the host egg is visible if the wasps have emerged.

BIOLOGY AND LIFE CYCLE: Females lay one or more eggs in the egg of a host insect. The larvae pupate inside the host egg, and adult wasps emerge seven to ten days after the egg is laid. Over fifty wasps can emerge from one egg. In warm weather many generations can be produced. Hosts include corn, cotton, cabbage, peas, tomatoes, soybeans, rice, citrus, ornamental plants, pecans, and forests.

HABITAT: Moth eggs. Parasitized eggs turn black. European corn borer, corn earworm, imported cabbage worm, diamond back moth, cabbage looper, pecan nut casebearer, tomato hornworm, and tobacco hornworm.

FEEDING HABITS: Little is known about the feeding habits of the adult wasps.

ECONOMIC IMPORTANCE: Very effective control of many troublesome pests in the landscape and in agriculture.

Trichogramma adult depositing egg in moth egg (BP)

Moth eggs after adult trichogramma wasps have emerged (B)

Trichogramma wasps hatching (B)

Trichogramma wasps ready for release (H)

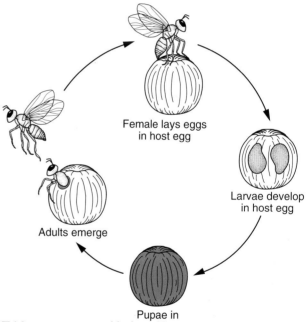

Female lays eggs in host egg

Larvae develop in host egg

Pupae in blackened host egg

Adults emerge

Trichogramma wasps

NATURAL CONTROL: These parasitoids are reared and shipped as larvae or pupae within the eggs of an alternate host.

ORGANIC CONTROL: None needed—highly beneficial.

INSIGHT: Man-made pesticides are the most destructive force limiting these helpful wasps. Trichogramma wasps are purchased on 1" tabs containing about 3,300 moths' eggs that contain wasp pupae. The adult wasps emerge from the eggs to parasitize troublesome insect eggs. Use a minimum of 10,000 eggs per acre on residential site per release. They can be stored for a week or less at 42°F.

A Malcolm Story

The twenty pecan trees on the small farm we purchased in 1957 produced a bumper crop, and we thought we had a bonanza on our hands. The second and third years, however, turned the bonanza into a bust. Little or no nuts were produced. Throughout the summer I watched the nutlets turn black and fall off the trees.

The extension office gave me the bad news: I had nut casebearers. Left alone, the casebearers could destroy between 50 percent and 90 percent of a pecan crop. Furthermore, they told me, the only way to get rid of them was to spray with arsenate of lead. That was against my organic farming principles, but sometimes principles get in a shoving match with economic realities. We needed that money from the pecan crop to make ends meet.

I went ahead and bought the poison. Then a new problem occurred to me. All our farm animals, including the milk cow, grazed under the pecan trees. Another call to the extension office told me I'd have to fence the animals away from the trees until after a rain. That bit of information gave my principles the little nudge they needed to win out. I returned the poison.

I still had the problem though, and I kept thinking there must be a safe, natural way to control those casebearers. A friend mentioned an ad he'd seen in *Organic Gardening* magazine. It advertised a microscopic wasp called trichogramma that was parasitic to moth eggs. He also told me that the nut casebearer might be the larva of a moth.

Once more I turned to the extension office. Yes, they said, the casebearer did turn into a moth. Furthermore, they knew that the adult moth deposited eggs between May 1 and May 6. They didn't know anything about the trichogramma wasp, so I called the man who was advertising the Trich-O. While he didn't know anything about casebearers, he did tell me about the success others had had by using the tiny wasps to control the cotton boll worm, another moth larva.

It was the middle of April, and I was excited and impatient to see if I'd found a solution to my problem. I immediately ordered a batch of the wasps and released them. Since I knew the moth was going to deposit eggs around May 1, I ordered another batch to be released then. I kept an eye on the trees, and that year the nut crop was greatly improved. Maybe the little wasps were doing their job!

Every year after that, I released a batch of wasps in the middle of April and another on May 1. I never lost more than 10 percent of a crop, and I wasn't the only one. Soon word got around that there was a safe, easy method to control the casebearer. Friends and neighbors tried the wasp, and all reported a measure of success.

I felt pretty proud of myself for making this discovery, but not everyone was quite as impressed. One day I was telling a friend in Gonzales, Texas, about my natural casebearer control. He was an agricultural extension entomologist, and all the time I was talking he was shaking his head. "Charlie," I asked, "don't you believe the wasps work?" "No," he said, he'd tried them and just couldn't see good enough results. He had released 50,000 wasps per tree on the day the casebearer moth released its eggs.

I left Charlie's office puzzled. Then it occurred to me that I was making two releases instead of one and probably, as a result, getting better coverage and allowing for any moths that deposited eggs early or late.

During one of his visits, I told Robert Rodale about my experience, and he asked me to write it up for *Organic Gardening* magazine. As soon as the article was published, there was a flood of phone calls and letters from all over the South requesting more information. I still get calls and letters from people who have solved their casebearer problems with an almost invisible wasp. I have used Trich-O since 1962 on two different pecan groves, and in all that time, I've never had more than 10 percent loss due to the nut casebearer.

I believe my continued success is due to using totally organic methods on both farms. I have a stable environment. Unlike those who use chemical pest control, I never upset the natural predator-to-prey balance. Furthermore, in the two weeks between April 15 and May 1, the wasps have a chance to reproduce in the area. They destroy other moth eggs, and when the casebearer deposits eggs, there is a bigger army of Trich-O wasps to attack the eggs and keep them from hatching into damaging larvae.

My experience and the experiences of others with the parasitic wasp and other parasite and predator insects show that these "good bugs" are a powerfully effective and completely safe method of pest control. They must, however, be a part of an organic whole. If they are used in a totally organic environment and applied with the best method and at the proper time, they will help Mother Nature do her stuff. The wasps are not like toxic insecticides to be applied once for a quick cure. Harmony and balance are the goal, and achieving the goal requires an overall organic program of providing what is needed when it is needed to sustain nature's great system.

TRUE BUG — see Bug

TUMBLEBUG — see Dung Beetle

TWIG BORER — see Peach Tree Borer

Twig girdler on stub after cutting the end of the branch away (B)

TWIG GIRDLER

COMMON NAME: Twig Girdling Beetle
SCIENTIFIC NAME: Order Coleoptera, family Cerambycidae, *Oncideres cingulata*
SIZE: Adult—⅜" to ⅝"

IDENTIFICATION: Adult is a gray-brown beetle with very long antennae. The body is covered with short hairs.
BIOLOGY AND LIFE CYCLE: Adult lays eggs on twigs, then cuts the twigs off to fall to the ground. Larvae hatch and live in and eat on the fallen branch or twig. They pupate in the spring, and the adult emerges in the summer.
HABITAT: Deciduous forests and in individual landscape trees. Apple, ash, oak, dogwood, elm, hickory, mimosa, pear, peach, pecan, and other trees.
ECONOMIC IMPORTANCE: Relatively little—just a curiosity.
NATURAL CONTROL: Birds and ichneumon wasps.
ORGANIC CONTROL: Destroy fallen twigs; the composting process will take care of the larvae.
INSIGHT: Twig girdlers can cut limbs up to 1½ inches in diameter.

TWOSPOTTED SPIDER MITE—see Spider Mite

TWOSPOTTED STINK BUG—see Predaceous Stink Bug

VELVET MITE

COMMON NAMES: Rain Bug, Scarlet Mite, Velvet Mite
SCIENTIFIC NAME: Order Acari, Family Trombidiidae
SIZE: ⅓"
IDENTIFICATION: Velvet-covered, bright pink to orange to red, pillow-shaped.
BIOLOGY AND LIFE CYCLE: Incomplete metamorphosis.
HABITAT: Mostly in sandy areas of the state.
FEEDING HABITS: Adults are found feeding on winged ants and winged termites after a shower during the summer. The nymphs have been found in the egg pods of grasshoppers.
ECONOMIC IMPORTANCE: Considered to be general predators.
NATURAL CONTROL: Unknown—by us at least.
ORGANIC CONTROL: None needed.
INSIGHT: These beauties of nature show off dramatically on the wet soil when the air is clean and the sun is bright after a summer shower.

VIOLIN SPIDER—see Brown Recluse Spider

Velvet mite (B)

WALKING STICK

COMMON NAMES: Devil's Darning Needle, Walking Stick

SCIENTIFIC NAME: Order Phasmatodea, family Phasmatidae, several species

SIZE: Adult—1" to 10"

IDENTIFICATION: Adults' bodies are very long, slender, wingless, and cylindrical. Resemble sticks or twigs. Usually brown or green; will sway in the breeze to imitate vegetation. Will sometimes fall to the ground and remain motionless. Always slow-moving. Males are much smaller than the females.

BIOLOGY AND LIFE CYCLE: Nymphs look like small adults. Black eggs are laid on the ground. One generation a year. Mating is in August. Overwinter in the egg stage and hatch in mid-summer.

HABITAT: Fruit trees, grassy vegetation, shrubs and trees.

FEEDING HABITS: Plant feeders, mostly at night. Can defoliate trees, but it's rare.

ECONOMIC IMPORTANCE: Usually not significant but can explode to cause severe plant damage.

NATURAL CONTROL: Parasitic wasps, flies, and birds.

ORGANIC CONTROL: Hand removal. They make interesting pets and are harmless to humans.

INSIGHT: These big insects are more interesting than destructive, even though they do eat plant foliage.

WASP—see Ichneumon Wasp, Mud Dauber, Paper Wasp, Texas Yellowjacket, Trichogramma Wasp

WATER BUG—see Cockroach

Walking stick (H)

Walking stick head and mouth parts (B)

Either a walking stick or a strangely designed praying mantis (B)

WEBWORM

COMMON NAMES: Fall Webworm, Webworm

SCIENTIFIC NAME: Order Lepidoptera, family Arctiidae, *Hyphantria cunea*

SIZE: Adult—½" to 1", larva—1" to 1⅛"

IDENTIFICATION: These caterpillars are pale yellow or beige, black-spotted, and covered with hairs. Adults are pure satiny white to dusty brown moths. They form loose, dirty white webs on terminal tree growth from spring through fall. Larvae eat the foliage within the web.

BIOLOGY AND LIFE CYCLE: Pupae overwinter in cocoons in the soil or tree bark. Adults emerge in early summer to lay eggs in large masses on the undersides of leaves. Eggs hatch after a few days and larvae feed as a

Webworm adult and egg mass (H)

Webworms in pecan tree (B)

group for about four to six weeks in mid-summer. White or pale yellow cocoons form in July. Can be several generations a year.

HABITAT: Pecan, ash, willow, persimmon, hickory, apple, walnut, mulberry, and other deciduous trees.

FEEDING HABITS: Larvae eat outer foliage of trees, especially pecans. They eat fast and furious and create an ugly mess in the foliage of trees.

ECONOMIC IMPORTANCE: Cosmetic damage to trees. Complete defoliation can badly stress trees.

NATURAL CONTROL: Protect the wasps, the birds, and the assassin bugs because they eat webworms.

ORGANIC CONTROL: Spray *Bacillus thuringiensis* products, always at dusk, as a last resort. Use one tablespoon of molasses per gallon of spray. Catch larvae in sticky tree bands.

INSIGHT: We have noticed an increase in this pest in direct relationship to the popularity of chemical lawn care companies and the use of aerosol wasp-killer sprays. Killing the beneficials has given the webworms a free rein.

A Malcolm Story

"Why don't you have webworms, Beck?" was the question always asked by friends and visiting farmers. We had eight acres scattered with twenty big pecan trees growing around the house, in the cow lot, the chicken yard, and around various buildings. We hadn't had a single webworm colony since first purchasing the place seven years earlier. It wasn't because they were scarce. Webworms were thick, especially those years, all over the state, and I knew that I wasn't blessed with the good fortune that webworms couldn't find me or were nice enough to leave me alone.

There had to be a reason my trees were free all those years. Having a big interest in nature and reading nature books, I did read where wasps preyed on larva such as webworms and on several occasions actually saw wasps attack and carry off green loopers. I believed the wasps were doing the job, but I wasn't sure. However, I soon got proof.

Having been an abandoned farm for several years with lots of old unpainted buildings and water hole nearby, our place was a perfect environment for the wasp. All kinds of wasps had nests built everywhere. One day my two younger brothers came out when I wasn't home and spent the day knocking down wasp nests with their slingshots. The wasps never bothered me, and I never bothered them, but the temptation was too great for the boys. The nests were the perfect target, and they only missed one or two. The boys' timing must have been perfect for knocking out future wasp generations, because to this day few wasp nests have been rebuilt. The very next year we had a webworm problem.

The wasps are interesting social insects, but they are not very prolific. The males and young queens arrive or hatch in late summer. Workers, males, and old queens die with the approach of winter. This leaves only the young queens, which hide in cracks, crevices, and tree bark throughout winter, emerging in the spring to start new colonies.

Other people have also found the wasp interesting and helpful. Once, when giving a talk on natural gardening to a group, I mentioned the wasp and a man in the crowd got all excited. He said, "I have a machine that will spray 100-foot-tall trees. That's what I do. I go up and down riverbottoms and spray trees for people. One day, while getting the rig ready to spray, I noticed a webworm colony in a low-hanging branch. A wasp flew in, captured a webworm, and flew off. I got interested and instead of cranking up the spray rig, I just watched. Within twenty minutes, the wasp had carried off every webworm."

About three years later, while talking to another gardening group, I told of my experience and the other man's story of the wasp. Again there was an old gentleman in the crowd who wanted to tell his story. He said, "I learned long ago the wasps were beneficial and preyed on webworms. But I noticed the wasp had a hard time getting through that web. So one day I decided to help them by taking a stick and tearing the web open. Sure enough, they would clean up a web a lot faster after I tore it. For years now I have been tearing the webs open for them. For a while it took fifteen to twenty minutes for the wasps to find the opened web; later it took them five minutes to find it. Now I can just walk out of the house with a stick and here they come."

We all laughed at this story's ending, but entomologists that study wasps claim they are the intellectuals of the insect world. They seem to have an ability to learn. The entomologist captured wasps and put them under a glass dome with a small escape hole. The wasps escaped, and each time they were caught and put back into the dome. They always looked for the opening and escaped again. No other insect they studied was able to learn or remember the escape hole.

I, too, find them pretty smart. While photographing them with a macro lens, I came within eight inches of a big nest. While I was taking time to get focused properly, they didn't bother me or fly. In fact, only one of them seemed to notice me. She watched for a while, then reached over and with a front leg tapped a neighbor on the back as if to draw his attention to me, then they both stared at me. I got the message and moved on.

As a child, I always played around pecan trees, and during the season my pockets were always full of nuts to munch on. Back then, I remember seeing an occasional webworm but never the problem of the 1950s, at least in our area. That was about the time people were learning to spray or were becoming prosperous enough to own spray equipment. I believe spraying with the wrong thing, a poison that kills too many beneficial insects, caused the webworm to eventually explode into a nuisance. I don't approve of persistent broad-spectrum insecticides, but I do believe there is a time and place for dusting and spraying. And a heavy webworm infestation is one of those times.

The adult webworm moth deposits large clusters of eggs, and without some natural check, their populations really multiply. The webworm's natural enemies aren't nearly so prolific as they once were, and years of spraying with the wrong materials have really allowed the webworm to gain a big lead. This makes us want to spray more.

Bacillus thuringiensis is a natural organism that destroys only the webworm and other lepidopterous caterpillars. It does not harm you, the wasp, the assassin bug, the praying mantis, the birds, or any of the rest of nature. Bt is being widely used in agriculture and, if properly used, works excellently on webworms.

The first time I tried it, it didn't work very well. I sprayed at about ten o'clock on a bright sunny day. I didn't realize the webworms were asleep in the web and wouldn't be feeding until dark. They must eat it before it will affect them, and by nightfall the Bt had probably degraded. So now I spray either late in the evening or on a damp cloudy day, and it is 100 percent effective.

WEEVIL

COMMON NAMES: Snout Beetle, Weevil
SCIENTIFIC NAME: Order Coleoptera, family Curculionidae, many species
SIZE: Adult—$\frac{1}{10}$"to $\frac{5}{8}$"
IDENTIFICATION: Adult weevils have a head that is elongated into a snout. Antennae are elbowed and clubbed. Mouthparts are attached to the end of the snout. Those having a long curved snout are called curculios. Usually a dull, dark color. Many weevils are flightless because their wing covers are fused.

Weevil on corn (B)

BIOLOGY AND LIFE CYCLE: Complete metamorphosis—eggs, larvae, pupae, and adults. Eggs are laid in or on the host plant. Larvae feed and pupate usually within the plant, and the adults later emerge to lay eggs. From one to several generations a year. Some larvae overwinter in the soil. Some species have whitish grubs that feed on roots and pupate in the soil.

HABITAT: Blackberries, blueberries, strawberries, azaleas, rhododendron, and other ornamental plants.

FEEDING HABITS: Feed on fruits, nuts, grains, plant roots, and leaves of ornamental and food crops. Larvae do the most serious damage to plant roots.

ECONOMIC IMPORTANCE: Can be quite damaging to ornamentals, food crops, and stored grain.

NATURAL CONTROL: Birds and predatory insects.

ORGANIC CONTROL: Spray foliage with garlic tea. Apply beneficial nematodes to soil to control larvae. Diatomaceous earth in stored grain or seed will help eliminate the problem.

INSIGHT: There are thousands of species of weevils.

WHEEL BUG—see Giant Wheel Bug

WHITEFLY

COMMON NAMES: Sweet Potato Whitefly, Whitefly
SCIENTIFIC NAME: Order Homoptera, family Aleyodidae, several species
SIZE: Adult—⅟₂₅" to ⅟₁₆"
IDENTIFICATION: Adults are tiny white mothlike insects. Larvae are flat, legless, translucent scales. Both are found on the undersides of leaves. Eggs are tiny yellow or gray cones.
BIOLOGY AND LIFE CYCLE: Adults and nymphs feed on the undersides of leaves and secrete a honeydew that

Whitefly adults (H)

Whitefly destroyed by beneficial fungi (ARM)

leads to sooty mold. Females lay eggs that hatch in two days to become tiny scalelike larvae that later pupate. Life cycle takes only twenty to thirty days. Many generations a year.

HABITAT: Greenhouses, gardens, and field crops. They like tropicals—gardenias, privet, citrus, hibiscus, vegetables like tomatoes, and crops like cotton.

FEEDING HABITS: Nymphs and adults suck plant juices and weaken plants. They especially like plants in the tomato and squash families.

ECONOMIC IMPORTANCE: Heavy infestations weaken plants and spread viral diseases.

NATURAL CONTROL: Native parasitic wasps, lacewings, lady beetles, and pirate bugs. Beneficial fungus called *Beauvaria bassiana.*

ORGANIC CONTROL: Spray garlic tea or garlic-pepper tea and seaweed. Release the parasitic wasp *Encarsia formosa* indoors. Manure compost, molasses, and citrus oil spray works very well.

INSIGHT: These pests are more troublesome in phosphorus-deficient soils. Use lots of colloidal phosphate and you probably won't see many of these pests. The pests are commonly found in tropical plants in pots. The lack of mychorrhizal fungi on plant roots is a strong contributor to the presence of this pest.

WHITEFLY PARASITE

COMMON NAMES: Eulophid Wasp, Whitefly Parasite
SCIENTIFIC NAME: Order Hymenoptera, family Eulophidae, *Encarsia formosa*
SIZE: Less than ⅟₂₅"
IDENTIFICATION: Adult wasps have a black head and thorax and yellow abdomen.
BIOLOGY AND LIFE CYCLE: Females lay fifty to one hundred eggs singly in whitefly nymphs. Parasitized whitefly nymphs turn black. Sweet potato whiteflies turn brown. Small wasps the size of a pinhead emerge from mature whitefly nymphs through a small hole.

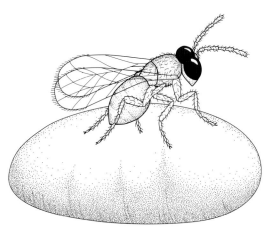

Whitefly parasite

Woolly bear after parasites (now in cocoons) have emerged (B)

WOOLLY BEAR

COMMON NAMES: Banded Woolly Bear, Tiger Moth, Woolly Bear

SCIENTIFIC NAME: Order Lepidoptera, family Arctiidae, *Pyrrharetia isabella*

SIZE: Adult—2¼", larva—1½"

IDENTIFICATION: Black, very fuzzy caterpillar. Red-brown band in the center on the body. Hairs are short, stiff, and bristly. Orange stripe. If more than one stripe, a cold winter is supposedly on its way. Commonly seen crossing roads in the spring and fall. They curl into a ball when disturbed. Adults are white or yellowish moths.

BIOLOGY AND LIFE CYCLE: Adult is the Isabella tiger moth. Caterpillars hibernate and spin a hairy cocoon in the spring. Adults emerge from the cocoon to lay eggs. The larvae hatch and undergo six molts, crawl around awhile, find a protected place to pupate, turn into adults that then lay eggs, which hatch into larvae that actively crawl around looking for a place to overwinter. Two generations a year.

HABITAT: Dandelion, plantain, and low-growing weeds and grasses. Meadows, pastures, uncultivated fields, road edges, and urban landscapes.

FEEDING HABITS: Feed on low-growing herbaceous plants of many kinds, mostly wild. Will sometimes but rarely attack ornamentals and food crops.

ECONOMIC IMPORTANCE: Little that we know of.

NATURAL CONTROL: Parasitic wasps, birds, and flies.

ORGANIC CONTROL: None needed.

INSIGHT: Folklore says that the more red stripes, the longer the winter will be.

YELLOWJACKET—see Paper Wasp, Texas Yellowjacket

YELLOW MEALWORM—see Mealworm

HABITAT: Greenhouses. This species cannot survive cold winters.

FEEDING HABITS: Adult whitefly parasites also kill whitefly nymphs by direct feeding. Eggs hatch into worms inside whitefly nymphs.

ECONOMIC IMPORTANCE: Control of whiteflies and aphids. They are most effective at 65–80°F with high light intensity and relative humidity of 50–70 percent.

NATURAL CONTROL: None needed—beneficial insect.

ORGANIC CONTROL: None needed.

INSIGHT: Whitefly parasites can help control pests that cause serious damage to tomatoes, cucumbers, and ornamental plants. They attack the whitefly in its immature stages, laying eggs in the third and fourth stages while feeding on the first and second stages. Early, preventative applications of *Encarsia formosa* prior to heavy infestations is recommended. They are expensive and should only be used as part of an overall organic program.

Widespread spraying of pyrethroids and other synthetic toxic pesticides on cotton crops has destroyed this beneficial natural control and cost the farming industry millions of dollars. Use one to five insects per square foot of plant area, one to eight per plant in greenhouses. There are several other species of *Encarsia* that are effective in field crops.

WIREWORM—see Click Beetle

Yellow sticky trap used for monitoring (H)

Logan releasing lady beetles (H)

APPENDIX A

Beneficial Insects

HABITATS AND BENEFITS OF SOME OF THE MOST HELPFUL BENEFICIALS

Beneficial	Preferred Habitat	Benefit
Assassin bug	Flowering plants of ornamentals and food crops	Controls aphids, Colorado potato beetles, small flying insects, caterpillars, leafhoppers, Mexican bean beetles
Bee	Beehives and flowers	Pollinates flowers, produces honey
Damsel bug	Vegetation of all kinds	Controls aphids, caterpillars, thrips, plant bugs, leafhoppers, treehoppers
Damselfly	Ponds, pools, water features	Controls mosquitoes, gnats, other flying insects
Doodle bug	Sandy soil	Controls ants, other small crawling insects
Dragonfly	Ponds, pools, water features	Controls mosquitoes, gnats, other flying insects
Giant wheel bug	Shrubs, trees	Controls moths, squash bugs, cucumber beetles, caterpillars
Ground beetle	Drainage ditches, rock gardens, ornamental and vegetable gardens, greenhouses	Controls aphids, flea beetles, cabbageworms, slugs, cutworms, leafhoppers
Hover fly	Herbs and flowers	Controls caterpillars, thrips, corn earworms, aphids, mealybugs, scale, leafhoppers
Ichneumon wasp	Woodlots, flowers	Controls caterpillars, beetles, moths, borers
Lacewing	Fencerows, woodlots, night-lights	Controls aphids, scale, thrips, mites, mealybugs, whiteflies, moths, loopers, beetles, leafminers
Lady beetle	Hedgerows, leaf litter, gardens, wildflowers, other protected places	Controls aphids, Colorado potato beetle eggs, spider mites
Longlegged fly	Ornamental and vegetable gardens	Controls many small, soft-bodied insects
Minute pirate bug	Pollen and nectar plants	Controls caterpillars, thrips, mites, aphids
Mud dauber	Flowering plants, food crops, barns and garages	Controls spiders, crickets, cicadas, flies, leafhoppers
Praying mantis	Wood areas, grass strips, fencerows, vines	Controls aphids, beetles, leafhoppers, caterpillars, flies and wasps
Spider	Beehives, wood scraps, fencerows, gardens	Controls many insect pests
Spined soldier bug	Vegetable gardens	Controls borers, moths, caterpillars, beetles
Tachinid fly	Herbs and flowers	Controls cutworms, stink bugs, beetles, corn borers, squash bugs, caterpillars, cabbageworms, sawflies, grasshoppers
Wasp	Orchards, vegetable gardens, ornamental gardens	Control of casebearers, caterpillars, and corn earworms

PLANTS THAT ATTRACT BENEFICIAL INSECTS

Alyssum—hover flies, lacewings, pirate bugs, wasps, tachinid flies.

Caraway—hover flies, true bugs, lacewings, wasps, tachinid flies.

Coriander—hover flies, pirate bugs, wasps, tachinid flies.

Coreopsis—hover flies, lacewings, lady beetles, wasps, bees.

Cosmos—hover flies, lacewings, lady beetles, pirate bugs, wasps.

Goldenrod—soldier beetles, lady beetles, bigeyed bugs, wasps, bees.

Lantana—hover flies, wasps, bees.

Liatris—true bugs, wasps, bees.

Roses—hover flies, wasps, bees.

Sunflowers—hover flies, lady beetles, wasps.

Tansy—hover flies, lady beetles, pirate bugs, wasps, bees.

Yarrow—hover flies, pirate bugs, wasps, bees.

BENEFICIAL INSECT RELEASE SCHEDULE

Quantities given are for each acre or residential lot.

April–May

Trichogramma wasps—10,000 to 20,000 eggs weekly for six weeks.

Green lacewings—4,000 eggs weekly for four weeks.

Lady beetles—as needed on aphid-infested plants.

May–September

Green lacewings—2,000 eggs every two weeks.

SOURCES OF BENEFICIAL BUGS

A-1 Unique Insect Control, 5504 Sperry Drive, Citrus Heights, CA 95621, (916) 961-7945, fax (916) 967-7082, www.a-1unique.com

American Insectaries, Inc., 30805 Rodriguez Road, Escondido, CA 92026, (760) 751-1436, fax (760) 749-7061

Arbico, P.O. Box 4247, Tucson, AZ 85738, 1-800-827-2847

Beneficial Insect Co., 244 Forest Street, Fort Mill, SC 29715, (803) 547-2301

Beneficial Insectary, 14751 Oak Run Road, Oak Run, CA 96069, (530) 472-3715

BioAg Supply, 710 South Columbia, Plainview, TX 79072, (806) 293-5861, fax (806) 293-0712, 1-800-746-9900

Biocollect, 5481 Crittenden Street, Oakland, CA 94601, (510) 436-8052

Biofac, P.O. Box 87, Mathis, Texas 78368, (512) 547-3259

BioLogic, Springtown Road, P.O. Box 177, Willow Hill, PA 17271, (717) 349-2789

Buena Biosystems, P.O. Box 4008, Ventura, CA 93007, (805) 525-2525

Gardener's Supply Co., 128 Intervale Road, Burlington, VT 05401, 1-800-863-1700

Gardens Alive, 5100 Schenley, Lawrenceburg, IN 47025, (812) 537-8650

Gulf Coast Biotic Technology, 72 West Oaks, Huntsville, TX 77340, 1-800-524-1958

Harmony Farm Supply, P.O. Box 460, Graton, CA 95444, (707) 823-9125

Hydro-Gardens, Inc., P.O. Box 25845, Colorado Springs, CO 80936, 1-800-634-6362

Kunafin Trichogramma Industries, Route 1, Box 39, Quemado, TX 78877, 1-800-832-1113, fax (830) 757-1468

M&R Durango, P.O. Box 886, Bayfield, CO 81122, 1-800-526-4075

Mellinger's Nursery, 2310 W. South Range Road, North Lima, OH 44452, 1-800-321-7444

Nature's Control, Medford, Oregon (541) 899-8318

New Earth, Inc., 9810 Taylorsville Road, Lewisville, KY 40299, (502) 261-0005

N-VIRO Products, Ltd., 610 Walnut Ave., Bohemia, NY 11716, (516) 567-2628

Oxnard Pest Control Association, 632 Pacific Ave., P.O. Box 1187, Oxnard, CA 93032, (805) 483-1024 fax (805) 487-6867

Peaceful Valley Farm Supply, P.O. Box 2209, Grass Valley, CA 95945, (916) 272-4769

Planet Natural, P.O. Box 3146, Bozeman, MT 59772, (406) 587-5891, (800) 289-6656

Rincon-Vitova Insectaries, Inc., P.O. Box 1555, Ventura, CA 93022, (805) 643-5407, 1-800-248-2847

Tri-Cal Biosystems, P.O. Box 1327, Hollister, CA 95024, (408) 637-0195

Worm's Way, Inc., 3151 South Highway 446, Bloomington, IN 47401, 1-800-274-9676

Growing Organic Roses, Pecan Trees, and Fruit Trees

We couldn't cover all the plants that grow in Texas, but the following programs for roses and fruit trees illustrate the basic approach. These are the plants that generate the most questions among gardeners.

ORGANIC ROSE PROGRAM

Yes, you can grow organic roses—which is good since they are one of the best medicinal and culinary herbs in the world. When they are loaded with toxic pesticides and other chemicals, that use is lost (or at least it should be). If you are drinking rose hip tea after spraying the plants with synthetic poisons, you're nuts! For best results with roses, here's the ultimate program.

Selection

Choose adapted roses such as antiques, Austins, and well-proven hybrids.

Planting

Prepare beds by mixing the following into existing soil to form a raised bed: 6 inches compost, ½ inch to 1 inch lava sand, ¼ inch to ½ inch Texas greensand, 20 pounds alfalfa meal, 20 pounds cottonseed meal, 40 pounds soft rock phosphate, 20 pounds Sul-Po-Mag or K-Mag, 5 pounds sulfur per 1,000 square feet, and 10 pounds cornmeal per 1,000 square feet. Soak the bare roots or rootball in water with 1 tablespoon of seaweed per gallon and 1 tablespoon of natural apple cider vinegar or biostimulant. Settle soil around plants with water—no tamping.

Mulching

After planting, cover all the soil in the beds with ½ inch of earthworm castings, followed by 2 or 3 inches of shredded hardwood bark or other coarse-textured mulch. Don't pile the mulch up on the stems of the roses.

Watering

If possible, save and use rainwater. If not, add 1 table-spoon of natural apple cider vinegar per gallon of water. If all that fails, just use tap water. But don't overwater. Avoid salty well water.

Fertilizing

Round 1 (February 1–15): 20 pounds of organic fertilizer (e.g., Garden-Ville, GreenSense, Bradfield, Maestro-Gro, Sustane, or Bioform Dry, or natural meals or manure compost) per 1,000 sq. ft.; 80 pounds lava sand per 1,000 sq. ft.; 5 pounds sugar or dry molasses per 1,000 sq. ft.

Round 2 (June 1–15): 20 pounds organic fertilizer per 1,000 square feet; 80 pounds Texas greensand per 1,000 square feet. In acid soils, use a high calcium product instead.

Round 3 (September 15–30): 20 pounds 100 percent organic fertilizer per 1,000 square feet, 20 pounds Sul-Po-Mag or K-Mag per 1,000 square feet. In acid soils, use a high calcium product instead.

Spraying

Schedule the first spraying just before bud break in the spring. Follow with additional sprayings as necessary. For best results spray Garrett Juice at least once a month.

- Compost tea—follow label directions; if homemade, 1 cup per gallon of water.
- Blackstrap molasses—1 ounce per gallon of water.
- Seaweed—1 ounce (liquid) per gallon of water; 1 teaspoon (dry) per gallon or follow label directions.
- Natural apple cider vinegar—1 ounce per gallon of water.

Optional ingredients:

- Citrus oil—2 ounces per gallon of water.
- Garlic tea—1 cup per gallon or follow label directions.
- Baking soda or potassium bicarbonate—1 rounded tablespoon per gallon or substitute liquid bio-stimulants (Agrispon, AgriGro, Medina, or similar product).

Insect Release

Trichogramma wasps—three weekly releases of 10,000 to 20,000 eggs per acre or residential lot starting at bud break.

Green lacewings—four weekly releases of 4,000 eggs per acre or residential lot.

Lady beetles—release of 1,500 to 2,000 adult beetles per 1,000 square feet at the first sign of shiny honeydew on foliage.

ORGANIC PECAN AND FRUIT TREE PROGRAM

Yes, you can maintain pecans organically and, no, you don't have to spray toxic pesticides. Plant adapted varieties. Texas has many environments—hot in the south, cold in the north, wet in the east, and dry in the west—and each of these environments requires different species. Plant the tree in a wide, ugly hole (not a small round hole), backfill with soil from the hole (no amendments), settle the soil with water (no tamping), add a 1-inch layer of lava sand and compost, and finish with a 3- to 5-inch layer of coarse-textured mulch. Don't stake the tree, wrap the trunk, or cut back the top. Mechanical aeration of the root zone of existing trees is beneficial, but tilling, disking, or plowing destroys feeder roots and should never be done.

Spraying

Schedule the first spraying of Garrett Juice when the bud starts to swell and show the color (additional sprayings are optional); the second, after flowers have fallen; the third, about June 15; the fourth, the last week in August.

- Compost tea—Follow label directions; if homemade, 1 cup per gallon of water.
- Molasses—1 to 2 tablespoons per gallon.
- Seaweed—1 to 2 tablespoons (liquid) per gallon; 1 teaspoon (dry) per gallon or follow label directions.
- Natural apple cider vinegar—1 tablespoon per gallon.

Optional ingredients:

- Citrus (orange) oil—2 ounces per gallon.
- Garlic tea—¼ to 1 cup per gallon or follow label directions.
- Baking soda or potassium bicarbonate—1 rounded tablespoon per gallon.
- Liquid biostimulants (Agrispon, AgriGro, Medina, or similar product)—follow label directions.
- Fish emulsion—2 to 3 tablespoons per gallon (may not need when using compost tea).

Fertilizing

Once soil health has been achieved, the following schedule can probably be cut to one application a year. Large-scale pecan orchards can use manure or compost at 2 tons per acre per year along with plantings of green manure cover crops. Lava sand and Texas greensand can be applied any time of the year.

Round 1 (February 1–15): 20 pounds 100 percent organic fertilizer (e.g., Garden-Ville, GreenSense, Maestro-Gro, Bradfield, Sustane, Bioform Dry, or natural meals or manure compost) per 1,000 square feet; 80 pounds lava sand per 1,000 square feet; 2 to 5 pounds sugar or dry molasses per 1,000 square feet.

Round 2 (June 1–15): 20 pounds 100 percent organic fertilizer per 1,000 square feet; 80 pounds Texas greensand per 1,000 square feet. In acid soils, use a high calcium product instead.

Round 3 (September 15–30): 20 pounds 100 percent organic fertilizer per 1,000 square feet; 20 pounds Sul-Po-Mag per 1,000 square feet. In acid soils, use a high calcium product instead.

Insect Release

Trichogramma wasps—three weekly releases of 10,000 to 20,000 eggs per acre or residential lot starting at bud break.

Green lacewings—four weekly releases of 4,000 eggs per acre or residential lot.

Lady beetles—release of 1,500 to 2,000 adult beetles per 1,000 square feet at first sign of shiny honeydew on foliage.

Pruning

Very little is needed or recommended.

NOTE:
Citrus oil should always be mixed with compost tea, molasses, humate, or other organic materials when used to spray plant foliage for buffering purposes. Citrus by itself can burn plants. Citrus oil can be mixed with water only when used to spray insects indoors or otherwise not on plants.

Basic Organic Program

The main points of difference between organic and nonorganic approaches are as follows:

ORGANIPHOBIC APPROACH

Lawn height low and cut often
Grass clippings caught and removed
High-analysis fertilizer 4 to 7 times per year
High-nitrogen artificial fertilizers—no organic matter
Fertilizer based on plant needs
Fertilizers with few or no trace minerals
Attempt to control nature
Treatment of symptoms (insects, diseases)
Synthetic toxic pesticides
Sprays used as preventatives
Beneficial insects discouraged
Only EPA-labeled products

ORGANIC APPROACH

Lawn height higher and cut less often
Grass clippings left on the ground
Low-analysis fertilizers three times per year
Low-nitrogen, natural, 100 percent organic fertilizer
Fertilizer based on soil needs
Fertilizers loaded with trace minerals
Works within nature's laws and systems
Treatment of soil and actual problems—
    the reasons for the pests
Soil and plants improved for natural pest resistance
Only preventative is soil improvement
Beneficial insects used as major tool
Teas, homemade mixtures, and labeled products

BASIC ORGANIC PROGRAM

Testing the Soil

Have soil tested to determine available levels of organic matter, nitrogen, sulfur, phosphorus, calcium, magnesium, potassium, sodium, chloride, boron, iron, manganese, copper, and zinc. A Texas lab that offers organic recommendations is Texas Plant and Soil Lab in Edinburg (210) 383-0739.

Planting

Prepare new planting beds by scraping away existing grass and weeds; adding a 4- to 6-inch layer of compost, 40 to 80 pounds of lava sand, 40 to 80 pounds of Texas greensand, 20 pounds of organic fertilizer, 5 pounds of sugar per 1,000 square feet; and tilling to a depth of 3 inches into the native soil. Excavation and additional ingredients such as concrete sand, topsoil, pine bark, and synthetic fertilizer are unnecessary and can even cause problems. More compost is needed for shrubs and flowers than for groundcover.

Fertilizing

Apply an organic fertilizer two to three times per year. During the growing season, spray turf, trees and shrub foliage, trunks, limbs, and soil monthly with a mixture of manure compost tea, molasses, natural vinegar, and seaweed. The commercial version of this mixture is called Garrett Juice. Annually add 80 pounds of lava sand per 1,000 square feet.

Mulching

Mulch all shrubs, trees, and ground cover with 1 to 3 inches of compost, native tree trimmings, or shredded hardwood bark to inhibit weed germination, decrease watering needs, and mediate soil temperature. Mulch vegetable gardens with 8 inches of alfalfa hay or rough-textured compost. Avoid hay (grass) unless it is organically grown because of the risk of persistent broadleaf herbicide.

Watering

Adjust schedule seasonally to allow for deep, infrequent waterings in order to maintain an even moisture level. Apply about 1 inch of water per week in the summer and adjust from there.

Mowing

Mow lawns weekly, leaving the clippings on the ground to return nutrients and organic matter to the soil. General mowing height should be 2½ inches or taller. Put occasional excess clippings in compost pile. Do not bag clippings or let clippings leave the site. Do not use line trimmers around trees.

Weeding

Hand-pull large weeds and work on soil health for overall control. Mulch all bare soil in beds. *Avoid synthetic herbicides*, especially pre-emergents, broadleaf treatments, and soil sterilants. These are unnecessary toxic pollutants. Spray broadleaf weeds with a mix of full-strength (20 percent or more) vinegar, molasses, and citrus oil.

Pruning

Remove dead, diseased, and conflicting limbs. Do not overprune. Do not make flush cuts. Leave the branch collars intact. Do not paint cuts except in the spring on oaks in oak-wilt areas. It's better to simply avoid pruning in the spring.

Controlling Insects

Aphids, spider mites, whiteflies, and lacebugs—use strong water blasts for heavy infestations. Release lady beetles and green lacewings regularly until natural populations exist. A spray of seaweed and garlic-pepper tea (recipe below) is an effective control.

Caterpillars and bagworms—Release trichogramma wasps. Spray *Bacillus thuringiensis* at dusk as a last resort.

Fire ants—manure compost tea, citrus oil, and molasses; beneficial nematodes. Garden-Ville Fire Ant Control.

Grubworms—beneficial nematodes and sugar help, but maintaining soil health is the primary control.

Mosquitoes—*Bacillus thuringiensis* 'Israelensis' for larvae in standing water; garlic-pepper tea spray for adults. Lavender and eucalyptus also repel mosquito adults.

Slugs, snails—hot pepper, cedar flakes, diatomaceous earth.

Fleas, ticks, chinch bugs, roaches, crickets—spray or dust diatomaceous earth products; spray citrus and release beneficial nematodes.

Controlling Diseases

Black spot, brown patch, powdery mildew, and other fungal problems are best controlled by prevention—through soil improvement, avoidance of high-nitrogen fertilizers, and proper watering. Spray with compost tea, seaweed, vinegar, blackstrap molasses, and baking soda (potassium bicarbonate is better). Treat soil with corn-meal. Alfalfa meal and mixes containing alfalfa are also good disease fighters. Cornmeal applied at 20 pounds per 1,000 square feet is even better.

Making Compost

Compost is nature's own living fertilizer that can be made at home or purchased ready to use. A compost pile can be started any time of the year and can be in sun or shade. Good ingredients include leaves, hay, grass clippings, tree trimmings, food scraps, bark, sawdust, rice hulls, weeds, nut hulls, and animal manure. Mix the ingredients together in a container of wood, hay bales, hog wire, or concrete blocks or simply pile the material on the ground. The best mixture is 80 percent vegetative matter and 20 percent animal waste, although any mix will compost. Since oxygen is a critical component, the ingredients should be a mix of coarse- and fine-textured material to promote air circulation through the pile. Turn the pile once a month if possible; turning it more often speeds up the process but releases nitrogen to the air. Another critical component is water. A compost pile should be roughly the moisture of a squeezed-out sponge to help the living microorganisms thrive and work their magic. Compost is ready to use as a soil amendment when the ingredients are no longer identifiable. The color will be dark brown, the texture soft and crumbly, and the smell similar to that of the forest floor. Rough, unfinished compost can be used as a top-dressing mulch around all plantings.

ORGANIC RECIPES

Citrus Oil Mix

Chop orange, grapefruit, or other citrus skins or cut them in very small pieces, then place in a pan of water. Simmer fifteen minutes. Cool thoroughly.

Compost Tea

Compost tea is effective on many pests because of certain microorganisms that are produced in the dark liquid. You can use any container, but plastic buckets are easy for the homeowner. Fill the container half full of compost and finish filling it with water. Let the mix sit for ten to fourteen days; then dilute and spray on the foliage of any and all plants. How much to dilute the dark compost tea before spraying it depends on the compost used. A rule of thumb is to dilute the concentrated leachate down to one part compost liquid to four to ten parts water. The final spray liquid should look like iced tea. Be sure to strain the solids out with old pantyhose, cheesecloth, or row cover material. Diluted compost tea is good for fruit trees, perennials, annuals, vegetables, roses, and other plants that are regularly attacked by insect and fungal pests. It is also very effective on blackspot on roses and early blight on tomatoes. Full-strength tea makes an excellent fire ant mound drench. Add molasses (one cup per gallon of mix) or citrus oil or both for even more power. Compost tea and other organic sprays are the most effective when sprayed at dusk.

Garlic-Pepper-Seaweed Tea

In a blender with water, liquefy 2 bulbs of garlic and 2 cayenne or habanero peppers. Strain away the solids. Pour the garlic-pepper juice into a gallon container. Fill the remaining volume with water to make one gallon of concentrate. Shake well before using and add ¼ cup of the concentrate to each gallon of water in the sprayer. To make garlic-seaweed tea, simply omit the pepper and add another bulb of garlic, then add 1 tablespoon of seaweed and molasses to each gallon.

Garden-Ville Fire Ant Control Formula

Mix equal portions of molasses, manure compost tea, and citrus oil. Add a tablespoon of humate and natural vinegar per gallon of final mix. Use 2 to 4 ounces per gallon of water for soft-skinned insects, 5 to 6 ounces per gallon for hard-shelled insects.

Garrett Juice

To make this basic foliar-feeding spray, mix the following ingredients per gallon of water:

1 cup manure compost tea or liquid humate
1 ounce liquid seaweed
1 ounce blackstrap molasses
1 ounce natural apple cider vinegar

For more serious disease infestations, add the following to the mixture above:

¼ cup garlic tea
1 rounded tablespoon baking soda or potassium bicarbonate

For more serious insect infestations, add citrus oil at 1 ounce per gallon of spray.

Tree Trunk Goop

Mix one part manure compost, one part diatomaceous earth, and one part soft rock phosphate (or fireplace ashes). Mix the material with water in a bucket, washtub, wheelbarrow, then paint on the trunks of fruit trees and others with borer or other insect problems. This mixture is also effective for all trunk or limb injuries.

NON-MEDICAL DEVICE FOR TREATING POISONOUS BITES

For some reason, brown recluse spiders *(Loxoceles reclusa)* seem to be on the increase, as are bites from these spiders. You can use boric acid products, citrus sprays, or pyrethrum to kill brown recluse spiders indoors. Brown recluse spider bites are very dangerous because there is no anti-venom and severe tissue damage or limb loss is possible. The bites are not painful at first but become extremely painful as the toxin spreads. If you get bitten you should know about the following method of treatment. Anecdotal evidence and articles in professional journals indicate that a significant electric shock will completely neutralize brown recluse spider bites and all other poisonous bites.

According to the medical journals listed below, this method is a safe and effective treatment for bites from brown recluse spiders, black widow spiders, rattlesnakes, copperheads, coral snakes, scorpions, wasps, bees, and other stinging animals. A person who has been bitten or stung by a poisonous animal should always see his or her physician as soon as possible, as should people with allergic reactions to bites or stings. Tetanus shots should be current and wounds must be properly cleaned and disinfected.

We are not medical doctors and cannot endorse the use of the device described below, but if you decide on your own to use it, here are the specifications and procedures that have been covered in the medical journals and used by many doctors.

Specifications

Power emittance: 25,000 volts powered by a 9-volt battery.

According to the articles in the medical journals listed below that suggested use of this device for treating snake bites, the following procedure should be used. Place one electrode on the skin as close to the bite as possible; put the other electrode on the skin to use as a ground, and make sure that both electrodes are firmly touching the skin. Push the spring-loaded trigger ON to release the current. Hold in contact with skin for two seconds, then release for ten seconds. Do this five times, leaving one electrode on the bite or sting while rotating the device around the wound. For bee stings and insect bites, hold in contact with the skin for two seconds and release for ten seconds. Do this twice.

The following sources suggest using this method of treatment:

"Shocking Snake-bites in Africa," by Robert L. Wenninger, M.D. (*Lancet*, July 26, 1986). This article discusses high voltage shock treatment for snake bites.

"Treatment of Venomous Bite by High Voltage Direct Current," by Carl D. Osborn, M.D. (*Journal of the Oklahoma State Medical Association* 83, no. 1 [January 1990]: 9–14). This journal concludes that "high voltage, low amperage direct current shock appears to be an effective, basically safe, mildly uncomfortable first aid emergency measure or supplement to conventional therapy for venomous bites and stings of all kinds."

"Treatment of Spider Bites by High Voltage Direct Current," by Carl D. Osborn, M.D. (reprinted from the *Journal of the Oklahoma State Medical Association* 84, no. 6 [June 1991]: 257–260).

"Multiple HVDC Shocks as First Aid or Therapy for Venomous Bites and Stings," by Carl D. Osborn, M.D. (*Journal of the Oklahoma State Medical Association* 85, no. 7 [July 1992]: 331–333).

The author of this article concludes: "HVDC (High Voltage Direct Current) is an effective therapy for venomous spider bites, and limits venom damage and reduces pain. Specific information of the vector has not been necessary for good results. The benefits of treatment outweigh the discomfort of shocks for short duration. The author hopes the utility of this method will be confirmed by other physicians."

These articles make strong claims that an electric shock of 25,000 volts will probably help greatly to neutralize the toxin of any biting or stinging animal. The articles do not recommend 50,000-volt stun guns, car batteries, or electric fences. We do not recommend any of these products or make claims as to their effectiveness, but if you are interested in finding out more, contact Cliff Mackey at P.O. Box 123, Claremore, Oklahoma 74018, (918) 341-6715. He will tell you how to get such a device but will make absolutely no claims on its use. Neither will we; you're on your own. You can thank us later.

Ant Baits

1. 1 teaspoon creamy peanut butter
   1 pat of butter
   1 tablespoon of any light syrup
   1 teaspoon boric acid

Blend the ingredients over a low heat until smooth; don't burn. Put the finished bait into lids or other small containers that will function as bait stations.

2. 1 part boric acid
   20 parts sugar or apple mint jelly

Add enough water to make a thin paste and put in the bait stations.

3. 4 parts flour
   2 parts sugar
   1 part boric acid

Add enough water to make little cakes. Put the cakes in the bait stations.

4. 1 teaspoon boric acid
   6 tablespoons sugar
   2 cups water

Thoroughly dissolve the sugar and boric acid in the water and then soak cotton balls with the solution. Make bait stations by punching holes in small plastic tubs with lids. Put soaked cotton balls inside.

Roach Baits

1. 1 part Arm and Hammer laundry detergent
   1 part sugar

Place the dry mix in bait stations.

2. 10 parts Arm and Hammer laundry detergent
   10 parts sugar
   1 part boric acid or less

Place the dry mix in bait stations.

For all these baits, it's best to use something that pets can't easily lick. Short pieces of a straw with one end taped shut or a piece of PVC pipe (1–2" diameter) with one end taped shut make good bait stations that can be taped to vertical surfaces. Commercial bait stations are available at feed stores and hardware stores.

BIBLIOGRAPHY

Arnett, Ross H., Jr., and Richard L. Jacques, Jr. *Simon and Schuster's Guide to Insects*. New York: Simon and Schuster, 1981.

Beck, Malcolm. *The Garden-Ville Method: Lessons in Nature*. San Antonio, Tex.: Garden-Ville, 1993.

Borror, Donald J., and Richard E. White. *Peterson Field Guides—Insects*. Boston: Houghton Mifflin, 1970.

Callahan, Phil. *Tuning into Nature*. Old Greenwich, Conn., 1975.

Carr, Anna. *Rodale's Color Handbook of Garden Insects*. Emmaus, Penn.: Rodale Press, 1979.

Common Names of Insects and Related Organisms. Lanham, Md.: Entomological Society of America, 1989. Available from the Standing Committee on Common Names of Insects, 9301 Annapolis Road, Lanham, MD 20706; (301) 731-4535.

Garrett, Howard. *Plants for Texas*. Austin: University of Texas Press, 1996.

Hoffman, Michael P., and Anne C. Frodsham, *Natural Enemies of Vegetable Insect Pests*. Ithaca, N.Y.: Cornell Cooperative Extension, 1993.

Lane, Richard P., and Roger W. Crosskey, eds. *Medical Insects and Arachnids*. New York: Chapman and Hall, 1993.

Lollar, Amanda. *The Bat in My Pocket*. Santa Barbara, Calif.: Kapra Press, 1992. Available from Bat World, 217 N. Oak, Mineral Wells, TX 76067; (940) 325-3404.

McGavin, George C. *Insects*. New York: Smithmark Publications, 1992.

Malais, M., and W. J. Ravensberg. *The Biology of Glasshouse Pests and Their Natural Enemies: Knowing and Recognizing*. The Netherlands: Koppert Biological Systems, 1992.

Metcalf, Robert L., and Robert A. Metcalf. *Destructive and Useful Insects—Their Habits and Control*. 5th ed. New York: McGraw-Hill, 1993.

Michalak, Patricia S., and Linda A. Gilkeson. *Rodale's Successful Organic Gardening: Controlling Pests and Diseases*. Emmaus, Penn.: Rodale Press, 1994.

Milne, Lorus, and Margery Milne. *National Audubon Society Field Guide to North American Insects and Spiders*. Knopf, 1980.

Olkowski, William, Sheila Daar, and Helen Olkowski. *Common Sense Pest Control*. Newtown, Conn.: Taunton Press, 1991.

Pope, Thomas, Neil Odenwald, and Charles Fryling, Jr. *Attracting Birds to Southern Gardens*. Dallas: Taylor Publishing, 1993.

Pests of Landscape Trees and Shrubs. Publication 3359. Oakland, Calif.: University of California, Division of Agriculture and Natural Resources, 1994.

Tuttle, Merlin. *America's Neighborhood Bats: Understanding and Learning to Live with Them*. Austin: University of Texas Press, 1988.

Tuttle, Merlin, and Donna L. Hensley. *The Bat House Builder's Handbook*. 1994. Distributed for Bat Conservation International by the University of Texas Press, P.O. Box 7819, Austin, TX 78713-7819.

Tveten, John, and Gloria Tveten. *Butterflies of Houston*. Austin: University of Texas Press, 1996.

Zak, Bill. *Critters*. Dallas: Taylor Publishing, 1984.

INDEX

Boldface page numbers indicate illustrations